LEARN C++
BY MAKING GAMES

LEARN C++
BY MAKING GAMES

ERIK YUZWA

FRANÇOIS DOMMINIC LARAMÉE

CHARLES RIVER MEDIA
Boston, Massachusetts

Cover Design: The Printed Image

CHARLES RIVER MEDIA
25 Thomson Place
Boston, Massachusetts 02210
617-757-7900
617-757-7969 (FAX)
crm.info@thomson.com
www.charlesriver.com

This book is printed on acid-free paper.

Erik Yuzwa and François Dominic Laramée. *Learn C++ by Making Games.*
ISBN: 1-58450-455-2

Library of Congress Cataloging-in-Publication Data
Yuzwa, Erik.
  Learn C++ by making games / Erik Yuzwa, François Dominic Laramée.
     p. cm.
  ISBN 1-58450-455-2 (pbk. with cd-rom : alk. paper)
  1. C++ (Computer program language) 2. Computer games--Programming. I. Laramée, François Dominic. II. Title.
  QA76.73.C153Y89 2006
  005.13'3--dc22

Printed in the United States of America
06 7 6 5 4 3 2 First Edition

I want to dedicate this book to my
wife Eliza and our two sons Noah and Isaac.
I'd also like to thank the Almighty for blessing me
with so much in my life, and helping me find my way home.

Contents

Acknowledgments

A book of this size and nature is definitely not a "lone wolf" venture, and many were involved to deliver this tome into your hands.

I would like to thank my wife Eliza and our two sons for their patience and understanding while I chiseled away at the manuscript, most often into the wee hours of the morning.

I would also like to thank all the great people at Charles River Media /Thomson Delmar Learning, including Lance Morganelli and Jenifer Niles in particular, for providing me a great opportunity to write this book.

A big "merci beaucoup" to François Laramée, who wrote some sections of the book that provide excellent explanations of the things I was not sure how to describe coherently.

I would also like to dedicate this book to you, the reader, for taking the opportunity to seize the moment and learn the C++ language. My hat's off to you, and I look forward to playing any games you might create!

Introduction

WHO SHOULD READ THIS BOOK

This book is written for a variety of individuals all interested in learning how to use the C++ language to develop software. Although the material has a bit of a slant toward discussing the development and creation of games-based programs, the concepts and topics discussed throughout this book can benefit any and every software developer interested in the C++ language!

HOW THIS BOOK IS ORGANIZED

This book is structured with the intent to enable you to learn the foundations of the C++ language. Each major section and individual chapter builds upon the previous material with the goal of instructing the beginner on picking up the C++ language. The text is presented in a slightly tutorial format, which allows you to progress at your own pace.

The following brief overview can help you chart your path through this book:

Part I: You are introduced to the fundamentals of the C++ language, which includes learning about the basic data types of the language.

Part II: After the initial introduction to the language, in this section of the book you will wade further into matters of creating/defining variables, basic mathematical operators, and the various loop structures you have at your disposal.

Part III: C++ software tends to be a fairly complex mass of programming that requires structure. This section is devoted to learning how to use functions to make your code more readable and maintainable, along with breaking up your source code into several files for easier readability.

Part IV: Eventually, when working with the C++ language you will come across situations in which other data structures are required. This section of the book discusses concepts like using collections to store multiple copies of a data type.

Part V: With the foundation of C++ firmly applied, you are ready to learn about one of the fundamental pillars of the language: pointers. You will cover the basics here, but will be applying pointers throughout the rest of your C++ programming.

Part VI: In this section of the book, you will learn about object-oriented programming (OOP) concepts the C++ language directly applies with its design. Topics such as classes, objects, inheritance, virtual methods, and polymorphism are introduced here.

Part VII: One of the common tasks of games and the C++ language is the ability to read and write data to files. This section of the book discusses these concepts, broadly known as "serialization."

Part VIII: You have been learning a great deal of the C++ language thus far, and in this section of the book, you will be applying this knowledge toward the usage of the Simple DirectMedia Layer to display graphics and handle basic input.

Part IX: In the final section of this book, you will be introduced to some of the more advanced topics of the language, along with using SDL to create a simple demo.

At the end of every Chapter is a list of review material in the form of some questions and exercises. This extra content is presented in a fashion to both slightly challenge the reader, as well as to further iterate what was explained during the Chapter. To verify your responses, the answers to the odd numbered questions have been included at the rear of this book. The use of these review exercises is also a chance to see some real-world application of any theory presented during the Chapter.

CONTACTING THE AUTHOR

I am always interested to hear from you about what you think of this material. You can send me email at *book@wazooinc.com*, or feel free to post topics and/or help other readers in the forums for this book at *http://forums.wazooinc.com*. Your kind feedback will benefit other readers and improve the material presented.

Part

I

Fundamentals of C++ Programming

This section of the book introduces the fundamental concepts of programming and the basic building blocks of the C++ programming language. Readers with no prior programming experience will be exposed to the "frame of mind" that this kind of work requires, while all readers will become acquainted with C++'s source files, built-in data types, text strings, screen output, and keyboard input. We conclude this section with a very simple "game" of funny headlines to illustrate the concepts before moving on to C++'s more elaborate constructs.

1 Programming First Steps

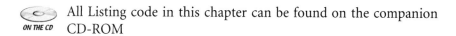 All Listing code in this chapter can be found on the companion
ON THE CD CD-ROM

Welcome to *Learn C++ by Making Games*. This chapter introduces you to the fundamental concepts of computer programming and sets you up with the tools you need to develop your own simple programs and games. At the end of this chapter, you will be ready to begin exploring the syntax of the C++ programming language and to compile your own programs.

THE FIRST LAW OF COMPUTER PROGRAMMING

Before going any further, a word to the wise that all programmers, novices, and gurus alike, would do well to remember:

TIP

The First Law of Computer Programming: Computers Are Not That Smart.

In fact, despite all the hype about "artificial intelligence" over the past couple of decades, computers are rather obtuse. Computers are tools that do exactly what programmers tell them to do, no more, no less; they just seem intelligent because they are able to obey instructions amazingly fast. Even Deep Blue, the supercomputer that became the first machine to defeat a reigning human World chess champion (Gary Kasparov, in 1997) only did so by using most of its tremendous processing power to examine (in painstaking detail) the consequences of nonsensical moves that a novice human player would have dismissed out of hand. Deep Blue is also an extremely specialized machine: for all of its chess expertise, it cannot play any other game because it does not know the rules, and it would be at a loss to explain why crossing a street without looking for oncoming traffic first might be hazardous to one's health.

Furthermore, computers take everything literally. They are unable to guess your intentions or fix even the most blatant programming mistakes. Indeed, one of computer science's most important theorems states that it is absolutely impossible for a computer to determine whether a syntactically valid program that is being fed to it will ever complete its execution, or whether it will run until the heat death of the universe without producing a result. Put in rather coarse terms, this theorem, often known as the *halting problem*, proves that nobody can possibly write a program that will analyze another program and fix it, at least not reliably. Programming will remain a (sometimes frustrating) human activity for as long as computers exist.

Anything your program tells the computer to do, it will do without asking questions, whatever the consequences. Some early microcomputers provided instructions that allowed programmers to modify the names of the operating system's commands in memory, even to change the voltage in the computer's circuits. The designers presumably installed safeguards; otherwise, a malicious (or merely reckless) programmer could quite literally have ordered his computer to fry its own brain.

WHY DO YOU NEED PROGRAMMING LANGUAGES?

Computers are also unable to use contextual information or common sense to resolve ambiguous orders. This is why you cannot communicate with them in anything resembling natural human languages.

For example, take the phrase "Time flies like an arrow." A fluent English speaker will have no trouble understanding its meaning: We are comparing the passage of time to the flight of an arrow, swift and inexorably unidirectional. However, from a purely syntactic and grammatical point of view, this phrase could also be interpreted as meaning:

- When measuring the speed of flies, you should use the same kind of chronometer that you would choose to measure the speed of arrows.
- A particular species of insect known as the "Time Fly" is known to enjoy eating arrows, or maybe to fall in love with them.
- There exists a particular news magazine that travels through the air under its own power, and does it in exactly the same manner as a Royal Canadian Air Force prototype jet fighter of the 1950s.

As a human reader, you can immediately dismiss these alternative interpretations as nonsensical, but a computer requires very complicated software knowledge bases, patiently crafted by linguists and full of exceptions and contradictions, to make that sort of distinction. Moreover, the science behind computer understanding of natural human languages is far from perfect, as any call to a voice-activated directory assistance service is bound to demonstrate. (Indeed, a perfect machine interpretation of something as "disordered" as a human language is provably impossible to attain.)

For these reasons, you need special languages to communicate with computers and give them orders they will be able to fulfill predictably. These programming languages follow strict rules of syntax and grammar that leave absolutely no room for ambiguity: whatever the programmer tells the computer to do, the computer will do. (Whether that happens to be what the programmer *meant* to tell the computer to do is an entirely different problem.)

WHY CHOOSE C++?

Over the years, hundreds of programming languages have been invented: machine and assembly languages, procedural languages, functional languages, logic languages, scripting languages, object-oriented languages, and so forth. Why, out of all of them, choose C++?

C++ is ubiquitous. There are C++ compilers available on just about every computer platform in existence, and a vast majority of commercial games are developed in C++.

C++ is object-oriented. As you will see in Part VI of this book, object-oriented programming is an effective way to organize large-scale projects that would otherwise become increasingly complex. Since commercial games involve several person-years of programming effort and hundreds of thousands of lines of code, C++'s built-in facilities for encapsulation, inheritance, and other features that make it easier to work in teams and reuse code will save every game development team a considerable amount of time, effort, and trouble.

C++ delivers high performance. Games routinely push the hardware to its limits. For a game programmer, a language that introduces so much overhead that it slows the game and reduces its quality is unacceptable; the optimizations that C++ compiler writers have developed over the years have made it one of the fastest of all programming languages in common use.

SOME IMPORTANT DEFINITIONS

Like all fields of human activity, computer programming has developed its own specialized vocabulary. Here are the definitions of a handful of common terms you will be using repeatedly throughout this book:

■   An *algorithm* is an ordered set of actions designed to accomplish a certain task. The method for long division that you learn in elementary school is an algorithm; so are cooking recipes, college application procedures, and the sequence of motions required to throw a curveball.

■   A *program* is a sequence of computer language instructions that implement one or more algorithms.

■   *Source code* is the text of a program as created by the programmer. Source code is legible to human eyes, but the computer cannot execute it directly.

■   A *compiler* is a special program that takes source code and translates it into object code the computer can understand and execute.

■   *Object code* is a program that has been translated into machine-readable form by a compiler. It consists of sequences of binary numbers and therefore cannot be read by human programmers. Object code is also known as an *executable program*, or simply an *executable*.

■   A *function* is a logically self-consistent and somewhat independent part of a program. Every C++ program contains at least one function (called main); as you progress through the book, you will develop programs containing an increasing number of functions.

■   A *library* is a collection of functions that can be added to a program. C++ includes many built-in libraries that all programmers can use; other libraries can be purchased from third-party vendors, downloaded from the Internet, or developed by the programmer himself.

■   A *bug* is a mistake in a program. Many years ago, an insect flew into a computer and caused a malfunction; the programmer who discovered it coined the term that has been used ever since. The three main categories of bugs are the *syntax error* (akin to a spelling mistake in English), the *grammatical error* (akin to a nonsensical phrase), and the *logic error* (a perfectly valid instruction that causes an error because the programmer did not properly express what he meant).

Compilers are able to catch syntax and grammar bugs and will refuse to produce object code out of source code that contains them. However, logic errors will generally only be discovered at runtime, when the program delivers unexpected results, although some compilers will warn the programmer if the source code contains certain constructs that are usually associated with logic errors.

When you reach Part VI of the book, you will be introduced to a considerable amount of additional vocabulary related to object-oriented programming.

THE PROGRAMMER'S TOOLKIT

To benefit from this book and write your own games, you will need a *compiler*, a *source code editor*, and a special library called *SDL*, the Simple DirectMedia Layer.

Compilers

Compilers come in all shapes and sizes, and different readers of this book are likely to want to program under a variety of operating systems and hardware configurations. Discussing them all would be far beyond the scope of this book; an ANSI standard-compliant C++ compiler is what you need.

If you are enrolled in a college programming course, your instructor will be able to tell you about your options and explain how to set up your programming environment properly. If you are studying C++ independently, you will need to acquire and install a compiler that is compatible with your computer and operating system. Various commercial options exist; if you prefer to work with a free compiler, you might want to visit the Web site *The Free Country*, which maintains a list of freely downloadable C++ compilers at *www.thefreecountry.com/compilers/cpp.shtml*.

Note that, generally, free compilers provide fewer features than commercial alternatives. Many commercial compilers come with their own programming environments that assist you in editing, building, and debugging (fixing) programs, whereas the free alternatives only provide the bare necessities. As a result, it may be easier to work through the examples with a commercial compiler and its programming environment, especially as we advance to more complex applications.

In any case, make sure to follow the compiler provider's instructions for installation and setup, and then test your installation by following the instructions in the section, "Your First Program."

Source Code Editor

To write your source code, you will need a program that can create simple text files. Under Windows®, *Notepad* will do fine; under Linux, *emacs* and *vi* are among the many options. Most commercial programming environments also provide their own source code editors that allow automatic source code formatting, easy search and replace features, integration with source control systems, and so forth.

As a general rule, however, word processors are not the ideal choice for source code creation, because compilers can't recognize the special characters the word processor inserts into files. If you do decide to use a word processor, make sure you save all source code as text-only files.

The Simple DirectMedia Layer (SDL)

SDL is a multiplatform library that supports graphics, sound, and input devices under a variety of operating systems. You will not encounter SDL until Part VIII of this book, once you have learned enough C++ to start coding graphical games, so you do not need to install it right away. You will also only use a minute fraction of SDL's capabilities; the SDL Web site contains a considerable amount of documentation that you will be able to browse should you decide to develop more complex SDL applications once you have finished reading this book.

To download and install the version of SDL that is most suitable to your own programming environment, visit *www.libsdl.org*.

If you are running a Windows operating system, feel free to use the SDL install provided on the book's accompanying CD-ROM.

YOUR FIRST PROGRAM

It is now time for you to take a peek at your first C++ program. You will also take this opportunity to test your compiler's installation and configuration. To do so, follow the instructions in this short algorithm:

1. Launch your source code editor and create a file called `hello.cpp`. "Hello" is the name of your program; the .cpp extension is used to identify the file as C++ source code. (Make sure the editor does not append another extention to the file, because the compiler will not be able to recognize a file called `hello.cpp.txt`, `hello.txt`, or `hello.doc` as source code.)
2. Type the following text into the file, making sure the line that begins with the pound sign is aligned *left*. Listing 1.1 provides further details.

LISTING 1.1.   Hello World.

```cpp
/***********************************
Learn C++ by Making Games
Example 1.1
***********************************/

#include <iostream>
using namespace std;

int main()
{
  cout << "Hello, world!" << endl;
  return 0;
}
```

ON THE CD

Alternatively, you could open the file example1_1.cpp on the companion CD-ROM and copy its contents into hello.cpp. You could also use example1_1.cpp directly (this is what the book will do from now on), but for this one you probably should create a .cpp file yourself and type in the text just to make sure your source code editor is set up properly for when you will create your own programs.

3. Save the hello.cpp file.
4. Compile the file, using the commands and formats specified by your compiler's manufacturer. For example, if you are using the free Borland C++ toolkit (version 5.5) under Windows, you will need to launch a command prompt window and type in:

```
bcc32 hello.cpp
```

Figure 1.1 is a screenshot of the compilation process using the free Borland C++ toolkit under Windows XP.

5. If the compiler generates an error, make sure you have not made a mistake in transcribing the text; as mentioned earlier, programming languages tend to be rather unforgiving of imprecise syntax or grammar. Fix the problems and try again until compilation succeeds.
6. Run the program by typing its name at the command prompt or by clicking on the executable file's icon, depending on your system setup. You should see a little "Hello, World!" message appear on screen, as in Figure 1.2.

FIGURE 1.1   Compiling the "Hello, World!" program.

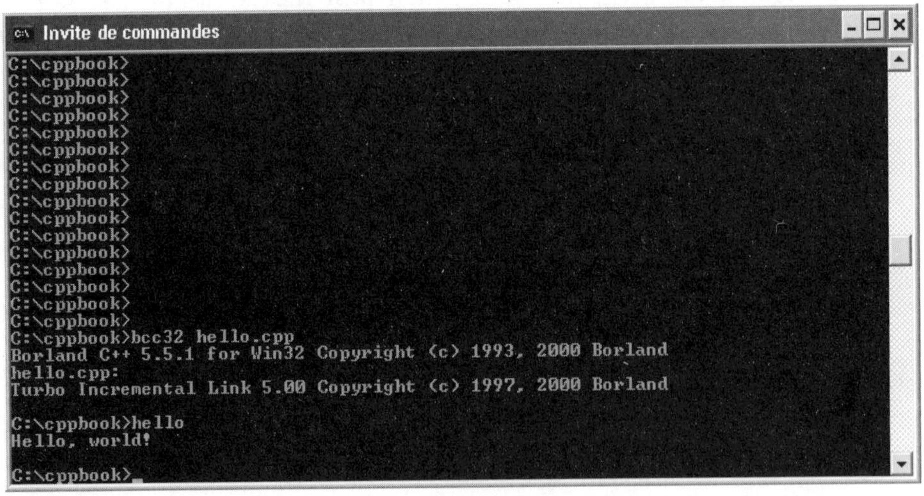

FIGURE 1.2   Execution of the "Hello, World!" program.

PROGRAM STRUCTURE: FILES, NAMESPACES, AND BLOCKS

Now, let us take a quick look at the contents of the "Hello, World!" program from Listing 1.1. First, you can start with the four lines enclosed by the slashes as shown in Listing 1.2.

LISTING 1.2   Hello World.

```
/************************************
Learn C++ by Making Games
Example 1.1
************************************/
```

In C++, everything enclosed within /* and */ is a *comment*. Comments are ignored by the compiler, so you can put whatever you want in there: your name, a description of your program, a copyright notice, and so forth. Indeed, if you remove these four lines and compile the program again, nothing will change in the result. The next section, "Programming Style," discusses comments in more detail.

Next comes the line shown in Listing 1.3.

LISTING 1.3   Hello World.

```
#include <iostream>
```

This is a *preprocessor directive* that tells the compiler that you will be using functions declared in the `iostream` library, which provides keyboard input and text output. You will be learning more about input/output functionality in Chapter 3, and you will revisit the `#include` directive in Part III concerning functions and libraries.

Next, you declare the *standard namespace* with the line shown in Listing 1.4.

LISTING 1.4   Hello World.

```
using namespace std;
```

To understand the need for a namespace, consider Springfield, Massachussetts, and Springfield, Illinois. Both cities bear the same name, so if you want to identify one without risking confusion with the other, you have to specify its home state every time. However, if everyone involved in a conversation is aware that the topic of discussion will be current events in Illinois, then repeating "Springfield, Illinois" time and time again is unneccessary. The same kind of phenomenon is at play here: by declaring that you will be using the standard namespace, you are "importing" all of the names that exist in that space into your program and will be able to use them without specifiying that they come from the standard namespace every time—just as if you were saying that, from now on, all city names that are mentioned would refer to cities located in Illinois.

With simple programs like the one you are writing now, declaring a namespace is not strictly required, but it is always good practice. You will briefly revisit namespaces in Part III of this book.

Then, you reach the program's main function shown in Listing 1.5.

LISTING 1.5 Hello World.

```
int main()
{
  cout << "Hello, world!" << endl;
  return 0;
}
```

The first line states that you are declaring a function called `main()`, and that this function will be returning a value of type integer. Every program has a `main()` function; this is where execution automatically begins when there is more than one function in the program. The reason for the parentheses will become clear when you learn more about function parameters in Part III.

The rest of the program is enclosed within a pair of curly brackets, { and }. Everything within such a pair is a *C++ block*, a collection of statements that belong together and are sometimes treated as one. You will be covering more examples of blocks in Part II.

The first line within the block is a statement that tells C++ to print some text to the screen. The `cout` statement is part of the `iostream` library, which you have included into the program with the `#include` directive; without the `#include`, the compiler would generate an error and tell you that it did not know what `cout` meant, just like you might not know what the White House is if you had never heard of the United States. (Go ahead, try it: remove the `#include` directive and try to compile the program again.)

Finally, the `return` statement tells C++ that it is time to exit the `main()` function, which will end the program and return control to the operating system. All functions require a `return` statement; the number following it in this case is the function's *return value*. There will be more talk about return values in Part III.

It is a lot to take in at once, but do not worry: You will get back to each of these topics in its own time. For now, just familiarize yourself with the structure of the program, make sure you can compile it, and maybe play around with the text to be printed on screen.

PROGRAMMING STYLE

Now, even though you may never have seen a computer program before today, you will certainly agree that the source code in Listing 1.6:

LISTING 1.6   Hello World.

```
int main()
{
  cout << "Hello, world!" << endl;
  return 0;
}
```

appears to make more sense than the code snippet shown in Listing 1.7.

LISTING 1.7   *Hello World.*

```
    int
main

(
    ){cout
<<"Hello, world!"<<endl;return 0;}
```

Interestingly enough, from the compiler's perspective, the preceding two code snippets are the same!

Indenting Programs

With very few exceptions (notably the fact that preprocessor directives must be left aligned), C++ does not care how you format and indent your source code. However, the same cannot be said of the other human beings who will read your programs, whether they are your instructors, your coworkers, or your teammates. Making sure code is as clear as possible is very important: Imagine being forced to scan through 5,000 lines of badly mangled C++, written by a complete stranger, to try to find a critical bug!

ON THE CD

There are no absolute standards for program indentation, but this book follows a relatively common convention. Observe the code samples in the book and on the companion CD-ROM; you will notice that blocks are aligned in a certain way to allow the reader to trace the flow of execution easily, the same information always appears in the same way, and so forth. Remember, other people may need to understand your programs someday—and if you revisit your old code six months from now, you will be glad you wrote it cleanly, too!

Commenting Your Code

Even at the best of times, C++ is not as easy to understand as human languages are. To make it easier for others to read your code (or to help yourself remember why you made a particular choice weeks or months after the fact), you should comment your code liberally.

There are two ways to add comments to your C++ programs:

■ Everything between /* and */ is a comment, no matter if it is a couple of characters or several pages' worth of text.
■ Everything that follows a pair of slashes (e.g., //) until the end of the current line is a comment.

Some examples are shown in Listing 1.8.

LISTING 1.8   Examples of comments.

```
/* This is a comment
   that is split over
   several lines */

// This is a single-line comment

cout << "Hello!";  // This part of the line is a comment
```

TIP

Comments can be used as debugging tools. If your program is producing erroneous results and you want to determine which piece of code is the culprit, you may want to comment out a few lines at a time and observe the program's behavior. For example, Listing 1.9 contains a cout *statement that will be ignored because the // has turned it into a comment.*

LISTING 1.9   Commented output.

```
// cout << "Hello!";
```

Finally, be careful that you do not accidentally comment out something valuable. The code snippet in Listing 1.10 will compile but will not do anything. Why?

LISTING 1.10   Bug.

```
/* A mistake /*
cout << "Hello!" << endl;
```

The reason is that the comment's opening marker, /*, is not matched by a closing */ pair. Look at the end of the comment line: Instead of closing the comment, we have inadvertently typed the /* pair that normally begins another comment. Since the new pair is itself within a comment, it is ignored, and so is everything else until the next */ appears in the source code. Since in this case we have no */ pair at all, the entire code snippet is treated as a comment!

Comment Frequency

Of course, since comments are ignored by the compiler, you can have as few or as many of them in your code as you want, including none. From the compiler's perspective, it will not change a thing. Comments are all about programmer convenience.

Therefore, you should add comments whenever it makes sense for you to do so; for example, to explain a tricky bit of code to a future reader, or to leave notes for yourself regarding work that remains to be done. The code included in this book and the accompanying CD-ROM is commented rather heavily because it is designed to teach you how to program. As a rule, you are better off erring on the side of caution by writing too many comments, because source code has a tendency to live for a long time and go through many hands before it is retired. For example, much of the software that was originally written in the 1960s was still in use at the turn of the millenium, and new generations of programmers had to upgrade this code to avoid the so-called Y2K bug long after its original authors had reached the end of their careers.

SUMMARY

Computers are powerful tools, but programming them requires a methodical approach. Since computers are unable to handle ambiguity, you cannot communicate with them using human languages; instead, hundreds of formal programming languages have been developed over the years.

C++ is a widespread object-oriented programming language that provides high performance and portability between systems.

In this chapter, we took a first look at a C++ program and its structure.

Finally, we hinted at the importance of using proper style when writing source code: Consistent indentation and liberal amounts of relevant comments will make the code more understandable to colleagues, teammates, and even to the author once the writing of the code is no longer fresh in memory.

EXERCISES

1.1 What is the difference between a human language and a computer language?
1.2 What is the difference between an algorithm and a program?

1.3 What is the relationship between source code, object code, and compilers?

1.4 Which of the following are valid ways to comment out the word *Rabbit*?

/*rabbit*/
//rabbit
// /* */ rabbit
rabbit //
 rabbit /*
 rabbit /*

2 Identifiers, Variables, and Constants

In This Chapter

- C++ Identifiers
- C++ Keywords
- Basic Data Types
- Literals
- Variables
- Constants
- Storage Modifiers
- More Constants: Enumerated Types
- The `typedef` Keyword
- Character Strings
- Programming Style: Naming Conventions

ON THE CD All Listing code in this chapter can be found on the companion CD-ROM

In this chapter, we will begin to investigate the syntax of the C++ language by looking at *identifiers*, which are the names you can give to memory locations, pieces of code, and other program-space entities. We will then look at C++'s *data types* and the various pieces of data you can declare in your programs. At the end of this chapter, you will be able to reserve memory for *variables*, create *constants* that will make your programs clearer, and understand how to choose identifiers that carry meaning and simplify program understanding.

C++ IDENTIFIERS

In the early days of programming, before high-level languages like C++ were invented, programmers had to write machine code by hand. Among other things, this meant that they had to refer to memory addresses explicitly—an impractical thing, since memory addresses typically look like 0xED32125A and most programs need to manipulate dozens (or thousands) of pieces of data.

It soon became obvious that a better solution would be required as programs grew in complexity. In C++, as in all other contemporary programming languages, the solution is to give memory addresses meaningful names called *identifiers*, which are easier to remember and to understand than the addresses themselves. (After all, it is easier to remember the name of the Louvre than to memorize its street address of: 99, rue de Rivoli, in Paris, France.)

In C++, the rules governing identifiers are fairly simple:

- An identifier must begin with a letter or an underscore character.
- Every character afterwards must be an underscore, a letter, or a digit.
- Identifiers are case-sensitive. For example, myname and MyName are two different identifiers.
- Several identifiers are reserved as keywords by the language and cannot be redefined by programmers; see the next section for details.

Table 2.1 lists examples of valid and invalid identifiers.

TABLE 2.1   Valid and Invalid Identifiers

Identifier	Valid?	If Invalid, Why?
anIdentifier	Yes	
xyz123	Yes	
_keyboard	Yes	
length_of_rectangle	Yes	
123xyz	No	An identifier cannot begin with a digit.
address home	No	The @ character is not a legal component of an identifier.
$amount	No	C++ does not allow the dollar sign in identifiers.

There is no upward limit to the length of an identifier, and longer identifiers do not necessarily mean that the amount of memory they are associated with is larger; only the data type determines the amount of memory associated with an identifier.

Also note that, while it is legal to begin an identifier with an underscore, it is rarely a good idea for a programmer to do so. By convention, this form is usually reserved to system variables and functions.

C++ KEYWORDS

As mentioned earlier, C++ reserves certain identifiers as language keywords. Programmers cannot redefine these keywords or the compiler will generate an error. The list of keywords appears in Table 2.2.

TABLE 2.2   C++ Keywords

asm	do	if	signed	typename
auto	double	int	sizeof	union
bool	dynamic_cast	long	static	unsigned
break	else	mutable	static_cast	using
case	enum	namespace	struct	virtual
catch	explicit	new	switch	void
char	export	operator	template	volatile
class	extern	private	this	wchar_t
const	false	public	throw	while
const_cast	float	register	true	inline
continue	for	reinterpret_cast	try	protected
default	friend	return	typedef	
delete	goto	short	typeid	

Note that all of these keywords are lowercase; also note that not all compilers implement every keyword yet, so it is possible that yours might allow you to redefine one or more of the keywords, but then your program would not be portable.

BASIC DATA TYPES

Many of C++'s keywords are used to define elementary data types. Table 2.3 is a list of these types.

TABLE 2.3   Basic Data Types

Type	Data It Is Designed to Contain
bool	Boolean truth value; i.e., the keywords true and false.
char	A single character.
wchar_t	A single "wide character"; i.e., a Unicode character.
short	Relatively short integer numbers. Equivalent to short int.
int	Integer numbers.
long	Relatively long integer numbers. Equivalent to long int.
float	Single-precision floating-point numbers.
double	Double-precision floating-point numbers.
long double	Very large floating-point numbers.
void	No data at all.

Types char, short, int, and long can be qualified as either signed or unsigned, which changes the range of values they can represent. What that range might actually *be*, however, is implementation-dependent; among the integer types, for example, all the C++ standard requires is that an int must hold at least as much memory as a short, and a long must hold at least as much memory as an int. In theory, nothing prevents a particular compiler from defining all of these types as being the same. In practice, int and float typically hold 32-bit values, double is usually 64-bits, and char is nearly always 8-bits. Check your compiler's documentation for details.

When signed or unsigned is used by itself, without long, int, short, or char, it means signed int or unsigned int.

LITERALS

A *literal* is a value that has no name, never changes, but belongs to a certain data type. Examples of literals include:

- The integer literals 12, 0, and −100
- The char literals "a," "z," and "D"
- The boolean literal `false`

char **Literals**

In C++, literals of type char are represented as a single character enclosed in single quotes. For example, 'a' and 'z.'

However, there are exceptions:

- The single quote character itself is represented by the sequence '\'' (quote, back-slash, quote, quote) with the backslash-quote pair \' in the middle known as an escape sequence. Generally speaking, a backslash located before a character tells C++ that this character should not be interpreted in the usual fashion.
- Other examples of escape sequences include the newline character \n, the tab-ulator \t, the double quote \" , the question mark \?, the null character \0, and the backslash character \\.

float **and** long **Literals**

By default, an integer literal will be assumed to be of type int, and a floating-point literal to belong to type double, as long as the value of the literal fits within the boundaries of the relevant type as defined by the compiler. To force a literal to belong to a different type, we can append a type indicator to the literal:

- To force a literal to be of type long, add a lowercase l to the end of the number, as in `123451`.
- To force a literal to be of type float, add a lowercase f to the end of the number, as in `1.234f`.

Scientific Notation

It is possible to represent floating-point literals in scientific notation by using a lowercase e to replace the 10 usually employed in mathematics. Note that C++ requires the exponent part of any floating-point number written in scientific notation to be an integer. For example:

- 3.2×10^4 is written as 3.2e4.
- -1.31×10^{-2} is written as −1.31e−2.
- 1.4e0.3 is invalid because the exponent part is not an integer.

VARIABLES

A *variable* is an identifier that gives a name to an area of memory. In C++, each variable has a type and it must be declared to the compiler before it can be used.

Listing 2.1 has some examples of valid variable declarations.

LISTING 2.1 Variable declarations.

```
// to declare a single integer variable
int theTemperature;

// to declare a boolean variable
bool isMarried;

// to declare a single unsigned long integer
unsigned long population;

// to declare several variables at the same time, separate
// them with commas in the declaration statement
float account1, account2, account3;
```

Variables can be declared anywhere in a program, but most often just before they are used for the first time. When the compiler encounters a variable declaration statement, it reserves some space in memory for the variable (the amount of memory depends on the variable's data type) and associates the variable's name with this space.

Note that every variable declaration statement ends with a semicolon. The same will be true of every other C++ statement. Don't forget the semicolon or the compiler will generate an error.

Initializing Variables

You can choose to initialize your variables to some arbitrary value when you declare them. (Actually, this is very good practice, because until you explicitly store some value in a variable, it can contain anything at all. If you use an uninitialized variable in your code, the results can be unpredictable.)

To initialize a variable, add the equal sign and the value to the declaration statement as demonstrated in Listing 2.2.

LISTING 2.2   Declarations.

```
// a bunch of initialized variables
int myAge = 34;
bool hasChildren = true;
double interestRate = 0.125;
float stockPrice = 35.35f;
```

CONSTANTS

Another type of C++ identifier is the *constant*, which (as its name suggests) is a piece of data that never changes during execution. To declare a constant, follow the variable rules you just learned, but add the keyword const in front of the declaration as shown in Listing 2.3.

LISTING 2.3   Const.

```
// constant declarations
const float PI_RATIO = 3.1415926f;
const unsigned short PLAYERS_ON_TEAM = 10;
```

The difference between a variable and a constant is that the compiler will generate an error if any instruction in the program tries to modify the value of the constant. Thus, declaring constants is a type of safeguard: The compiler will find the error, so you will not have to do so at runtime.

NOTE

Note that all constants must be initialized as soon as they are declared—since they are constants and cannot be changed, if they were not initialized immediately, they could never acquire any value at all later!

Constants and Literals

There are many reasons why you might want to declare constants in your programs instead of using literals. For example:

To give intuitive meaning to a value. It is easier to understand the constant CALGARY_POPULATION than to guess that a certain literal in the millions is referring to the number of people living in Cowtown.

To save time and avoid mistakes. Typing the constant name PI 100 times is much faster than typing 3.141592653589793f 100 times, and also much less likely to lead to error.

To differentiate between identical values. Suppose you are programming a baseball game. In baseball, there are nine players to a side, and a game normally lasts nine innings. Without constants, it may be more difficult for a reader to guess whether a specific instance of the number 9 in the source code is referring to players, innings, or something entirely unrelated to either.

To facilitate maintenance. The baseball game we just mentioned probably refers to the number of teams in the league many times, in all areas of the code. If the league ever expands or contracts its ranks, it will be easier to change the initialization of a single constant than to hunt down dozens of lines of code and change the value by hand every time.

Using Constants

Once a constant has been declared and initialized, it can be used anywhere a literal could be, including in initializing variables. An example is shown in Listing 2.4.

LISTING 2.4   Constant example.

```
const int STARTING_SCORE = 1000;
int myScore = STARTING_SCORE;      //myScore is now 1000.
```

Preprocessor Constants

There is another way to declare constants in C++, which is inherited from its predecessor language, C. It is through the preprocessor directive #define with an example provided in Listing 2.5.

LISTING 2.5   #Define.

```
#define MY_CONSTANT 5

//set the myVariable variable to the value of MY_CONSTANT
//which is 5
int myVariable = MY_CONSTANT;
```

Note that the syntax is different this time: the #define directive requires neither the equal sign nor the semicolon (and will in fact generate an error at compilation if you add either one).

Like the #include directive we encountered in Chapter 1, #define performs its magic before the compiler translates the source code into object code; in this case, #define actually replaces the identifier MY_CONSTANT with the literal 5 in the source code before feeding it to the compiler.

The main differences between a `#define` constant and a `const` constant are that the `#define` constant does not have an explicit type of its own, and it is not stored in memory. Since types are an important part of C++, and since you may need to refer to constant data in memory from time to time, it is recommended to use the `const` constants in most cases, but the two categories are often interchangeable.

STORAGE MODIFIERS

Although they are rarely used in games, two additional modifiers (besides `const`) can apply to variables: `register` and `volatile` shown in Listing 2.6.

LISTING 2.6   Storage modifiers.

```
register int superFastInt;
volatile float temperatureFromThermometer;
```

- `register` tells the compiler that the variable should, whenever possible, be stored in a CPU register instead of main memory, for the sake of performance. This modifier is rarely used these days, as compilers are often much better at optimizing the use of registers, cache, and main memory than programmers themselves.
- `volatile` tells the compiler that the value of the variable can change at any time, outside of the programmer's control, and that the compiler should double-check the value every time the variable is referred to in the program. A good example of a `volatile` variable would be one that is connected to the gamepad: you never know when the player will press a button, so you can never assume that every button is free even if you just checked it half a second ago.

Note that while it is technically possible to declare a piece of data as both `const` and `volatile`, which would seem to imply that the program cannot change it but that some external process (like the gamepad) could do it at any time, most compilers will treat this piece of data as constant and ignore the volatile part.

MORE CONSTANTS: ENUMERATED TYPES

So far, all the constants that have been defined have been names given to specific values. However, sometimes, what are needed are the names themselves, and the values are of little importance. For this purpose, C++ provides the *enumerated type*.

Enumerated types are simply lists of names that carry some meaning within the program. For example, in a card game, you might want to define constants to represent the four suits. You could do it as shown in Listing 2.7.

LISTING 2.7   Card defines.

```
const int spades = 0;
const int clubs = 1;
const int diamonds = 2;
const int hearts = 3;
int myCard = diamonds;     // a card
```

Or, with an enumerated type, you could do it as demonstrated in Listing 2.8.

LISTING 2.8   Other card defines.

```
enum { spades, clubs, diamonds, hearts };
int myCard = diamonds;
```

Internally, the two are equivalent: in C++, enumerated constants are considered integers; the first constant in an enumerated list is given the value zero by default, and all the others receive values one higher than their predecessor. However, in this case, you are no longer manipulating the numbers explicitly, although the variable myCard is still of type int.

You can go one step further and *create a brand new type* for the cards by changing the declaration of the enumeration, shown in Listing 2.9.

LISTING 2.9   New type.

```
enum eCardSuits { spades, clubs, diamonds, hearts };
eCardSuits myCard = diamonds;
```

You have given the type name eCardSuits to the enumeration, and now the variable is of type eCardSuits, which is somewhat more explicit than type int. (You could still have declared myCard to be of type int, and C++ would not have complained: remember that enumerated constants are integers.)

Finally, it is also possible to initialize enumerated constants to values of your choice (as long as they are integers) instead of letting C++ decide. For example, the following declaration of a set of constants to represent temperatures would be perfectly valid, and can serve as shorthand for defining them all individually (while providing a new type in the process) shown in Listing 2.10.

LISTING 2.10   Constant set.

```
enum eTemperatures { frigid = -20, cold = 0, chilly = 10,
comfy = 20, hot = 30 };
```

THE `typedef` KEYWORD

In the previous section, you created new enumerated data types that are interchangeable with integers. It is also possible to create all sorts of other new type names with the `typedef` keyword, an example of which is shown in Listing 2.11.

LISTING 2.11 `typedef` example.

```
typedef double tMoneyValue;
tMoneyValue myAccountBalance = 200000.0;
```

You will use `typedef` later when you come across more advanced data types, like the pointers in Part V.

CHARACTER STRINGS

The last data type we will study in this chapter is the *character string*, which is used to store text.

String Literals

In C++, string literals are written between double quotes. Since a string is a collection of characters, anything that can be represented by a `char` variable (including escape sequences) can appear within a string. Examples of string literals include:

- "This is a string"
- "This is a line\nAnd this is another"

String Variables

The data type for strings is `string`. However, it is not an elementary data type like `int` or `float`, but rather a *class*, and each string variable, a C++ *object*. You will learn more about classes, objects, and the many features of the `string` type in Part VI; for now, you can treat strings like any other variable, but make sure you declare usage of the standard namespace, as in Example 2.1 shown in Listing 2.12, or the compiler may not recognize the `string` type.

LISTING 2.12

```
/***********************************
  Learn C++ by Making Games
  Example 2.1
 ***********************************/
```

```
#include <iostream>
using namespace std;


int main()
{
  const string myString = "This is chapter 2.";

  cout << myString << endl;
  return 0;
}
```

 C++ also supports the old C-style strings implemented as character arrays; you will learn more about them in Part IV. More detail on this object is also provided in Part IX of this book.

PROGRAMMING STYLE: NAMING CONVENTIONS

While C++'s rules regarding identifiers are very flexible, it is always a good idea to select a standard for the naming of the variables, constants, and other components in your programs. If all variable names, for example, are built according to the same template, it will be easier to identify them in the source code and to avoid frustrating mistakes.

Perhaps unfortunately, there are no industry-wide standards in this area, although some methods have become more popular than others. This book will follow these rules:

Variables: All variable names begin with a lowercase letter. Words are concatenated together without a separating underscore. The first letter of every word after the first will be capitalized. Ex.: aVariableName.

Constants: Constant names are written in all caps, with underscores between words. Ex.: NUMBER_OF_LIVES.

Enumerated types: Like variables, but the name of the type will begin with a lowercase "e." Ex.: eCardSuits.

Typedef types: Like enumerated types, but the first letter will be a "t." Ex.: tMoneyAccount.

Other rules governing the naming of functions, structures, and classes will become obvious as these concepts are introduced later in the book.

Meaningful Names

It goes without saying that you should choose identifier names that carry meaning. A variable intended to store the number of lives that the player of a game has accumulated should be called `numberOfLives`, not `vader123`; otherwise, the program will quickly become unmanageable.

SUMMARY

This chapter introduced C++ identifiers, which are names given to items stored in memory. Identifiers are case-sensitive and begin with a letter or an underscore, followed by an arbitrary number of letters, digits, and underscores. C++ reserves about 50 keywords that can't be redefined as identifiers by the programmer. While C++ allows a great deal of freedom in naming identifiers, it is always a good idea to adhere to a standard to keep the program easy to read.

Among the various types of identifiers, variables are used to store data in memory while constants give names to immutable values. Both variables and constants (except the old C-style constants declared with the `#define` preprocessor directive) belong to data types like `int`, `char`, `float`, `double`, `long`, `short`, or `string`.

Enumerated types are collections of constants that are usually defined for the sake of having meaningful names to manipulate rather than for their values. You can also define your own data types using the `typedef` keyword.

EXERCISES

2.1   Are the following declarations valid or not? If not, why?

```
a)   const int accountNumber;
b)   long a, b, c;
c)   char grade1 = 'A', grade2 = 'C+';
d)   string playerName = "Anthony Player";
e)   short theFilm = 125;
f)   float interestRate = 5.25e-2;
g)   bool isMarried = false;
h)   int score1 = 10, score2 = 200, score 3 = 5;
i)   int float myAverage = 12.5;
j)   double goto = 15.2;
```

2.2   Why is it a good idea to initialize variables as soon as they are declared?

2.3   What is the difference between a literal and a constant?

2.4   Would the following code snippet compile without error?

```cpp
enum eColors { blue, red, green };
int paintCan = yellow;
```

2.5   Would the following code snippet compile without error?

```cpp
int myAge = 34;
int yourAge = MyAge;
```

3   Input and Output

In This Chapter

- Setting up the C++ Console
- Printing Messages to the Screen with cout
- Reading Data from the Keyboard with cin
- The cerr Error Stream

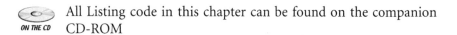 All Listing code in this chapter can be found on the companion

ON THE CD   CD-ROM

In this chapter, you will learn how to use the "console input-output" functionality provided by C++'s iostream library. In this context, "console" refers to a text window on your screen, not to a special-purpose game platform; depending on your compiler, operating system, and development environment, the console can be the window from which you have launched the program's execution, a new window created at program startup, or a special area of the integrated development environment. Whichever the case, you will be able to use the console to print messages to the user and to input data from the keyboard.

SETTING UP THE C++ CONSOLE

Technically, the C++ text input and output functionality is not a part of the core language. It has rather been packaged into a library called `iostream`, which we already encountered in Chapter 1. You must include this library and tell the compiler about the names of the functions and objects from the library that you will be using in your program before you can invoke any of them. If you try to write code that uses the `iostream` functions without including the library, the compiler will not understand what you are saying and will generate an error.

There are two ways to import the names of the `iostream` entities into your program.

Importing All of `iostream`

First, you can include the library and import all of its components, as shown in Chapter 1:

```
#include <iostream>
using namespace std;
```

This tells C++ to import the names of every entity declared in the standard namespace (`std`) into your program. Since everything in `iostream` is part of the standard namespace, this gives you access to all `iostream` components (plus much more) at one stroke and is therefore the most common way to do things.

Importing Individual `iostream` Components

Alternatively, you can declare only the components of the `iostream` library you want to make available to your program. Assuming that you need `cin`, `cout`, and `endl`, you would write the declarations shown in Listing 3.1.

LISTING 3.1   Individual declarations.

```
#include <iostream>
using std::cin;
using std::cout;
using std::endl;
```

The two colons between `std` and `cin`, `cout` and `endl` are called the *scope operator*; you will see this operator frequently in other contexts beginning in Part VI.

Since you are likely to want access to non-`iostream` entities that belong to the standard namespace in your programs, this method will seldom be the most appropriate, but it works.

PRINTING MESSAGES TO THE SCREEN WITH cout

All programs need to provide their users with textual feedback, whether in the form of computation results, questions to answer, menu choices, or messages of warning. The iostream library contains cout, an entity that handles all such screen output. cout is an *output stream*, a particular kind of object that is designed to send data elsewhere; in this case, to the screen.

Technically, cout sends its data to the system's standard output, not to the screen. It just so happens that, by default, the standard output is the screen on just about every system in existence. However, some operating systems (including Unix) allow the user to redirect the standard output, so instead of being sent to the screen the program's output will be diverted to a file or to another process' input stream; see your operating system documentation for details.

To send a message to the screen, write a statement as shown in Listing 3.2.

LISTING 3.2   cout.

```
cout << "This is my message!";
```

The << (a pair of smaller-than signs without any blank space between them) located between cout and the message is called an *insertion operator*, because it inserts a message into the stream. You can chain as many insertions as you want, on a single line or in many consecutive lines, provided that you *do not* separate them with a semicolon; after a semicolon, you must start a new insertion statement with cout again. Listing 3.3 provides some clarification.

LISTING 3.3   Insertion operator.

```
// Valid
cout << "One" << "Two" << "Three";
cout << "One"
     << "Two"
     << "Three";

// Invalid
cout << "One"; << "Two"; << "Three";

// Valid again
cout << "One";
cout << "Two";
cout << "Three";
```

TIP
Remember that the insertion operator looks like a double arrow pointing toward cout.

Virtually anything can be inserted into cout: literals, variables, constants, and many other C++ constructs that you will encounter in later chapters. A larger example is shown in Listing 3.4.

LISTING 3.4

```
/***********************************
 Learn C++ by Making Games
 Example 3.1: Experimenting with cout
***********************************/

#include <iostream>
using namespace std;

int main()
{
  // First, let's print a message
  cout << "Hello, world!";

  // Then, let's print a number
  cout << 34;

  // And we're done!
  return 0;
}
```

In this example, you have printed two literals: the string "Hello, world!" and the integer number 34. The statement structure is identical in both cases: the name of the stream that will receive the message (cout), the insertion operator, and then the message to be printed. Figure 3.1 shows the result of Example 3.1's execution:

Now, if you look at the screen shot carefully, you will notice that there is a slight bug in the program: the two messages are printed side by side, on the same line, without any separation. Why?

Using endl and '\n'

The answer is that C++ requires you to specify carriage returns explicitly; after all, it is entirely possible that you might have wanted to print more than one message on the same line, as you will soon do.

To force a line change, you have two options:

■ You can insert a newline character, '\n', into cout, either by itself or as part of a string literal, variable, or constant.

FIGURE 3.1   Two messages output on the same line.

■   You can insert the special constant endl into cout.
    Example 3.2 shown in Listing 3.5 details both methods in action.

LISTING 3.5

```
/***********************************
 Learn C++ by Making Games
 Example 3.2: More fun with cout
***********************************/

#include <iostream>
using namespace std;

int main()
{
  // First, let's print a message
  string myHello = "This is Chapter 3 already?";
  cout << myHello << endl;

  // Then, let's print a couple of integers
  int myScore = 100, yourScore = 75;
  cout << myScore << " " << yourScore << endl;

  // Then, let's mix and match content types
  const double primeRate = 4.85;
  cout << "Today's prime rate is " << primeRate << " percent.\n";
```

```
    // And we're done!
    return 0;
}
```

First, you insert the string variable myHello into cout, followed by an endl. This tells C++ to change lines before the next message. Note that the endl appears by itself, not within quotes; otherwise, C++ would print the message "endl" instead of changing lines!

Then, you output a complex message made up of an integer, a blank space, another integer, and an endl. Without the blank space, the two integers would be stuck together; instead of "100 75," it would read the single number "10075."

Finally, a third message is printed made up of a string literal, a double-precision floating-point constant, and another string that ends with the newline character '\n'. Note that the newline character is a part of the string; if you wanted to insert it into cout by itself, you would need to enclose it with single quotes as shown in Listing 3.6.

LISTING 3.6   Newline.

```
cout << message << '\n';
```

At the very least, you should insert an endl or a newline into cout at the end of each block of output; otherwise, there is a chance that C++ won't output the text immediately. This might be very awkward if the message you want to print is a prompt for the user to type in some data at the keyboard: if the message is not sent to the screen immediately, the user might not know that he is expected to provide data and might think the program has frozen.

Figure 3.2 shows what happens when Example 3.2 is executed.

The endl constant and the newline character can be used interchangeably, and you can even mix and match them within a single statement. Some programmers like to use newline when outputting string literals and endl in other cases, but it's a matter of personal taste.

If you insert multiple newlines or endls in a row, the output will skip as many lines as there are newlines and endls before printing the next message.

READING DATA FROM THE KEYBOARD WITH cin

cin ("console input") is to the keyboard what cout is to the screen: a special object that allows data input into the program.

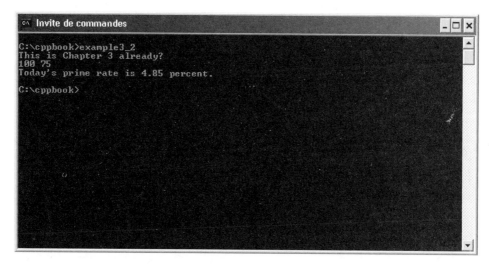

FIGURE 3.2   Messages output on different lines.

To read an integer, character, or floating-point value from the keyboard and store it into a variable, you will need to write statements like Listing 3.7.

LISTING 3.7   Reading.

```
int myChoice;
cin >> myChoice;

float temperatureMax, temperatureMin;
cin >> temperatureMax >> temperatureMin;
```

The >> operator (a pair of greater-than signs without any space between them) is called an *extraction operator*, because it extracts data from the cin input stream. The extraction operator works very much like the insertion operator, only in reverse; in the case of the temperature readings in Listing 3.7, the system will look for the first floating-point value entered on the keyboard, store it into temperatureMax (the first variable in the extraction chain), and then look for another value to store into temperatureMin.

Example 3.3 shows how to extract integers from cin, which is detailed in Listing 3.8.

LISTING 3.8

```
/*************************************
 Learn C++ by Making Games
 Example 3.3: Keyboard input
```

```
**********************************/

#include <iostream>
using namespace std;

int main()
{
  // Prompt the user for data
  cout << "Type in three integer numbers:" << endl;

  // Read in the three values
  int a, b, c;
  cin >> a >> b >> c;

  // Give feedback
  cout << "I understood: "
       << a << ", "
       << b << ", and "
       << c;

  // And let's try again
  cout << ". Now, type three more: " << endl;
  cin >> a >> b >> c;
  cout << "This time, I understood: "
       << a << ", "
       << b << ", and "
       << c;

  // And we're done!
  return 0;
}
```

Technically, cin extracts data from the system's standard input, not necessarily from the keyboard, although the two are most often the same. Some systems, like Unix, allow users to redirect standard input so a program can read its data directly from a file or from the output of another application.

The Keyboard Input Buffer

When you type data on the keyboard, C++ will wait until you press the Enter key before sending the line of text to the *keyboard input buffer*, a special area of memory where keyboard data is stored until needed. Only then will the cin requests be fulfilled, in order. (This gives you time to correct typing mistakes before sending the data to the program; however, once you press Enter, the data entry is final.)

The rules governing input stream data extraction are somewhat fussy:

- C++ uses white spaces (and carriage returns) between values as separators. As long as there is a blank space or more between two values, they will be considered separate. C++ will ignore any additional spaces.
- If there are enough values in the input buffer to satisfy all outstanding cin requests, and they are of the *right* types, everything will work out fine. If the values are of the *wrong* types, C++ may try to translate, but the results are unlikely to be satisfactory.
- If there are *more* values in the input buffer than currently needed, the leftovers will be kept until the *next* cin request comes in and used to satisfy it. Since the next cin request may come as a response to a completely different question to the user, this behavior can lead to disaster.
- If there are *not enough* values in the input buffer, C++ will use whatever is there and wait for another line of input to come in, thus "freezing" the program until the user supplies enough data.

Figure 3.3 shows the results of three different executions of Example 3.3.

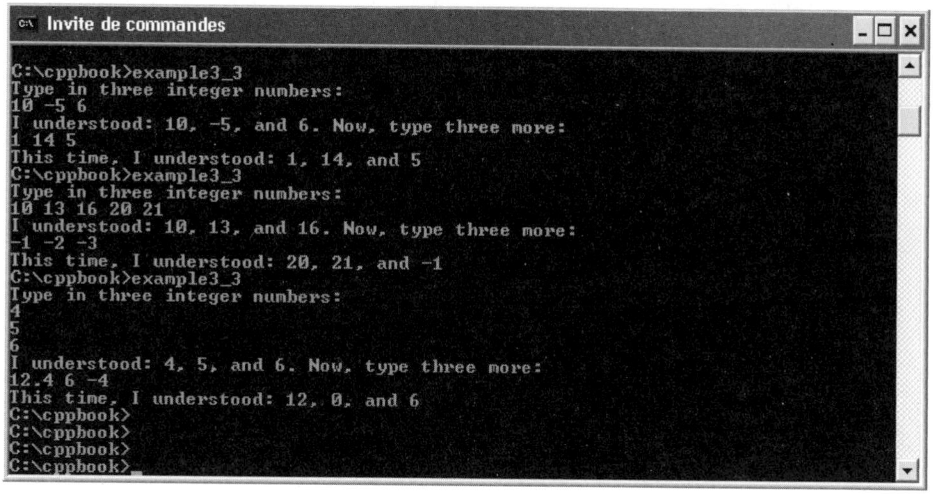

FIGURE 3.3 Keyboard input.

In the first instance, everything works out fine: in response to both of the program's prompts, the user provides the right types of data in the right amounts.

In the second case, however, the user has entered too much data at the first prompt (e.g., five numbers instead of three). Thus, the leftover numbers *20* and *21* stay in the input buffer and are sent to the program as part of the response to the second query. At the end of this second query, *–2* and *–3* are still in the buffer, ready to "pollute" the next cin request that comes along. (Since there are no more requests in this program, this data is lost forever since the contents of the input buffer are deleted at the end of execution.)

In the third case, the user types in the data required by the first request at the rate of one number per line. The program waits until it has enough data to fulfill the request before asking a second question. Then, the user types in a floating-point value instead of an integer and the entire process breaks down.

Input validation is always an important aspect of programming; we will discuss several relevant techniques later in the book.

Reading Strings

The >> operator is also able to extract strings from standard input, but only up to a point. Remember that >> uses blank spaces as a separator between values; therefore, it can only read "words," not complete sentences. To read an entire line of text into a string, you will have to use a function called getline; you will learn more about C++ functions in due time, but for now take a look at Example 3.4 detailed in Listing 3.9 and at its execution in Figure 3.4.

LISTING 3.9   Input.

```
/***********************************
 Learn C++ by Making Games
 Example 3.4: Reading strings
***********************************/

#include <iostream>
using namespace std;

int main()
{
  // Prompt the user for data
  cout << "Please enter two words:" << endl;

  // Read in the values
  string b, c;
  cin >> b >> c;

  // Give feedback
  cout << "I understood: "
       << b << ", and "
       << c << endl;

  // Now, let's read a whole line of text as a single entity
  cout << "Now, type in a whole line of text, "
       << "with as many blanks as you want:"
```

```
                    << endl;

        // getline() is a function; we'll talk more about them in Part 3
        string wholeLine;
        getline( cin, wholeLine );

        // In the cout statement below, remember that \"
        // is an escape sequence!
        cout << "I understood: \"" << wholeLine << "\"" << endl;

        // And we're done!
        return 0;
    }
```

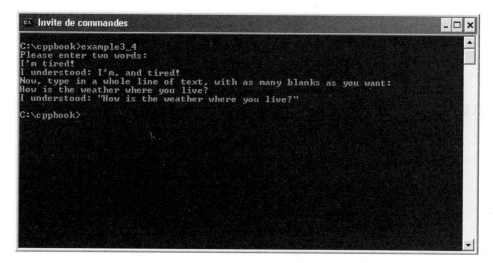

FIGURE 3.4   String input and output.

THE cerr ERROR STREAM

In addition to cout, the iostream library contains a second output stream, cerr, which is dedicated to error and warning messages. cerr behaves exactly as cout, and on most systems, messages inserted into cerr will be printed on screen, just as if they had been sent to cout. (In fact, messages sent to cout and to cerr may very well alternate in the same window.)

However, some systems, notably Unix, allow users to redirect cout's output one way and cerr's another; for example, by sending cout's messages to the screen and cerr's error messages to a log file for future processing. It is always good practice to use cout for normal program messages and cerr in case of abnormal program termination due to errors from which the program cannot recover; therefore, this book will be using `cerr` quite regularly.

SUMMARY

In this chapter, you learned how to display messages on screen and input data from the keyboard.

Standard output is performed using the `cout` object and the insertion operator, `<<`. To force a line change during output, you can insert a newline character or the special constant `endl` into `cout`.

Standard input is performed using `cin` and the extraction operator, `>>`. The input buffer follows strict rules of extraction, so improper data may lead to improper program execution. When reading whole lines of text, the extraction operator is insufficient; you must use the `getline()` function instead.

EXERCISES

3.1   Find the bug in this code snippet:

```
string myName = "Fred Rogers";
cout >> myName;
```

3.2   What is the difference between `cout` and `cerr`?

3.3   Will this program work?

```
#include <iostream>
int main()
{
  cout << "Hello, everyone!" << endl;
  return 0;
}
```

3.4   Why will this program generate an error?

```
#include <iostream>
using namespace std;

int main()
{
  const int NUMBER_OF_TEAMS = 10;
  cin >> NUMBER_OF_TEAMS;
```

```
  cout << "There are " << NUMBER_OF_TEAMS <<
      << " teams in our league." << endl;
  return 0;
}
```

3.5   Write a program that inputs three numbers from the keyboard and prints out all permutations of the numbers on screen.

3.6   Modify programming exercise 3.1 to use strings instead of numbers.

3.7   Write a program that enters the first and last names of a person and prints out a personalized welcoming message.

4 Game Project: Funny Headlines

In This Chapter

- The First Game
- Other Project Idea

 All Listing code in this chapter can be found on the companion CD-ROM

Even with the limited amount of C++ syntax in our arsenal, you can already develop a first simple game of Funny Headlines. This short program will also serve as a review example for Part I, bringing together variable declarations and input-output.

THE FIRST GAME

Funny Headlines is just about the simplest game that can be implemented in C++. It consists of two steps:

1. Asking the player a series of apparently unrelated questions.
2. Using the answers out of context to create weird (and hopefully entertaining) fake news headlines.

Let's examine the program, line by line, to review what was learned in Part I of the book.

First, you need to include the `iostream` library and declare that you will be using the standard namespace, so that `cout`, `cin`, and `endl` are available to the program as shown in Listing 4.1.

LISTING 4.1   Funny Headlines–part 1.

```
/***********************************
 Learn C++ by Making Games
 Project 4.1 - Game of Funny Headlines
 ***********************************/

#include <iostream>
using namespace std;
```

Then, you open the program's `main` function as shown in Listing 4.2.

LISTING 4.2   main().

```
int main()
{
```

You then send a greeting to the player and ask him a series of apparently unrelated questions. For each question, you declare a variable of the appropriate type, send a prompt to the user with a `cout` statement, and then input a value from the keyboard into the variable with a `cin` statement as detailed in Listing 4.3.

LISTING 4.3   Input.

```
// First, let's welcome the user
cout << "Welcome to the C++ News Network!" << endl << endl;

// Then, let's input several values to plug into our headlines.
// Note that the questions don't always match the names of the
// variables because we are trying to surprise the player.

string userName;
cout << "Please type in your first name: " << endl;
cin >> userName;

int smallNumber;
cout << "How many siblings do you have?" << endl;
cin >> smallNumber;
```

```
float largeNumber;
cout << "How much money would you like to earn every year?"
    << endl;
cin >> largeNumber;

string color;
cout << "Tell us your least favorite color:" << endl;
cin >> color;
```

There are a few more questions to ask the user, but this time the answer will be a string that may contain white spaces (for example, the full name of an actor), so you need to replace the simple cin statement with extraction operator with a get-line() function call as outlined in Listing 4.4.

LISTING 4.4 getline().

```
string amorphousObject;
cout << "Which vegetables have the weirdest shapes?" << endl;
getline( cin, amorphousObject );

string deadGuy;
cout << "Name a famous dead person:" << endl;
getline( cin, deadGuy );

string celebrityActor;
cout << "Who is your favorite actor?" << endl;
getline( cin, celebrityActor );

string politician;
cout << "Name a current world leader:" << endl;
getline( cin, politician );

string cartoonCharacter;
cout << "Who is your favorite cartoon character?" << endl;
getline( cin, cartoonCharacter );

string weirdGroup;
cout << "Name a hobby or a profession you find scary: " << endl;
getline( cin, weirdGroup );

string somethingGross;
cout << "Name a food item you detested as a child: " << endl;
getline( cin, somethingGross );
```

Now that you are done with the questions, it is time to assemble the answers into funny headlines with complex cout statements. If you insert endls into cout every time you need to change lines, insert an additional one or two to skip lines in the output as shown in Listing 4.5.

LISTING 4.5   Assembly.

```
// Finally, let's print out the headlines!
cout << endl << endl << endl
    << "And now, today's headlines from the C++ News Wire:"
    << endl;
cout << "-------------------------------------------------"
    << endl;

cout << "ALIENS SHAPED LIKE " << color << " " << amorphousObject
    << " INVADE THE EARTH, KIDNAP " << celebrityActor << ", "
    << "RESURRECT " << deadGuy << "!" << endl << endl;

cout << userName
    << " RELEASES NEW ALBUM! " << smallNumber
    << " COPIES EXPECTED TO BE SOLD!"
    << endl << endl;

cout << politician << " CAUGHT IN LOVE TRIANGLE WITH "
    << cartoonCharacter << " AND SECRET "
    << weirdGroup << " CULT LEADER!" << endl << endl;

cout << "WORLD'S LARGEST BABY BORN - WEIGHS " << largeNumber
    << " POUNDS, EATS " << smallNumber << " TONS OF "
    << somethingGross << " EVERY DAY!" << endl << endl;

// And we're done!
return 0;
}
```

That's it! You have a complete game; go try it out!

The complete source code for this project is included on the accompanying CD-ROM as Project4_1.cpp.

SUMMARY

In this chapter, you put together several concepts from Chapters 1 through 3 and assembled a simple word game out of them. Go ahead: compile the program, play with it, and then add your own headlines!

EXERCISES

4.1 Modify the program to allow the player to input a rank number of the kind of news they wish to see first. In other words, if the player enters a value of 1, then list the "serious" headlines before the "completely silly" ones.

4.2 Modify the program to display a line of dashes to separate each news item.

OTHER PROJECT IDEAS

Input a list of *10* names and high scores on the keyboard and print them as a nice, formatted table. Hint: You might want to use the tabulator character, '\t', or research your compiler's documentation about the formatting capabilities of cout.

Part

II

C++ Statements and Constructs

In this section, we will start manipulating data with C++ code, and will expand our programs beyond Part I's simple linear structures. We will discuss how to assign values to variables, perform arithmetic calculations, concatenate strings in memory, execute code if and only if some specific runtime condition is met, and use loop structures to execute the same code several times without having to resort to cutting and pasting statements. We will also study C++'s scope rules, which determine the life cycles of variables and constants.

At the end of this section, we will be able to write simple nonlinear programs, including a game of Nim, in which the object is to force the opponent to pick up the last of a pile of sticks—and since we will implement a simple computer player, we will also get our first taste of artificial intelligence!

5   C++ Operators

In This Chapter

- Assignment Operator
- Mathematical Operators
- The `static_cast` Operator
- Boolean Expressions and Logic Operators
- Relational Operators
- Bitwise Operators
- Shorthand Assignments
- Operator Priority

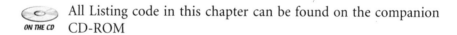 All Listing code in this chapter can be found on the companion
ON THE CD   CD-ROM

This chapter discusses C++'s *operators*, constructs that perform simple computations on data. You will study several categories of operators and identify which ones have priority over others. At the end of this chapter, you will be able to perform all sorts of mathematical calculations, evaluate the truth-values of expressions, and write complex statements that take into account operator precedence rules.

ASSIGNMENT OPERATOR

The *assignment operator* stores a value into a variable in memory. You have already encountered it: it is the equal sign (=) that you have been using to initialize variables and constants. The code snippet in Listing 5.1 shows a few examples of assignments involving variables of type `int`.

LISTING 5.1   Assignments.

```
int currentPlayer = 0;          // create and initialize
int otherPlayer = 3;            // create and initialize
currentPlayer = 2;              // currentPlayer is now 2
currentPlayer = otherPlayer;    // currentPlayer is now 3
otherPlayer = 0;                // otherPlayer is now 0,
// but currentPlayer is still 3.
```

An assignment statement should be interpreted as saying, "Take a copy of the value on the right-hand side of the assignment operator (in C++ parlance, the *rvalue*) and store it into the variable on the left side of the operator (the *lvalue*)." The assignment does not change the rvalue in any way, so any expression can become an rvalue, including a literal or a constant. On the other hand, since the purpose of an assignment is to change the lvalue, only variables can appear on the left side of an assignment. (Exception: When creating and initializing a constant, the constant is an lvalue, but only at this precise moment.)

Assignments do not create any lasting relationships between the lvalue and the rvalue. As you can see in the preceding code snippet, once you have copied the value of otherPlayer into currentPlayer, you can do whatever you want to otherPlayer and the change will not automatically propagate to currentPlayer. The two variables are separate in memory; you are just copying one into the other.

Swapping Values

You can further examine the properties of the assignment operator by developing a method to swap the values of two variables of type int, called homeTeamScore and awayTeamScore.

First, Listing 5.2 details a method that does not work.

LISTING 5.2   Swapping error.

```
// Initializations
int homeTeamScore = 100, awayTeamScore = 80;

// Try to swap
homeTeamScore = awayTeamScore;
awayTeamScore = homeTeamScore;
```

Why does this method fail? After all, you are telling the compiler to put awayTeamScore's value into homeTeamScore, and to put homeTeamScore's value into awayTeamScore, which is what you want, right?

The problem is that the computer completes the execution of the first assignment before looking at the second, so what happens is shown in Listing 5.3.

LISTING 5.3   Swapping—part 2.

```
homeTeamScore = awayTeamScore;  // homeTeamScore is now 80
awayTeamScore = homeTeamScore;  // We are copying 80 into
                                // awayTeamScore
```

homeTeamScore's old value, 100, is overwritten by the first assignment and lost. Thus, at the end of the snippet, both variables contain the same value. How do you avoid this problem? You must store a temporary copy of homeTeamScore as shown in Listing 5.4.

LISTING 5.4   Swapping—part 3.

```
// Initializations
int homeTeamScore = 100, awayTeamScore = 80;

// The right way to swap
// Start by making a temporary copy; temp will contain 100
int temp = homeTeamScore;

// Now give homeTeamScore its new value; both homeTeamScore
// and awayTeamScore will contain 80, as before
homeTeamScore = awayTeamScore;

// Now, retrieve the temporary value and store it into
// awayTeamScore; homeTeamScore is 100, awayTeamScore is 80.
awayTeamScore = temp;
```

Assignments and Types

The assignment operator works the same way with all basic data types, including string. However, make sure the type of the rvalue you wish to store into a variable is compatible with the variable's own type; otherwise, the compiler may generate an error or try to convert the rvalue, with sometimes bizarre consequences as shown in Listing 5.5.

LISTING 5.5   Error.

```
int myScore = 2.99;               // myScore is now worth 2
float monsterVelocity = "Speed";  // Compilation error
float f = 'r';                    // f contains 114, the ASCII code for
                                  // 'r'
```

C++'s provides automatic type conversions, called *typecasts*, between values that belong to basic data types. The conversion rules are:

■ When a floating-point value is stored into an integer variable, the decimal part is truncated.

- When an integer value is stored into a floating-point variable, the conversion will probably work, but some precision may be lost, depending on the relative sizes of the integer and floating-point types in memory.
- When a `char` value is stored into a variable of another integer or floating-point type, the *ASCII code* of the character is what is stored in the variable.
- Any integer or floating-point value other than 0 (including negatives) can be stored into a `bool` variable, where it will be converted to the value `true`. Any Boolean expression of value `true` can be stored into an integer or floating-point variable, where it will take on the value 1.
- Any integer or floating-point value equal to 0 can be stored into a `bool` variable, where it will be converted to the value `false`. Any Boolean expression of value `false` can be stored into an integer or floating-point variable, where it will be converted to the value 0.
- For the purposes of these rules, a `char` variable can usually be treated like an integer variable of size equal to one byte.

As you can see, this can quickly become confusing, and typecasts of this kind are usually to be avoided, except in the case of an integer value being stored into a sufficiently large floating-point variable (where there is no risk of loss of precision). However, later in this chapter, you will encounter a case where you will want to force a typecast yourself, using a specific operator for this purpose.

MATHEMATICAL OPERATORS

C++ provides a full set of operators to implement the standard arithmetic operations, and a few more mathematical functions that are specific to computer programming. Table 5.1 is a full list of these operators:

TABLE 5.1   C++ Mathematical Operators

Operator	Name	Purpose	Example
++	Post-increment	Add 1 to an lvalue after it has been evaluated.	n++;
++	Pre-increment	Add 1 to an lvalue before it is evaluated.	++n;
--	Post-decrement	Subtract 1 from an lvalue after it has been evaluated.	n--;
--	Pre-decrement	Subtract 1 from an lvalue before it is evaluated.	--n;

Operator	Name	Purpose	Example
*	Multiplication	Multiply two numbers.	n * 4;
+	Addition	Add two numbers.	4 + n;
-	Subtraction	Subtract one number from another.	n - 4;
-	Unary minus	Change the sign of a value.	-n;
/	Division	Divide one number by another. If the two operands are integers, apply integer division; otherwise, apply floating-point division.	n / 5;
%	Modulo	Remainder of the integer division of two numbers.	n % 3;

Example 5.1 shows a few arithmetic calculations; Figure 5.1 shows the results of a sample execution from Listing 5.6.

LISTING 5.6   Mathematical operators.

```
/************************************
 Learn C++ by Making Games
 Example 5.1: Arithmetic
 ************************************/

#include <iostream>
using namespace std;

int main()
{

    // Get two values from the keyboard
    cout << "Please type in two floating-point numbers:" << endl;
    double a, b;
    cin >> a >> b;

    cout << "The two values are: a = " << a
         << " and b = " << b << endl;

    // Print a few simple calculations
    cout << "a + b = " << a + b << endl;
    cout << "a - b = " << a - b << endl;
    cout << "a * b = " << a * b << endl;
    cout << "a / b = " << a / b << endl;
```

```
    // And we're done!
    return 0;
}
```

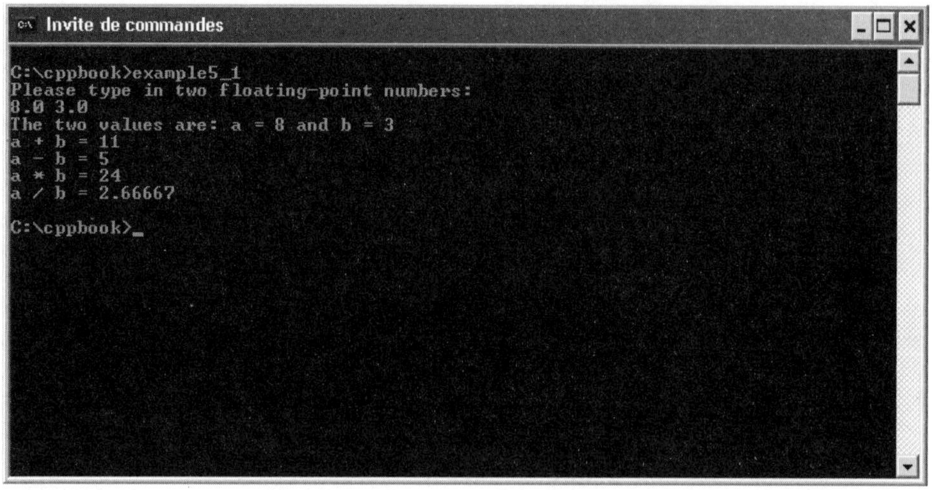

```
Invite de commandes

C:\cppbook>example5_1
Please type in two floating-point numbers:
8.0 3.0
The two values are: a = 8 and b = 3
a + b = 11
a - b = 5
a * b = 24
a / b = 2.66667

C:\cppbook>_
```

FIGURE 5.1 Arithmetic calculations.

You can also easily combine an assignment and an arithmetic operation of arbitrary complexity, as long as what appears on the left side of the assignment is an lvalue, like:

```
int a = ( b * 5 ) + ( 3 / c ) - 1;    // Valid statement
```

but not

```
(3 + a ) = 5;       // left side is not an lvalue
```

The Increment/Decrement Operators

The increment and decrement operators, ++ and --, are a kind of shorthand notation, combining an assignment and an addition or subtraction. Indeed, for a given variable n, the expressions n++ and ++n are equivalent to n = n + 1, while n-- and --n are equivalent to n = n - 1.

The reason for the existence of the shorthand is that C++ descends from the C programming language, which was designed to provide programmers with a great deal of access to the CPU, and since the instruction sets of all CPUs contain specific commands to increment and decrement values, an expression of the form n++ might be able to run a little faster than n = n + 1. (Contemporary compilers will usually be able to optimize the two into the same object code.)

The reason for the existence of *two* forms of the increment and decrement operators is that the variable being incremented or decremented is evaluated as part of the increment/decrement operation, and its value may be used in a calculation or assignment. Example 5.2 and Figure 5.2 show how this works from Listing 5.7.

LISTING 5.7   Increment operators.

```cpp
/**************************************
 Learn C++ by Making Games
 Example 5.2: Increment Operators
**************************************/

#include <iostream>
using namespace std;

int main()
{

   // Let's see what happens when we mix increments
   // with assignments and additions
   int a = 0;
   int b = 10;

   a = a + b++;
   cout << "a = " << a << ", b = " << b << endl;

   a = a + ++b;
   cout << "a = " << a << ", b = " << b << endl;


   // Now, let's try again, but in reverse
   a = 0;
   b = 10;

   a = a + ++b;
   cout << "a = " << a << ", b = " << b << endl;

   a = a + b++;
   cout << "a = " << a << ", b = " << b << endl;


   // And we're done!
   return 0;
}
```

```
cx Invite de commandes                                              - □ ×

C:\cppbook>example5_2
a  =  10,  b  =  11
a  =  22,  b  =  12
a  =  11,  b  =  11
a  =  22,  b  =  12

C:\cppbook>_
```

FIGURE 5.2 Mixing increments with assignments and additions.

As you can see from Figure 5.2, the first assignment statement, a = a + b++;, starts by evaluating b and adding its value (10) to a *before* incrementing b to 11. The second assignment *increments b first*, giving it the value 12, before evaluating it and adding its new value (12) to a.

The second pair of assignment statements reverses the process. The result (final values of 22 for a and 12 for b) is the same, but a's intermediate value is not. Choose your own forms of the increment and decrement operators carefully, as mixing them up can yield very tricky bugs to find.

The most common way to use n++, ++n, --n, *and* n-- *is by themselves, as independent expressions and statements, in which case there is no difference between the pre- and postforms of the operators:*

```
// two equivalent statements:
n++;
++n;
```

THE static_cast OPERATOR

Now, if you write the statement:

```
double quotient = 5 / 4;
```

you would expect quotient to contain the value 1.25, but that is not what happens: in fact, quotient will be assigned the value 1.0. Why?

The problem is that when a division has two integer operands, C++ *automatically applies integer division, no matter what the type of the lvalue into which the quotient is to be stored!* In the preceding case, since 5 and 4 are integers, C++ applies integer division (which yields quotient 1 and remainder 1) and *only then* typecasts the result to a double before storing it into the variable quotient.

How do you solve this problem? There are two ways. First, you can make sure that at least one of the division's operands belongs to a floating-point type by adding 0.0 to it. Since, for example, (5 + 0.0) is a floating-point expression, because the addition has a floating-point operand and returns a floating-point value, the division (5 + 0.0) / 4 will be a floating-point operation. However, this is an ugly hack and introduces an unnecessary addition.

The preferred way to solve this problem is to force an early typecast of one or more of the operands with the static_cast operator:

```
double quotient = static_cast<double>( 5 ) / 4;
```

The syntax of the static_cast operator is somewhat hairy so let's go through it slowly:

- First, the static_cast keyword.
- Then, the name of a type enclosed within < and >.
- Then, the expression whose type you want to change. This can be a literal, a variable, a constant, or any other complex expression as outlined in Listing 5.8.

LISTING 5.8   Casting.

```
// static_cast with a variable
int myInt = 5;
double myDouble = static_cast<double>( myInt );

// static_cast with a constant
const long BIG_NUMBER = 10000000;
myDouble = static_cast<double>( BIG_NUMBER );

// static_cast with an expression
myDouble = static_cast<double>( BIG_NUMBER + 2 * myInt );
```

CAUTION

Note that static_cast allows you to cast pretty much anything into anything else. You may want to use it to cast back and forth between, say, int and an enumerated type of your own, or between a basic type and a synonym you defined with typedef. In any case, C++ will use its best efforts to effect a conversion that makes sense, but if you mistakenly do something silly like try to cast a float into a char,

*the compiler will assume that you know what you're doing and let you proceed
with meaningless data.*

BOOLEAN EXPRESSIONS AND LOGIC OPERATORS

A Boolean expression can take one of two values: `true` and `false`. C++ provides
three operators that manipulate Boolean expressions and allow programmers to
compute arbitrarily complex truth-values. Table 5.2 introduces these operators,
while Tables 5.3 and 5.4 describe their behavior.

TABLE 5.2   Logic Operators

Operator	Name	Function	Example (using boolean variables a and b)
&&	AND	Logical Conjunction	`bool theAnd = a && b;`
||	OR	Logical Disjunction	`bool theOr = a || b;`
!	NOT	Logical Negation	`bool theNotA = !a;`

TABLE 5.3   Binary Logic Operator Truth Values

First Operand (a)	Second Operand (b)	a && b	a || b
true	true	true	true
true	false	false	true
false	true	false	true
false	false	false	false

TABLE 5.4   Unary "NOT" Truth Values

Operand (a)	!a
true	false
false	true

In short, an AND expression is true if *both* of its operands are true, an OR expression is true if *either* of its operands is true, and a NOT expression is true if its operand is *false*.

As you will see in Chapter 6, Boolean expressions are commonly used to control the execution of a program; for example, by choosing whether to execute a piece of code based on a condition or by repeating an operation as long as another condition holds true.

RELATIONAL OPERATORS

Relational operators implement comparisons between expressions. Table 5.5 lists the common relational operators available in C++.

TABLE 5.5   Relational Operators

Operator	Meaning
==	Equality.
!=	Inequality.
<	Smaller-than.
<=	Smaller-than or equal.
>	Greater-than.
>=	Greater-than or equal.

All relational operators return a truth-value (true or false) as their result. For example, 5 < 4 is false, while a == a is true.

Equality and inequality are fairly straightforward, but the exact meaning of the other (ordinal) relational operators depends on the data type:

- For Boolean values, false is defined as being smaller than true.
- A char value is considered smaller than another if its ASCII code is smaller. For example, 'z' is considered smaller than 'a'.
- Strings are compared one character at a time, using the rule for char values, until the first unequal character is found.

Of course, comparing values of different types is unlikely to yield meaningful results.

Floating-point calculations have limited precision, so testing values of type float or double for equality is rarely a good idea. Even a tiny imprecision of 0.00000001% will cause the equality test to fail.

One of the most common errors in C++ is the mix-up between the assignment operator, =, and the equality operator, ==.

The problem is that the equality operator is used to test for a truth-value, while the assignment operator returns the value that it stores into the variable—but as mentioned earlier in this chapter, any integer or floating-point value will automatically be typecast to a Boolean value in the right context.

Suppose you want to test whether the player's current score is 100, but instead of typing (score == 100), you type (score = 100). The assignment's return value is 100, which is automatically typecast into true since 100 is a nonzero value—therefore, your test will always be true as shown in Listing 5.9.

LISTING 5.9 Inequality/assignment.

```
int score;
// … do something with score …

bool sometimesTrue = (score == 100); // true if score is 100
bool alwaysTrue = ( score = 100 );   // always true since
                                     // 100 casts to true
```

Most current compilers will raise a warning if they encounter an assignment in a context where an equality test is expected, but remember that warnings don't stop the compilation process.

Here is a way to minimize the risk: when you are comparing a variable's value against a literal or a constant, write the literal or the constant on the left side of the equality test. Then, if you mistakenly type the assignment operator instead of the equality operator, the compiler will trap the error immediately, since you cannot assign anything into a literal or a constant as outlined in Listing 5.10.

LISTING 5.10 Testing inequality.

```
bool b = (13 == myScore); // Equality test, as intended
bool b = (13 = myScore);  // Compilation error
bool b = (myScore == 13); // Equality test, as intended
bool b = (myScore = 13);  // Assignment, always true!
```

BITWISE OPERATORS

C++ allows you to manipulate the individual bits of data inside `char` and integer variables, as if each was its own individual `bool` variable. This is not as useful as it once was; in the old days, memory was scarce, so packing as much data as possible into a single `int` was a worthwhile exercise, but today it is rarely worth the effort.

For the sake of completeness, Table 5.6 lists the bitwise operators and shows what happens when they are applied to `char` values.

TABLE 5.6 Bitwise Operators

Operator	Name	Action	Example using
				`char c1 = 'A'` (bitwise: 01000001) `char c2 = 'B'` (bitwise: 01000010)
|	Bitwise OR	Each bit is ORed	`char c3 = c1 | c2;` `// becomes bitwise 01000011: 'C'`
&	Bitwise AND	Each bit is ANDed	`char c4 = c1 & c2;` `// becomes bitwise 01000000: '@'`
~	Bitwise NOT	Each bit is reversed	`char c5 = ~c1;` `// becomes bitwise 10111110`
^	Bitwise XOR	Each bit is exclusive-ORed (becomes 1 if only one of the operand bits is 1)	`char c6 = c1 ^ c2;` `// becomes bitwise 00000011`
<<	Shift left	Each bit is shifted left; a 0 is introduced in the least significant position	`char c7 = c1 << 1;` `// everything shifted left one place, become bitwise 10000010`
>>	Shift right	Each bit is shifted right; a value equal to the old leftmost bit is inserted at left.	`char c8 = c1 >> 2;` `// everything shifted right two places, becomes bitwise 00010000`

CAUTION

Be careful not to confuse the logical operators !, && *and* || *with their bitwise counterparts* ~, &, *and* |.

SHORTHAND ASSIGNMENTS

In addition to the increment and decrement operators you saw earlier, C++ provides a large number of shorthand notations that combine an assignment with another operator. Table 5.7 is a list of these operators.

TABLE 5.7   Shorthand Assignments

Shorthand	Is Equivalent To:
a += 3;	a = a + 3;
a -= 4;	a = a - 4;
a *= 5;	a = a * 5;
a /= 2;	a = a / 2;
a %= 5;	a = a % 5;
a >>= 2;	a = a >> 2;
a <<= 3;	a = a << 3;
a |= 2;	a = a | 2;
a &= 2;	a = a & 2;
a ^= 3;	a = a ^ 3;

CAUTION

*Be careful when using shorthand notation with complex rvalues; the result may not be intuitive. For example, score *= monsters + 10 is equivalent to score = score * (monsters + 10), not to score = (score * monsters) + 10.*

Chained Assignments

It is also possible to assign the same value into multiple variables at the same time. For example, the statement in Listing 5.11 puts the value 100 into all three variables.

LISTING 5.11   Three variables.

```
myScore = yourScore = highScore = 100;
```

CAUTION

Be careful: it is easy to type:

```
int myScore = yourScore = 100; // chained assignments
```

when what you really mean is:

```
int myScore = yourScore + 100; // assignment of a sum
```

Both statements are legal in C++, so the compiler can't detect the mix-up!

OPERATOR PRIORITY

In arithmetic, multiplication and division have priority over addition and subtraction, so that a + b * c means a + (b * c) and not (a + b) * c. C++ follows these rules and adds more rules to cover its other operators. Table 5.8 lists the operators you have seen in this chapter, in decreasing order of priority; everything within a single box is considered to have the exact same priority.

TABLE 5.8   Operator Priority

Priority Category	Operators
Highest	Increment and decrement operators (++, --)
Bitwise NOT (~)	
Logical NOT (!)	
Unary minus (-)	Multiplication, division, modulo (*, /, %)
or plus (+)	Addition and subtraction (+, -)
	Shift left and shift right (<<, >>)
	Less than, more than, less than or equal, more than or equal (<, >, <=, >=)
	Equal, not equal (==, !=)
	Bitwise AND (&)
	Bitwise exclusive-OR (^)
	Bitwise OR (|)
	Logical AND (&&)
	Logical OR (||)
Lowest	All assignment operators

Within a priority category, the compiler is free to apply operators in any order it chooses, except for logical operators that always apply left to right.

And, of course, whenever you are in doubt about the order in which operators will be applied, or when you want to force an order that differs from the built-in priorities, or when you want to clarify a complicated expression, you are always free to introduce parentheses as you see fit.

SUMMARY

In this chapter, we learned about the basic operators available in the C++ language. Assignment operators allow us to store data into memory. Mathematical operators implement basic arithmetic functions. Logical and relational operators allow us to test data for certain conditions. Bitwise operators allow us to manipulate variables as if they were collections of Booleans, all at once. Shorthand assignment operators combine an assignment and an arithmetic or bitwise operation. Finally, you looked at the priority rules governing the order in which operators are applied.

EXERCISES

5.1   What is wrong with the statement int a == 5;?

5.2   Why is it a bad idea to test floating-point variables for equality with the == operator?

5.3   At the end of the following code snippet, what is the value of numPotions?

```
int numPotions = 0;
numPotions++;
int foundPotions = 3;
numPotions = foundPotions;
foundPotions++;
```

5.4   What is the difference between the bitwise and logical AND operators, & and &&?

5.5   Why would you want to use static_cast when dividing two int variables?

5.6   Using the priority rules described in this chapter, determine the values of these variables:

a) int myScore = 50 * 4 / 2 + 2 * 5 - 10;

b) bool myTruth = true && true || !true && (false || true);

c) bool myTest = 50 <= 10 && true;

5.7   Write a program that reads the names of two players from the keyboard, prints them, swaps them in memory, and prints them again.

5.8   Write a program that inputs three numbers a, b, and c, and prints out the results of the equations:

a) a2 + 2abc + b2 - 4

b) abc + 2c(a - b) + ac / b + -a

5.9   The logical exclusive-OR operation is defined as true when one and only one of its operands is true. As an equation, this can be represented as (a || b) && (!a || !b). Write a program that calculates and prints the truth table for logical exclusive-OR, calculating the truth values for all combinations of operands using variables. (Note: C++ prints out true as a 1 and false as a 0.)

6 Blocks and Variable Scope

In This Chapter

- Blocks
- Block Scope and Local Variables
- Using Variables within Embedded Scopes
- Hiding Variables
- Global Variables
- Justification for Scope Rules

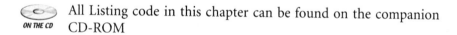 All Listing code in this chapter can be found on the companion
CD-ROM

In this chapter, you will learn the concept of *scopes*, which determine the "life expectancy" of variables. Scopes are intimately related to C++ *blocks*, which you have already encountered in previous chapters, and which are themselves crucial to the flow control statements that you will be studying in Chapter 7. At the end of this chapter, you will understand C++'s *scope rules* and be able to determine when a variable is born, when it is visible as far as code is concerned, and when it is destroyed.

BLOCKS

In C++, a *block* is an arbitrary number of statements enclosed within a pair of curly brackets, { and }. Blocks can appear anywhere individual fully formed statements can; every program contains at least one block, the one that contains the definition of the main() function. Here is an example of a piece of code that contains several blocks:

```cpp
int main()
{
  // We are within the main function's block
  // …

  {
    // We are within an embedded block
    // …
  }

  {
    // We are within another embedded block
    // …
  }

  return 0;
}
```

Blocks rarely appear by themselves like the ones in the preceding example. They are usually associated with the conditional statements and loops you will examine in Chapter 7, with the functions you will study in Part III, and with the classes and structures you will encounter in Part VI.

BLOCK SCOPE AND LOCAL VARIABLES

A variable that is declared within the boundaries of a block is said to have *block scope*, which means that the variable only "lives" as long as the program stays within the boundaries of the block. The variable is also called a *local variable*, because its meaning is local to the block and scope in question.

As soon as execution leaves the block within which a variable has been declared, the variable is destroyed and its name is forgotten; in C++ parlance, the variable is said to go *out of scope*. All the programs we have seen so far consisted of a single block (the main() function), so all the variables we have declared have stayed in scope until the program terminated, but the situation gets more complicated when there is more than one block involved. For example, the code snippet in Listing 6.1 will not compile because the variable myVar has gone out of scope and no longer exists by the time you try to print out its contents.

LISTING 6.1   Scope sample.

```
int main()
{
  // Let's begin a block with an opening curly bracket
  {
    // Declaring a variable within a block
    int myVar = 5;
  }
  // We have left the block, so myVar is out of scope

  cout << myVar; // Compilation error!

  return 0;
}
```

However, if you had declared myVar *before* entering the embedded block, the program would have compiled properly. Why? Because in that case, myVar would have belonged to the main function's primary block and it wouldn't have gone out of scope until program execution terminated, as detailed in Listing 6.2.

LISTING 6.2   Scope sample 2.

```
int main()
{
  // …
  // We declare a variable in the main function's scope
  int myVar = 5;

  // We do some work within an embedded block
  {
    // …
  }

  // myVar is still in scope, because it belongs to
      // the main program's block
  cout << myVar;  // Works properly

  return 0;
}
```

USING VARIABLES WITHIN EMBEDDED SCOPES

As you can see from the previous code sample, the variable myVar is not destroyed (or influenced in any way) when program execution leaves the inner block, because it has been declared outside of it. However, it would have been possible to refer to myVar's value or to change it within the inner block, because this inner block is part of myVar's scope, as demonstrated by Listing 6.3.

LISTING 6.3   Embedding scope.

```
int main()
{
  int myVar = 5;
  {
    myVar = 7; // Legal, since myVar is in scope
  }
  cout << myVar; // Prints out the number 7
}
```

Thus, in C++, any variable declared in a scope that surrounds other scopes is available in these inner scopes as well, but variables declared within the inner scopes are not available in the outer scope. (To memorize this, think of the one-way relationship between national laws and municipal bylaws. A country is like an "outer scope" that contains many "inner scopes" like cities, towns, and provinces. The laws of the country are like variables declared in the outer scope: they apply everywhere. The bylaws of a city are like variables declared in the inner scope: they apply locally but have no legal weight anywhere else.)

HIDING VARIABLES

There is one exception to the rule that says that a variable declared in an outer scope is visible within its embedded scopes. Consider the example outlined in Listing 6.4.

LISTING 6.4   Variable hiding.

```
int main()
{
  // Declaring a variable in the main scope
  int myVar = 5;

  // Declaring a variable in the inner scope
  {
    int myVar = 10;

    cout << myVar; // What is going to happen?
  }

  return 0;
}
```

In this program, you have declared *two variables of the same name* in two different scopes, one of which is embedded into the other. How will the program react? Will it print out the value of the first myVar that was declared, which is 5? Will it print out the value of the most recent declaration, which is 10? Or will it generate a compilation error because there are two variables of the same name that are in scope at the same time and it cannot choose between them?

The answer is that the innermost variable temporarily hides the other one, so the program will print out the number 10. However, as soon as the innermost variable goes out of scope, the outermost one becomes visible again, as in Example 6.1 and Figure 6.1, shown in Listing 6.5.

LISTING 6.5

```
/************************************
Learn C++ by Making Games
Example 6.1: Fun with scopes
************************************/

#include <iostream>
using namespace std;

int main()
{

  // Let's define a variable in the outermost scope
  int myVar = 5;

  // Now, let's define another variable that hides it
  {
    int myVar = 10;
    cout << "In the inner block: " << myVar << endl;
  }

  // Now that the inner variable has gone out of scope...
  cout << "In the outer block: " << myVar << endl;

  // And we're done!
  return 0;
}
```

As you can see from Figure 6.1, as soon as the inner variable goes out of scope, the original myVar becomes visible again and can be printed out. Example 6.2 shows a slightly more complicated case, and the results of its execution appear in Figure 6.2, taken from Listing 6.6.

FIGURE 6.1 Inner and outer variables.

LISTING 6.6

```
/************************************
 Learn C++ by Making Games
 Example 6.2: More scopes
 ************************************/

#include <iostream>
using namespace std;

int main()
{

  // Let's define a variable in the outermost scope
  int myVar = 5;

  // Now, let's manipulate it within an inner block
  {
    myVar += 10;
    cout << "First: " << myVar << endl;

    // Now, let's hide it
    int myVar = 75;
    cout << "Second: " << myVar << endl;
  }

  // Now, some manipulation in the outer block
  myVar++;
```

```
cout << "Third: " << myVar << endl;

// Now, a second inner block...
{
  int myVar = -2;
  cout << "Fourth: " << myVar << endl;
}

// And finally:
cout << "Fifth: " << myVar << endl;

// And we're done!
return 0;
}
```

Tracing the execution of this program reveals:

- First, you declare the outermost variable myVar and assign the value 5 to it.
- Then, you enter a scope and encounter a shorthand assignment/arithmetic operation involving myVar. Since the only myVar you know about at this point is the outermost variable, 10 is added to its value, which becomes 15. This is what appears in the first output line.
- Then, you create an inner myVar that hides the outermost variable until the end of the current block, and it is given the value 75. This is what appears in the second output line.
- Then, you leave the first inner block, so the inner variable (value: 75) goes out of scope. The outermost myVar (value: 15) again becomes visible. Note that the effects of the calculations that have been applied to the outermost variable inside the inner block are *not* reversed as you leave this block.
- Then, you increment the outermost myVar, which becomes 16. This is the value that appears in the third output line.
- Next, you enter another inner block, create another inner variable that hides the outermost myVar, and give it the value –2. This is the value that appears in the fourth output line.
- Finally, this second inner variable goes out of scope, and you are again left with only the outermost myVar to deal with. Its value is unchanged at 16 since the last increment, and this is the value that appears in the fifth output line.

Note that if two variables of the same name are declared in the same scope, the compiler will generate an error, whether the two variables are of the same type or not, as shown in Listing 6.7.

CAUTION

FIGURE 6.2 A more complicated example of C++'s scope rules.

LISTING 6.7 Compiler error.

```
int main()
{
  // Declaring a variable in the main scope
  int myVar = 5;

  // Doing some work in an inner scope
  {
    // ...
  }

  // Declaring another myVar in the main scope
  char myVar = 10; // Compilation error

  return 0;
}
```

GLOBAL VARIABLES

What if a variable is declared outside of *any* block, as in the snippet in Listing 6.8?

LISTING 6.8 Globals.

```
int myVar = 10; // Variable declared outside of any block
int main()
```

```
{
  cout << myVar << endl;
  return 0;
}
```

Such a variable is called a *global variable*, and is considered in scope everywhere until the end of the source file.

Global variables (or globals, for short) can also be made available in other source files, if the program contains more than one source file; we will see how in Part III.

All rules regarding variable visibility apply to global variables just as they do to local variables. For example, if a variable that has the same name as a global is declared within the `main()` function, the new variable will hide the global within `main()` until it goes out of scope.

However, if there are other functions in the program where the global is not hidden, figuring out which identifiers refer to the global and which refer to local variables can become a tracking nightmare. For this reason, many programmers make sure globals are never hidden; for example, by naming them with a category of identifiers they reserve exclusively for globals, as shown in Listing 6.9.

LISTING 6.9   Naming globals.

```
int globalScores;
int g_myVariable;
```

JUSTIFICATION FOR SCOPE RULES

At this point, you may wonder why C++ provides such detailed rules to handle two or more variables that have been given the same name—something that, intuitively, sounds like a very bad idea. Indeed, if all programs only contained a single `main()` function, it would be far easier to force programmers to give unique names to all their variables and to generate compilation errors if they failed to do so.

As your programs grow in complexity, they will come to include many functions, and later many source files and classes of objects. Commercial games routinely require the efforts of 10 or more programmers working on hundreds of source files for a period of years; even the relatively simple game that you will be coding in Part VI contains several thousand lines of code. In such cases, it quickly becomes impossible to come up with unique and meaningful names for every variable and for every piece of code—not to mention counterproductive. By localizing the meanings of names, the scope rules will greatly simplify your work.

SUMMARY

A C++ block is an arbitrary number of statements enclosed within curly brackets. A variable declared within a block is local to this block; it is also said to have block scope, or local scope.

Any variable declared within a block is also visible within blocks embedded in its home block, unless another variable of the same name is declared within an embedded block and hides it.

As soon as execution leaves a block, all variables declared within it go out of scope and are destroyed; any variables that were hidden by variables going out of scope become visible again at that point.

A variable declared outside of any block is a global variable, visible everywhere from then on in the program. Global variables are subject to the same hiding rules as any other variables.

EXERCISES

6.1   Is it possible for a variable to have no scope?
6.2   Is it possible for a variable to be declared outside of any blocks?
6.3   What happens to a variable that goes out of scope?

7 C++ Flow Control

In This Chapter

- Boolean Expressions
- The if Statement
- The Conditional Operator
- The switch Statement
- The while Loop
- The do-while Loop
- The for Loop
- Controlling Loops with continue and break

 All Listing code in this chapter can be found on the companion CD-ROM

So far, all of your programs have been strictly linear: Every instruction has been executed once and only once, and always in the same order. In this chapter, you will learn a number of statements that will allow you to implement more complex computational behaviors like *conditional execution* (e.g., choosing whether a block of code should run, based on a Boolean condition) and *looping* (e.g., running the same block an arbitrary number of times).

BOOLEAN EXPRESSIONS

The execution of each of the conditional statements and loops that you will be studying in this chapter depends on the truth value of a *Boolean expression*. C++ Boolean expressions include:

- The literals `true` and `false`.
- Variables and constants of type `bool`.
- The results of calculations involving the relational operators `==`, `!=`, `<`, `>`, `<=`, and `>=`.
- If `expr` is a Boolean expression, its negation (written as `!expr`) is also a Boolean expression.
- If `expr1` and `expr2` are both Boolean expressions, their conjunction (written `expr1 && expr2` and read as "expr1 and expr2") is also a Boolean expression.
- If `expr1` and `expr2` are both Boolean expressions, their disjunction (written `expr1 || expr2` and read as "expr1 or expr2") is also a Boolean expression.

As you saw in Chapter 5, the negation operator `!` has the highest priority of all operators involved in Boolean expressions, followed by the relational operators, then by the AND operator `&&`, then by the OR operator `||`. Therefore, an expression like `x==0 || x == 1` is equivalent to `(x == 0) || ( x == 1)`, while `!a && b < c` is equivalent to `!a && ( b < c )`. However, as a matter of style, you may want to use the parenthesized versions to make the code clearer, except in very special cases like `a || b || c || !d`.

You will see many more Boolean expressions as you progress through this chapter and throughout the rest of the book.

Short-Circuit Evaluation

One of the interesting features of C++ Boolean expressions is that they are evaluated left to right, but that evaluation stops as soon as the final truth value can be determined with certainty. For example, when evaluating the expression `true || a || b`, C++ will never check the truth value of either a or b, because the result of the disjunction is completely determined by the presence of the literal `true`.

This feature is called *short-circuit evaluation* and allows programmers to write elegant expressions that might otherwise cause disasters at runtime. For example, consider the Boolean expression shown in Listing 7.1.

LISTING 7.1 Boolean expression.

```
( myScore != 0.0 ) && ( yourScore / myScore < 1.0 ).
```

Expressions such as this start by testing some of their data for validity before performing useful calculations if the data is indeed valid. In this case, if `myScore` is not equal to 0.0, the left half of the conjunction is true, and so the ratio of `yourScore / myScore` is evaluated to determine who is in the lead and by how much. However, if `myScore` is equal to zero, the left half of the conjunction is false, which means that the final truth value of the expression can only be false as well, so C++ stops the calculation immediately—a great thing, because if it tried to calculate `yourScore / myScore`, the result would be a division by zero, which would cause a runtime exception and crash the program.

You will make use of the short-circuit evaluation feature extensively in this book, since it is a common and very handy idiom.

In the previous example, you tested a floating-point variable, `myScore`, for inequality. As mentioned before, this is rarely a good idea because of the imprecision associated with floating-point calculations. However, if you are testing the variable against a value that you have assigned to it yourself, like an initial score of 0.0, rather than against the result of a calculation, the risk disappears.

THE `if` STATEMENT

The first conditional statement that you will examine is the `if` statement, which executes a statement or a block of code if and only if some Boolean expression of arbitrary complexity is `true`. Its syntax consists of the keyword `if`, followed by a Boolean condition enclosed in parentheses, followed by a statement or a block of code to execute if the condition is true.

Example 7.1 is a very simple divination game that asks the player to guess which number the computer is "thinking about" and is shown in Listing 7.2.

This version of the divination game is not very challenging, since the computer is always thinking of the same number. You will make it a little more interesting when you introduce random numbers in Chapter 9.

LISTING 7.2

```
/************************************
   Learn C++ by Making Games
   Example 7.1: Divination Game, v. 1
************************************/

#include <iostream>
using namespace std;

int main()
{

   // Let's define the number that we want the
```

```
// player to guess as a constant
const int magicNumber = 8;

// Ask the player for his guess
cout << "Guess which number between 1 and 10 "
    << "I'm thinking about..." << endl;
int playerGuess;
cin >> playerGuess;

// Test and give feedback
if( playerGuess == magicNumber )
  cout << "Congratulations, you guessed right!" << endl;

// And we're done!
return 0;
}
```

The program will print a congratulations message, if the player types in the correct answer (i.e., the number 8).

NOTE

You have indented the cout statement to execute if the player has guessed right. This is to indicate to humanoid readers of the program that this statement is subordinated to the if, but as far as the compiler is concerned, the indentation is irrelevant.

In Example 7.1, the code that the if statement executes when the condition is true consists of a single cout statement. In Example 7.2, shown in Listing 7.3, the if clause contains a block of code.

LISTING 7.3

```
/*************************************
  Learn C++ by Making Games
  Example 7.2: Divination Game, v. 2
*************************************/

#include <iostream>
using namespace std;

int main()
{

  // Let's define the number that we want the
  // player to guess as a constant
  const int magicNumber = 8;
```

```
// Ask the player for his guess
cout << "Guess which number between 1 and 10 "
     << "I'm thinking about..." << endl;
int playerGuess;
cin >> playerGuess;

// Give some feedback if the guess is correct
if( playerGuess == magicNumber )
{
  cout << "Congratulations, you guessed right!" << endl;
  cout << "You're obviously too smart for me!" << endl;
}

// And we're done!
return 0;
}
```

Make sure not to forget the curly brackets if you want an if (or any other conditional or loop statement) to control a block of code. Without brackets, the if can only have a single statement under its control. And remember that C++ does not understand the meaning of indentation, so it will not be able to guess that both cout statements should belong to the if block in the following code snippet:

```
if ( myName == "Sam Fisher" )
    cout << "Hello, Sam...";  // Executed if myName is Sam Fisher
    cout << "Your mission is..." << endl; // ALWAYS Executed!
```

if-else Statements

Examples 7.1 and 7.2 provide some positive feedback to the player if he guesses right, but tell him nothing if he guesses wrong, which is not very user-friendly. Indeed, the best way to handle the situation would be to choose between two alternative messages depending on whether the guess is right or wrong. For cases like this one, C++ provides the *if-else statement*, which looks like this:

```
if( some condition )
{
  // A block of code to execute if the condition is true
}
else
{
  // Another block of code to execute if the condition is false
}
```

In Example 7.3, we use the `if-else` statement to give the player some feedback whether he guessed right or not, which is detailed in Listing 7.4.

LISTING 7.4

```
/***************************************
 Learn C++ by Making Games
 Example 7.3: Divination Game, v. 3
 ***************************************/

#include <iostream>
using namespace std;

int main()
{

  // Let's define the number that we want the
  // player to guess as a constant
  const int magicNumber = 8;

  // Ask the player for his guess
  cout << "Guess which number between 1 and 10 "
       << "I'm thinking about..." << endl;
  int playerGuess;
  cin >> playerGuess;

  // Give some feedback whether the guess is right or not
  if( playerGuess == magicNumber )
  {
    cout << "Congratulations, you guessed right!" << endl;
    cout << "You're obviously too smart for me!" << endl;
  }
  else
  {
    cout << "No, sorry, that's not it. Try again!" << endl;
  }

  // And we're done!
  return 0;
}
```

Both the `if` and the `else` blocks can contain any valid C++ statements, including another `if-else`. In Example 7.4 shown in Listing 7.5, you give the player a second chance if his first guess is wrong.

LISTING 7.5

```
/************************************
 Learn C++ by Making Games
 Example 7.4: Divination Game, v. 4
 ************************************/

#include <iostream>
using namespace std;

int main()
{

  // Let's define the number that we want the
  // player to guess as a constant
  const int magicNumber = 8;

  // Ask the player for his guess
  cout << "Guess which number between 1 and 10 "
       << "I'm thinking about...\n";
  int playerGuess;
  cin >> playerGuess;

  // If the guess is right, congratulate the player
  if( playerGuess == magicNumber )
  {
    cout << "Congratulations, you guessed right!\n";
    cout << "You're obviously too smart for me!\n";
  }
  // If the guess is wrong, let the player try again
  else
  {
    cout << "No, sorry, that's not it. Try again:\n";
    cin >> playerGuess;
    if( playerGuess == magicNumber )
    {
      cout << "Yes, this time you got it!\n";
    }
    else
    {
      cout << "No, that's not it either. "
           << "Better luck next time!\n";
    }
  }

  // And we're done!
  return 0;
}
```

Chained `if-else` Statements

In situations where you want to perform one of many actions depending on the many possible values of one or more Boolean expressions, it is possible to use a sequence of *chained if-else* statements. For example, if you wanted to give the player an assessment of his performance, you might do it with a series of `if-else` tests on his score, as in Example 7.5 detailed in Listing 7.6.

LISTING 7.6

```cpp
/*************************************
 Learn C++ by Making Games
 Example 7.5: Score assessment
*************************************/

#include <iostream>
using namespace std;

int main()
{

  // Let's read the score
  cout << "What score did you get?" << endl;
  int playerScore;
  cin >> playerScore;

  // Give an appropriate assessment
  if( playerScore >= 1000 )
    cout << "Excellent performance! Good job!";
  else if( playerScore >= 800 )
    cout << "Pretty good, you're getting better!";
  else if( playerScore >= 600 )
    cout << "Not bad for a rookie...";
  else if( playerScore >= 300 )
    cout << "Well, at least you're not getting fired...";
  else
    cout << "Did you fall asleep during the game?";

  cout << endl;

  // And we're done!
  return 0;
}
```

In this example, you first check whether the score is 1000 or more, which is considered excellent. If it is, you congratulate the player; otherwise, you enter the `else` clause, which is another test for a slightly lower score. You keep going until you find a test that succeeds or the final `else` statement is reached.

Technically speaking, nothing prevents you from using entirely unrelated Boolean conditions in each of a series of chained if-else statements, but since that would make your code harder to understand, you should use this approach with caution.

THE CONDITIONAL OPERATOR

C++ provides a shorthand notation that allows programmers to embed conditional statements into other statements. This *conditional operator*'s syntax is the following:

- First, a Boolean expression, usually written in parentheses.
- Then, a question mark, ?.
- Then, the value the conditional operator will return if the Boolean expression is true.
- Then, a colon, :.
- Finally, the value that the conditional operator will return if the Boolean expression is false.

For example, the if-else statement

```
if( myScore > yourScore )
  highScore = myScore;
else
  highScore = yourScore;
```

could be replaced with the one-line statement:

```
highScore = ( myScore > yourScore ) ? myScore : yourScore;
```

The conditional operator is usually reserved for such very simple cases, as it is somewhat less legible than an if statement.

THE switch STATEMENT

The switch statement is a powerful and versatile conditional branching mechanism. It begins by evaluating its argument, which can be any expression of type bool, int, char, or of an enumerated type, and then selects one of several execution branches according to the argument's value. Example 7.6 shows the switch statement's syntax shown in Listing 7.7.

LISTING 7.7

```cpp
/***************************************
Learn C++ by Making Games
Example 7.6: Switch statement
***************************************/

#include <iostream>
using namespace std;

int main()
{

  // Let's read the grade
  cout << "What grade did you get?" << endl;
  char theGrade;
  cin >> theGrade;

  // Give an appropriate assessment
  switch( theGrade )
  {
    case 'A':
      cout << "Excellent! ";
    case 'B':
    case 'C':
    case 'D':
      cout << "You get a passing grade.";
      break;
    case 'F':
      cout << "Sorry, you fail.";
      break;
    default:
      cout << "Sorry, I didn't understand you.";
      break;
  }

  cout << endl;

  // And we're done!
  return 0;
}
```

First, there is the switch keyword, followed by the argument (in this case, the char variable theGrade) enclosed within parentheses.

Then, you open a block that contains a set of case statements. Each case statement corresponds to one of the argument's possible values. For example, case 'A' in Example 7.6 serves the same purpose as an if test like if(theGrade == 'A').

Now, here is the tricky part: when C++ encounters a `case` statement that matches the argument's value, it begins executing *all of the non-case statements in the block from that point on, until either the block is finished or it encounters a* `break` *statement.*

In Example 7.6, if the user types in an A, execution branches in at the statement following `case 'A'`, which prints out the message "`Excellent!`" Then, the computer will keep looking for code to execute, skipping the other `case` statements; it eventually finds `cout << "You get a passing grade."` Finally, it reaches a `break` statement, which tells it to exit the switch block and to resume execution at the first statement following the block's closing bracket.

If the user had typed in a B, C, or D, the first executable statement the computer would have encountered is `cout << "You get a passing grade."` Thus, the user would have gotten the good news, only without the "`Excellent!`" mention. If she had typed in an F, execution would have branched in at the `cout << "Sorry, you fail."` statement, which is immediately followed by a `break`.

If you forget a break in a switch statement, the computer may execute code that was meant for a completely different case.

Finally, at the end of the switch block is a `default` case, a catchall for values of the argument that do not match any of the `case` statements. While the default case is optional, it is usually a good idea to include one and use it to warn the user about improper data, as you did in Example 7.6.

In cases where each `case` *statement is paired with its own* `break`, `switch` *behaves very much like a sequence of chained* `if-then` *statements. Thus,*

```
switch( myTeam )
{
  case homeTeam: cout << "Yea!"; break;
  case awayTeam: cout << "Boo!"; break;
  default: cout << "Huh…"; break;
}
```

would be equivalent to

```
if( myTeam == homeTeam )
  cout << "Yea!";
else if( myTeam == awayTeam )
  cout << "Boo!";
else
  cout << "Huh…";
```

THE while LOOP

Now that you are finished with conditional statements, it is time to look at C++'s loops, which are constructs that allow a block of code to be executed any number of times.

The first (and most common) of C++'s loops is the while loop, which executes a statement or a block *as long as a specific test condition is satisfied.* Its syntax is as follows:

- The while keyword, followed by a Boolean expression within parentheses, called a *test condition.*
- Then, a block of code (or a single statement) to execute as long as the test condition holds true.

The code snippet in Listing 7.8 is an example of a while loop that counts from 1 to 10 and prints out the numbers.

LISTING 7.8   while loop.

```
int iter = 1;
while( iter <= 10 )
{
   cout << iter << endl;
   iter++;
}
```

In Listing 7.8., you begin by establishing the loop's starting conditions, in this case by creating a *controlling variable* called iter that will store the numbers and by initializing it with the value 1.

Then, when you encounter the while statement, the computer evaluates the condition. In this case, since iter is equal to 1, the expression iter <= 10 is true, so you enter the while block, print out the number 1, and increment the iter variable, which is now 2.

Next, you return to the top of the while statement and re-evaluate the test condition. Since iter is now 2, iter <= 10 is still true, so you execute the block again, print out the number 2, and increment iter again.

Eventually, you will print the number 10 and increment iter to 11. At that point, when the computer re-evaluates the test condition, the result will be false, since 11 is greater than 10. At this point, the program's execution will break out of the loop and continue with the first statement following the while block's closing bracket.

NOTE

Note that if a while loop's test condition is false right from the start, its block will not be executed even once. For example, if you had mistakenly initialized iter to 20 instead of 1 in the snippet in Listing 7.8, the test would have failed the first time and you would not have printed anything.

Example 7.7 shown in Listing 7.9 upgrades the divination game by letting the user try again and again until he finds the right answer.

LISTING 7.9

```
/**********************************
 Learn C++ by Making Games
 Example 7.7: Divination with a loop
 **********************************/

#include <iostream>
using namespace std;

int main()
{

  // Let's define the number that we want the
  // player to guess as a constant
  const int magicNumber = 8;

  // Let's initialize the player's guess with a
  // bogus value that is not the right choice
  int playerGuess = -1;

  // Then, ask the player to guess until he
  // gets it right
  cout << "Guess which number between 1 and 10 "
       << "I'm thinking about...\n";

  while( magicNumber != playerGuess )
  {
    cin >> playerGuess;
    if( magicNumber == playerGuess )
      cout << "You're right! Congratulations!\n";
    else
      cout << "No, try again:";
  }

  // And we're done!
  return 0;
}
```

Infinite Loops

Any C++ loop will keep looping as long as its test condition holds true. Therefore, if the test condition never becomes false, the loop will never exit. For example, consider the snippet in Listing 7.10, which is designed to print the odd numbers between 1 and 100.

LISTING 7.10   Infinite loop.

```
int iter = 1;
while( iter != 100 )
{
  cout << iter << endl;
  iter += 2;
}
```

Instead of testing whether the controlling variable is smaller than or equal to 100, this loop mistakenly tests it only for equality—and since `iter` only takes on odd values, it will never become equal to 100 and the loop will run forever.

Infinite loops may happen for any number of reasons, but the most common include:

- A badly designed test condition, like the one shown in Listing 7.10.
- A controlling variable that never changes. If `iter` had stayed at 1 forever, the previous snippet would have printed an endless series of ones.
- Improper manipulation of a controlling variable within the loop block. If two or more statements had changed the value of `iter` in conflicting manners, the loop might have behaved erratically.

THE do-while LOOP

The `do-while` loop is very similar to the `while` loop. In fact, the only behavioral difference between the two is that the `do-while` loop's test condition is verified at the end of execution instead of at the beginning. As a result, a `do-while` loop's block is always executed at least once.

Example 7.8 is a rewriting of Example 7.7 with a `do-while` loop detailed in 7.11.

LISTING 7.11

```
/*************************************
 Learn C++ by Making Games
 Example 7.8: Divination with do-while
 *************************************/

#include <iostream>
using namespace std;

int main()
{

  // Let's define the number that we want the
```

```
// player to guess as a constant
const int magicNumber = 8;

// With do-while, we don't need to initialize
// the player's choice with a dummy value
// since we know that the loop's body will
// always be executed at least once
int playerGuess;

cout << "Guess which number between 1 and 10 "
        << "I'm thinking about...\n";

do
{
  // Ask the player for his guess;
  cin >> playerGuess;

  // Give feedback
  if( magicNumber == playerGuess )
    cout << "You're right! Congratulations!\n";
  else
    cout << "No, try again:";

} while( magicNumber != playerGuess );

// And we're done!
return 0;
}
```

THE for LOOP

The third and last of C++'s looping statements is the for loop, which combines an initialization, a test, and an update in a single line. The snippet in Listing 7.12 uses a for loop to read 10 numbers from the keyboard and print out the highest of them.

LISTING 7.12 for loop.

```
int theMax = -50000;
int theData;

for( int i = 0; i < 10; i++ )
{
  cout << "Type in number " << ( i + 1 ) << " of 10:\n";
  cin >> theData;
  if( theData > theMax )
    theMax = theData;
}
```

The `for` line contains, enclosed within parentheses and separated by semi-colons, three different statements:

■   The initialization of a control variable. In this case, the control variable i was also declared within the `for` line, but that is not required.
■   The test condition `i < 10`.
■   A statement that updates the control variable, in this case an increment.

As usual, the block associated with the loop is executed as long as the test condition is true. Thus, this `for` loop is equivalent to the `while` loop outlined in Listing 7.13.

LISTING 7.13   Rewritten `for` Loop as a `while` loop.

```
int i = 0;
while( i < 10 )
{
  cout << "Type in number " << ( i + 1 ) << " of 10:\n";
  cin >> theData;
  if( theData > theMax )
    theMax = theData;
  i++;
}
```

It is also possible to have more than one initialization and more than one update statement within the same `for` loop; simply separate them with commas, as shown in Listing 7.14.

LISTING 7.14   Multiple initialization.

```
int index;
char c;

for( index = 1, c = 'A'; index <= 26; index++, c++ )
{
  cout << "In the alphabet, letter number " << index
       << " is " << c << endl;
}
```

However, it is usually impossible to *declare* two variables of different types in a `for` statement. Most compilers will generate an error if you write this:

```
for( int index = 1, char c = 'A'; index <= 26; index++, c++ )
```

because of the two declarations.

Another thing to keep in mind is that while the C++ standard says that variables declared in a `for` statement should go out of scope at the end of the `for` loop, not every compiler follows this standard. Microsoft Visual C++, for example, has a command-line option that determines whether the variables will go out of scope. A standard-compliant compiler would let you write something like this:

```
for( int iter = 0; iter < 10; iter++ )
{
  // do some work
}

for( int iter = 45; iter > 0; iter-- )
{
  // do some more work
}
```

but a noncompliant compiler will generate an error, saying that you are trying to redeclare a variable iter that is still in scope.

CONTROLLING LOOPS WITH continue AND break

Two more statements can modify the flow of control within any loop:

- The break statement immediately terminates the loop. Execution continues with the first statement following the loop's closing bracket.
- The continue statement terminates the *current iteration* of the loop. The program's execution continues with the next evaluation of the test condition. The snippet in Listing 7.15 gives examples of both statements.

LISTING 7.15   continue and break.

```
int i = 0;
while( true )
{
  i++;
  if( i == 7 )
    continue;

  if( i == 10 )
    break;

  cout << i << endl;
}
```

Normally, the while(true) construct would force an infinite loop. However, when variable i takes on the value 10, the break statement will force termination of the loop.

Meanwhile, when `i` becomes 7, the `continue` statement will force termination of the current loop iteration before the `cout` statement. As a result, the snippet will print the numbers between 1 and 9, except 7.

SUMMARY

C++ provides several conditional statements: `if`, `if-else`, the conditional operator, and `switch`. Each executes code if certain Boolean test conditions are met.

The language also includes three types of loops: the `while` loop, which may run any number of times (including zero), the `do-while` loop that executes its code block at least once, and the `for` loop that provides certain convenience features. Within a loop, the `break` statement terminates the loop early, and the `continue` statement terminates the loop's current iteration.

EXERCISES

7.1 What is the difference between a `while` loop and a `do-while` loop?

7.2 What is short-circuit evaluation?

7.3 What is the purpose of the `break` statement in a `switch` block? In a loop block?

7.4 What is the best way to avoid accidentally writing an assignment statement when you mean to write a test for equality?

7.5 What happens if we execute this code snippet?

```
int iter = 25;
while( iter > 0 );
{
  cout << iter << " " << iter * iter << endl;
  iter--;
}
```

7.6 Write a calculator program that selects an operation (_, -, * or /) from a menu, inputs two operands, and prints the result.

7.7 Write a program that inputs three numbers and prints them out in increasing order.

7.8 Upgrade Example 7.7 or Example 7.8 so the user is expected to find a number between 1 and 100, and the computer tells him after each guess whether the answer is higher, lower, or equal to his guess.

8 Game Project: Single-Pile NIM

In This Chapter

- The Game of NIM
- Game Architecture
- Important Data
- Who Goes First?
- Human Player Moves
- Computer Player Moves
- Endgame Conditions
- Complete Source Code

 All Listing code in this chapter can be found on the companion CD-ROM

For the second major project, you will be implementing one of the many forms of the game of NIM. Invented, according to Wikipedia, over 100 years ago by C. L. Bouton of Harvard University, who also developed a complete mathematical analysis of the game, NIM was chosen because it can be coded quickly and provides an exceptionally simple way to implement a "smart" computer opponent.

Before delving into the source code, you may want to compile the game, found in Project8_1.cpp, which is located in the Chapter 8 folder on the companion CD-ROM, and play a few games against your computer.

THE GAME OF NIM

The NIM variant you will be coding is a two-player game in which players take turns removing sticks from a single pile. There are 22 sticks in the pile at the start of the game, and each player must take between 1 and 4 sticks from the pile during each turn. The player who takes the last stick wins.

The Winning Strategy

Suppose there are five sticks left in the pile and it is your turn. How many sticks should you remove: one, two, three, or four?

Unfortunately, your choice does not matter because the situation is hopeless. If you remove a single stick, there will be 4 sticks left in the pile, and your opponent will be able to take them all and win during his next turn. If you remove the maximum of 4 sticks, you leave the opponent with a single stick to take for the win. Clearly, unless your opponent makes a silly mistake, he will win the game during his next turn no matter what you do.

Therefore, an optimal strategy for NIM is to make sure it will be the opponent's turn to play when the number of sticks in the pile falls to 5. In general, if you manage to leave a *multiple of 5* sticks in the pile in time for any of the opponent's turns, you are guaranteed to win the game if you keep playing optimally: no matter what the opponent plays, you will be able to leave him with a smaller multiple of 5 for his next turn, and then to repeat the trick until the pile is exhausted.

Mathematically, this strategy translates to the following rules:

■ If the remainder R of the division of the number of sticks in the pile by 5 is nonzero, then take R sticks from the pile, leaving the opponent with a multiple of 5 sticks.
■ If the remainder is zero, the position is hopeless unless the opponent makes a mistake, so any move is as good or as bad as any other.

Table 8.1 shows an example in which Player A takes the first turn.

TABLE 8.1 A Sample NIM Game

Moves	Sticks left in the pile
Initial configuration.	22
22 modulo 5 is 2, so Player A takes 2 sticks.	20
Player B takes 1 stick.	19
19 modulo 5 is 4, so Player A takes 4 sticks.	15 $\rightarrow$

Moves	Sticks left in the pile
Player B takes 2 sticks.	13
13 modulo 5 is 3, so Player A takes 3 sticks.	10
Player B takes 4 sticks.	6
6 modulo 5 is 1, so Player A takes 1 stick.	5
Player B takes 2 sticks.	3
3 modulo 5 is 3, so Player A takes 3 sticks.	0; Player A wins.

Note that since there are 22 sticks in the pile at the beginning of the game, whoever plays first has a guaranteed victory if he or she plays flawlessly.

GAME ARCHITECTURE

The game will consist of four major components:

- First, you must let the human player decide whether he wants to play first or whether he wants to let the computer do the honors. This component must verify that the player has made a valid choice, and let him try again if he has entered incorrect data.
- Then, you must implement a routine that will allow the human player to enter the number of sticks he wants to take during his turn. You also need to validate this data against the rules of the game (i.e., the choice must be a number between 1 and 4 sticks, and no more than the number of sticks left in the pile) and let the player try again if he enters an illegal move.
- Then, you will need a simple "artificial intelligence" routine to generate moves for the computer.
- Finally, you will need a component that alternates between the two players, checks whether the game is over, and announces the winner.

Each of these components will be described in detail in its own section, with snippets from the source code inserted whenever appropriate.

IMPORTANT DATA

The game's implementation will require several variables and constants.

First, you will define two Boolean constants to represent the players. You could have used `true` and `false` directly in the code, but the identifiers `HUMAN_PLAYER` and `COMPUTER_PLAYER` will be much more expressive.

```
const bool HUMAN_PLAYER = true;
const bool COMPUTER_PLAYER = false;
```

You will also require a variable that will contain the identity of the current player at any given time. This variable will also have type `bool`, since it will take on the values of the two constants `HUMAN_PLAYER` and `COMPUTER_PLAYER` at various times during the game.

```
bool currentPlayer;
```

Finally, you will need two integer variables: `nimSticks`, initialized at 22, will hold the number of sticks left in the pile, and `currentPlayerMove` will hold the number of sticks the current player will be taking during his turn.

```
int nimSticks = 22;
int currentPlayerMove = 0;
```

In the full source code, these variables are not all declared at the same time. Instead, each is declared when it first becomes necessary.

WHO GOES FIRST?

The first thing to do before starting the game is to determine which of the two sides will take the first turn, a decision that you will leave in the hands of the human player.

This algorithm will be as follows:

- Ask the player to enter a single character to signify his choice: 'C' in upper- or lowercase if he wants the computer to move first, 'P' in upper- or lowercase if he wants to take the first turn himself.
- If the player makes an improper choice (i.e., he types any other character), give him feedback and let him try again, as many times as needed to produce a valid answer.

This type of algorithm, where a certain job has to be performed at least once but possibly an arbitrary number of times, is perfectly suited to implementation with a `do-while` loop, so this is the technique we will be using, as illustrated by the pseudo-code snippet in Listing 8.1.

LISTING 8.1   Input loop algorithm.

```
do
{
  // Prompt the user
  // Read his choice from the keyboard
} while( // the choice is incorrect );
```

The code that implements this algorithm is in Listing 8.2.

LISTING 8.2   Input loop.

```
char firstPlayer;           // the human player's choice
bool validPlayer = false;   // is this choice valid?

do
{
  // Prompt and data entry
  cout << "Who plays first: [P]layer or [C]omputer?" << endl;
  cin >> firstPlayer;

  // Let's analyze the player's choice
  switch( firstPlayer )
  {
    // First, if the player has chosen to go first
    case 'P':
    case 'p':
      validPlayer = true;
      currentPlayer = HUMAN_PLAYER;
      break;

    // Then, if the player has chosen to let the
    // computer go first
    case 'C':
    case 'c':
      validPlayer = true;
      currentPlayer = COMPUTER_PLAYER;
      break;

    // Finally, if the player has made a mistake
    default:
      cout << "Invalid entry; please try again. ";
      break;
  }
} while( !validPlayer ); // Repeat as long as necessary
```

Within the do-while loop, you use a switch statement to look at the player's choice. The first two cases, case 'P' and case 'p', are valid choices that indicate that the human player wants to go first, so you assign the `currentPlayer` variable with the `HUMAN_PLAYER` constant value and raise the `validPlayer` Boolean flag by setting it to `true`. The next two cases are similar, except that they give the first turn to the computer. Finally, any choice that is not 'P,' 'p,' 'C,' or 'c' is caught by the `default` case, which simply prints an error message.

Then, you reach the `do-while` loop's test condition, which is satisfied if `!validPlayer` is true, which means that `validPlayer` is false. Look at the snippet's second line; you have initialized `validPlayer` to `false` (since there was not a proper choice at that point) and you have only changed its value if the human player has typed in one of 'C,' 'c,' 'P,' or 'p.' Therefore, unless you have a definite answer, the program will iterate through the loop one more time.

By the time you exit this loop, you will know with certainty who is supposed to play first, and you can then enter the *core game loop*, which will run until there are no sticks left in the pile as outlined in Listing 8.3.

LISTING 8.3   Main loop algorithm.

```
// CORE GAME LOOP: as long as there are sticks left,
// we'll need to get moves from the opponents
while( 0 != nimSticks )
{
  // Get moves from the players, etc.
}
```

HUMAN PLAYER MOVES

The routine that allows the player to enter her moves is similar in structure to the one you just saw: You must prompt the player, read her choices at the keyboard, validate them, and let her try again if the move is illegal. Therefore, you will be using another `do-while` loop, but this time the validation will take the form of an `if` statement that checks whether the number of sticks entered by the player is legal.

There are two rules to determine whether a move is legal:

- It must be between 1 and 4 sticks.
- It must not be larger than the number of sticks remaining in the pile.

In Listing 8.4, the `validHumanMove` flag is raised only if a move satisfies all the rules.

LISTING 8.4   Move processing.

```
if( currentPlayer == HUMAN_PLAYER )
{
```

```
    // If it is the human player's turn, ask for
    // a number of sticks between 1 and 4
    // and validate like we did for the choice of
    // starting player above
    bool validHumanMove = false;
    do
    {
      cout << "How many sticks do you want to remove [1-4]?";
      cin >> currentPlayerMove;

    // A move is valid if the number is between 1 and 4
      validHumanMove = ( currentPlayerMove > 0 &&
            currentPlayerMove < 5 &&
                     currentPlayerMove <= nimSticks );

    // If the move is invalid, give an error message
      if( !validHumanMove )
        cout << "Between 1 and 4, and no more than there are "
            << "in the pile, please." << endl;

    } while( !validHumanMove );
  }
```

COMPUTER PLAYER MOVES

You will give the computer opponent intelligence by implementing the perfect NIM strategy discussed earlier. Fortunately, to do so is easy as demonstrated in Listing 8.5: all you will need is the modulo operator, %.

LISTING 8.5   Computer move.

```
    // A little piece of artificial intelligence :)
    // based on the mathematical analysis of the
    // game that we discussed in the chapter

    // Ideally, we'd like to leave a multiple of 5
    // sticks in the pile after the computer's turn
    int idealMove = ( nimSticks % 5 );
```

The ideal move is to take as many sticks as the remainder of the division of nimSticks by 5, because that would leave the opponent with a pile containing a multiple of 5 sticks, which is a losing position. However, if you are already in a losing position, the remainder is 0, which is an illegal move; in that case, there are no good moves available and you can play anything as outlined in Listing 8.6.

LISTING 8.6   More computer moves.

```
// If that's impossible, the position is lost,
// so any move is as good or as bad as another
if( 0 == idealMove )
  currentPlayerMove = 1;
else
  currentPlayerMove = idealMove;

// Announce the computer's move to the player
cout << "I am taking " << currentPlayerMove
     << " sticks from the pile." << endl;
```

ENDGAME CONDITIONS

Once the current player has entered a move, you must verify whether the move has just won the game. If so, you need to print out a message of congratulations as shown in Listing 8.7.

LISTING 8.7   Congratulations message.

```
// Do we have a winner?
if( 0 == nimSticks )
{
  // If so, who has just taken the last stick?
  if( HUMAN_PLAYER == currentPlayer )
  {
    cout << "You win. Congratulations!" << endl;
  }
  else
  {
    cout << "I win! Better luck next time..." << endl;
  }
}
```

If the game is not over, you must let the other player take a turn. Since the two players are represented by Boolean constants, you will use a simple trick to alternate between players: simply negate the currentPlayer Boolean variable as shown in Listing 8.8.

LISTING 8.8   Switching players.

```
// If there are sticks left in the pile, it is
// now the other player's turn
else
{
```

```
        currentPlayer = !currentPlayer;
    }
```

And you iterate the core game loop again, until there are no sticks left in the pile.

COMPLETE SOURCE CODE

Here is the complete source code for the NIM game, which is detailed in Listing 8.9.

LISTING 8.9   Nim source.

```
*************************************
Learn C++ by Making Games
Project 8.1 - Simple Nim
*************************************/

#include <iostream>
using namespace std;

int main()
{
  // Let's start with a welcoming message
  cout << "Welcome to the Game of Single-Pile Nim!" << endl;
  cout << "-------------------------------------" << endl
       << endl;

  // Let's define constants to identify the sides
  const bool HUMAN_PLAYER = true;
  const bool COMPUTER_PLAYER = false;

  // Let's define some variables that will help us let
  // the human player decide who goes first:
  // Himself/herself or the computer
  char firstPlayer;            // the human player's choice
  bool validPlayer = false;    // is this choice valid?

  // Once the game has begun, we'll need to know the
  // identity of the current player at all times
  bool currentPlayer;

  // Now, let's ask the human player who goes first
  // We have to do this at least once, and maybe more
  // if the first choice is bad, so we'll use a do-while loop
  do
  {
    // Prompt and data entry
```

```cpp
  cout << "Who plays first: [P]layer or [C]omputer?" << endl;
  cin >> firstPlayer;

  // Let's analyze the player's choice
  switch( firstPlayer )
  {
    // First, if the player has chosen to go first
    case 'P':
    case 'p':
      validPlayer = true;
      currentPlayer = HUMAN_PLAYER;
      break;

    // Then, if the player has chosen to let the
    // computer go first
    case 'C':
    case 'c':
      validPlayer = true;
      currentPlayer = COMPUTER_PLAYER;
      break;

    // Finally, if the player has made a mistake
    default:
      cout << "Invalid entry; please try again. ";
      break;
  }

} while( !validPlayer ); // Repeat as long as necessary

// Now that we know who plays first, we can start
// the game by initializing the heap of sticks
int nimSticks = 22;

// CORE GAME LOOP: as long as there are sticks left,
// we'll need to get moves from the opponents
while( 0 != nimSticks )
{
  // How many sticks are there left in the pile?
  cout << "There are now " << nimSticks
       << " in the pile." << endl;

  // A variable to hold the number of sticks that
  // the current player wants to take
  int currentPlayerMove = 0;

  // Let's get a move from the current player
  if( currentPlayer == HUMAN_PLAYER )
  {
```

```
      // If it is the human player's turn, ask for
      // a number of sticks between 1 and 4
      // and validate like we did for the choice of
      // starting player above
      bool validHumanMove = false;
      do
      {
        cout << "How many sticks do you want to remove [1-4]?";
        cin >> currentPlayerMove;
        validHumanMove = ( currentPlayerMove > 0 &&
              currentPlayerMove < 5 &&
                      currentPlayerMove <= nimSticks );
        if( !validHumanMove )
          cout << "Between 1 and 4, and no more than there are "
              << "in the pile, please." << endl;
      } while( !validHumanMove );
    }

    else // currentPlayer is automatically COMPUTER_PLAYER
    {
      // A little piece of artificial intelligence :)
      // based on the mathematical analysis of the
      // game that we discussed in the chapter

      // Ideally, we'd like to leave a multiple of 5
      // sticks in the pile after the computer's turn
      int idealMove = ( nimSticks % 5 );

      // If that's impossible, the position is lost,
      // so any move is as good or as bad as another
      if( 0 == idealMove )
        currentPlayerMove = 1;
      else
        currentPlayerMove = idealMove;

      // Announce the computer's move to the player
      cout << "I am taking " << currentPlayerMove
          << " sticks from the pile." << endl;
    }

    // Now that we know how many sticks the current
    // player wants to take, we remove them from the
    // pile
    nimSticks -= currentPlayerMove;

    // Do we have a winner?
    if( 0 == nimSticks )
    {
```

```
      // If so, who has just taken the last stick?
      if( HUMAN_PLAYER == currentPlayer )
      {
        cout << "You win. Congratulations!" << endl;
      }
      else
      {
        cout << "I win! Better luck next time..." << endl;
      }
    }

    // If there are sticks left in the pile, it is
    // now the other player's turn
    else
    {
      currentPlayer = !currentPlayer;
    }
  } // end of the while( 0 != nimSticks ) loop


  // And we're done!
  return 0;
}
```

SUMMARY

In this chapter, you used loops, conditional statements, Boolean expressions, constants, and variables to build a complete game of NIM. You also took the opportunity to introduce some data entry and validation techniques that apply to a wide variety of games and programs, and showed the essential structure of a game, specifically how to write a core game loop that iterates until one side has won.

If you have not done so already, compile the game's source code, which can be found in the Project8_1.cpp file in the Chapter 8 folder of the book's companion CD-ROM, and play with it.

EXERCISE

8.1 Alter the game by allowing the player to specify a pile of sticks larger than 22. The games rules do not need to be altered, but it is interesting to see the effect on game strategy by the player and the computer.

OTHER PROJECT IDEAS

Expand the NIM game by allowing the human player to determine some of the game's parameters at runtime:

- The number of sticks in the initial pile.
- The maximum number of sticks one player can pick up in any turn.
- Whether to play human-vs.-human or human-vs.-computer.

Make sure the rest of the code is updated accordingly, especially the computer player's move selection routine.

Use C++'s built-in random number generator (which you will learn more about in Chapter 9) and develop a game of hi-lo, in which the player must guess whether the next random number generated will be higher or lower than the last. Limit the random numbers to a small range (like 1–13) and instead of presenting them to the user as numbers, write a `switch` statement that prints significant strings (like playing card names) instead. Keep track of the longest streak of correct guesses made by the player. Then, upgrade the game to allow the player to bet on each guess, keeping track of the amount of money he has in his account.

Part

III

Functions and Structured Programming

The programs we wrote in Part II are relatively small and simple by today's standards, but they are already rather difficult to read: there is simply too much code in the main program, and this code is not particularly versatile. And remember that there are only a few dozen lines of source code in these programs; imagine how difficult it would be to understand a 5,000-line program written like this! To solve these problems, C++ provides a way to split a program into logical structural elements, called *functions*, that can be developed independently and simplify programs enormously.

In this part of the book, we will learn how to use the many functions provided by the standard C++ libraries (including the built-in random number generator), how to create our own functions to give structure to our programs, how to pass parameters to functions to change their behaviors, how to return values from functions, and how to speed up program execution with inline functions. We will also learn how to further improve program structure by splitting programs into multiple source and header files and by creating function prototypes.

9

Function Fundamentals

In This Chapter

- What Is a C++ Function?
- The C++ Library Structure
- Calling Library Functions
- Some Important Library Functions

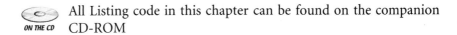 All Listing code in this chapter can be found on the companion
CD-ROM

This chapter introduces the concept of a *function* and generalizes the work you did with iostreams by presenting *C++'s standard library*. At the end of the chapter, you will be able to tap into C++'s wealth of built-in functions to enhance your code and speed development.

WHAT IS A C++ FUNCTION?

In C++, a function is an independent block of code with its own name. You use functions to split programs into small, self-consistent chunks that can be developed independently. So far, you have only seen one function, called `main()`; every program has at least a `main()` function, but most include many other functions of all shapes and sizes.

The rules governing the design and use of functions are:

- The function must have a *name*, which must be a legal identifier.
- A function may accept any number of *parameters*, including none. Parameters are values that are passed to the function from outside and are manipulated by its code. The list of parameters is enclosed within parentheses; the parentheses are always required, even if the parameter list is empty.
- Each function has a *type* that corresponds to the type of the value it returns. The main() function always returns a value of type int; other functions can return values of all basic data types, including user-defined types, and several kinds of values we will study later, like pointers, objects, and structures, but not arrays. A function that returns nothing has type void.
- Each function must have a unique *signature*. A function's signature is made up of its type, its name, and the types of its parameters; furthermore, it is illegal for two functions to differ only in their return type.
- A *function call* is a statement that includes a function's name and a list of parameter values enclosed within parentheses. The number and the types of the parameters must match those in the function's signature; otherwise, C++ may attempt an automatic type cast, but as usual, the results may not be satisfactory.
- Before a function may be called, it must be either *defined* (i.e., written in full) or *prototyped* (i.e., its signature must be announced to the compiler). All built-in libraries include prototypes of all their functions.

Other programming languages have different rules to define what is and is not a function. Other names for function-like constructs in various languages include method, procedure, subprogram, and subroutine.

The rest of this chapter will present several library functions that are provided with every C++ implementation. You will learn how to create your own functions and prototypes in Chapter 10.

Some authors make a distinction between a function's parameters, which are formal constructs that refer to the types of data the function expects to receive, and its arguments, which are the actual values being passed to it. In this book, the terms parameter and argument are used interchangeably.

THE C++ LIBRARY STRUCTURE

C++'s *libraries* contain hundreds of functions that you can use within your programs. Each library (of which there are dozens) includes a number of functions and constants that handle related tasks. For example, the math library includes functions that implement many trigonometric and algebraic operations, while the iostream library deals with keyboard input and screen output.

Unlike the built-in keywords like while and return, library functions are not automatically understood by the compiler. If you want to use a library function in a program, you must first *include* the appropriate *header file*, as you have been doing for iostreams for several chapters. The code snippet in Listing 9.1 tells the compiler that we plan to use some math, string, and iostream functions in the program.

LISTING 9.1   Including.

```
#include <math>
#include <string>
#include <iostream>
using namespace std;
```

The order in which libraries are included in a program is unimportant. All that matters is that libraries must be included before any of their functions are called in the program—which usually means that all #include statements will appear at the very top of the source file.

Some compilers must be told where the standard libraries are stored on the hard drive before they can produce executable programs that refer to library functions. Please read your compiler's documentation to learn how to set this up properly.

Why does C++ use libraries (and so many of them) instead of including everything as built-in keywords? First, to reduce executable program size; very few programs use more than a tiny fraction of the libraries' capabilities, and forcing every executable to include lots of code it does not need would be a waste of resources. Second, because the library inclusion mechanism is very powerful and allows programmers to add their own libraries to the system or to buy additional libraries from third-party vendors; for example, most compilers come with system-dependent libraries to handle graphical user interfaces.

CALLING LIBRARY FUNCTIONS

To take advantage of a library function's services, all you need to do (once the proper header file has been included) is to write a function call. Example 9.1 in

Listing 9.2 reads two numbers a and b from the keyboard and calculates the value of a raised to the bth power.

LISTING 9.2

```
/***************************************
 Learn C++ by Making Games
 Example 9.1: Library Function Calls
 ***************************************/

#include <iostream>
#include <math>
using namespace std;

int main()
{
  // First, get the data
  cout << "Type in a number A and an exponent B:" << endl;
  double a, b;
  cin >> a >> b;

  // Then, make the function call
  double theResult = pow( a, b );

  // And give feedback to the reader
  cout << "A to the Bth power is " << theResult << endl;

  // And we're done!
  return 0;
}
```

The function pow() calculates the powers of numbers. It belongs to the math library, which you have included in the program, accepts two arguments of type double (first the number to be elevated, then the exponent), and returns a value of type double (the result). Therefore, its signature looks like:

```
double pow( double, double );
```

It is possible to see pow's actual prototype and to check out what other functions are included in the math library by looking at the header file math.h, which is stored in your compiler's standard header file directory on disk. However, all C++ library files are highly optimized and extremely hard to read, so you are much better off reading the compiler's documentation for details.

Since a function call returns a value, you can use function calls anywhere a value of the same type is appropriate. In Project 8.1, you used a switch statement to decide whether the player or the computer should have the first move in a game of NIM as shown in Listing 9.3.

LISTING 9.3   NIM snippet.

```
switch( firstPlayer )
{
  // First, if the player has chosen to go first
  case 'P':
  case 'p':
    validPlayer = true;
    currentPlayer = HUMAN_PLAYER;
    break;

  // Then, if the player has chosen to let the
  // computer go first
  case 'C':
  case 'c':
    validPlayer = true;
    currentPlayer = COMPUTER_PLAYER;
    break;

  // Finally, if the player has made a mistake
  default:
    cout << "Invalid entry; please try again. ";
    break;
}
```

In this `switch` statement, there are two cases for the player (one for a capital 'P', one for a lowercase 'p') and two for the computer. This could have been reduced to a single case for each side by switching on the value of the `char`-valued function `toupper`, which takes a character and returns its uppercase equivalent. This function belongs to the `ctype` library and has the signature:

```
char toupper( char );
```

and therefore can be used anywhere a `char` value is expected; for example, as an argument for a `switch` statement. By using this function, you could transform the code snippet in Listing 9.3 into something as shown in Listing 9.4.

LISTING 9.4   NIM switch.

```
switch( toupper( firstPlayer ) )
{
  // First, if the player has chosen to go first
  case 'P':
    validPlayer = true;
    currentPlayer = HUMAN_PLAYER;
```

```
      break;

      // Then, if the player has chosen to let the
      // computer go first
      case 'C':
        validPlayer = true;
        currentPlayer = COMPUTER_PLAYER;
        break;

      // Finally, if the player has made a mistake
      default:
        cout << "Invalid entry; please try again. ";
        break;
  }
```

You can even pass a function's return value as an argument to another function. Suppose you need to calculate the mathematical function *cos x^y* for two arbitrary values *x* and *y*. You have already seen that *x^y* can be written as pow(x, y) in C++. The math library also contains a cosine function that takes a double argument and returns a double value; its signature is

```
double cos( double );
```

Therefore, you could write a single statement to implement our calculation:

```
double theBigResult = cos( pow( x, y ) );
```

SOME IMPORTANT LIBRARY FUNCTIONS

There are literally hundreds of functions in the standard libraries, and most compiler vendors add hundreds or thousands more in their own system-dependent libraries, so an exhaustive look at all of them is far beyond the scope of this book. In later chapters, you will be looking at specific libraries that handle string manipulation, data files, timers, and graphics (with the Simple DirectMedia Layer, which is not part of the C++ standard); for now, you will concentrate on math and random numbers.

The Math Library

C++'s math library contains a number of valuable constants and functions. Table 9.1 lists some of the most useful.

TABLE 9.1   Math Constants and Functions

M_PI	A #define constant that contains the value of PI, rounded to about 20 decimals.
M_E	Another #define constant that holds the value of the e constant, the base of the natural logarithms.
M_SQRT2	The square root of 2.
double acos(double), double asin(double), double atan(double), double cos(double), double sin(double), double tan(double)	The six main trigonometric functions: cosine, sine, tangent, and their inverses.
double log(double), double log10(double)	Logarithms (natural and in base 10).
double floor(double), double ceil(double)	Floor and ceiling; e.g., a number rounded down or up.
int abs(int), long labs(long), double fabs(double)	Absolute value.

Random Numbers

The stdlib library includes a *pseudo-random number generator*, which allows you to write programs that roll dice, deal cards, and work with probabilities.

The "pseudo" in pseudo-random means that the sequence of numbers generated by the process, while appearing random to the human eye, is actually entirely predictable, because each entry is calculated from its predecessor using a fixed algorithm. However, for your purposes, the difference between a true random number generator and the pseudo-random generator provided by C++ is insignificant.

To use the random number generator, you must:

- Include the stdlib library. Note that many, but not all, compilers will do it for you automatically.
- Initialize the generator by calling the srand() function, which returns nothing and takes a single unsigned integer parameter called the *seed*. srand() should only be called once.
- Every time you need a random number, call the rand() function, which takes no arguments and returns a value of type int between 0 and RAND_MAX, a constant that is system-dependent but never smaller than 32,767.

Typically, you will want to provide `srand()` with a seed that changes with every execution of the program, so that the sequence of random numbers will never be the same twice. A perfect example is the result of the `time()` function, which returns the number of seconds that have elapsed since January 1, 1970. Example 9.2 in Listing 9.5 shows how to use `time()` as a seed; the parameter `NULL` being passed to `time()` is a special *pointer constant* we will encounter again in Part V of this book.

LISTING 9.5

```
/***********************************
 Learn C++ by Making Games
 Example 9.2: Random Number Generator
 ***********************************/

#include <iostream>
#include <stdlib>
#include <ctime>

using namespace std;

int main()
{
  // First, seed the random number generator
  srand( time( NULL ) );

  // Then, roll a standard six-sided dice 10 times
  for( int i = 0; i < 10; i++ )
  {
    int theDice = ( rand() % 6 ) + 1;

    cout << "I have rolled a dice and got a " << theDice
        << endl;
  }

  // And we're done!
  return 0;
}
```

Example 9.2 also shows an example of a very common technique employed when calling `rand()`. When a random number between 0 and a certain value *N* is needed, the easiest way to calculate it from the value *R* returned by `rand()` is to take the remainder of the division of *R* by *N*. Then, an addition or a subtraction can be performed to shift the range of random values to whatever is required; for example, to roll a standard six-sided dice, adding 1 to the result of a random number generation between 0 and 5 will produce a random number between 1 and 6:

```
int theDice = ( rand() % 6 ) + 1;
```

SUMMARY

C++'s standard libraries include hundreds of functions and constants that can be used to speed development. To use a library function in a source code file, the library's header file must first be included. Then, the programmer can write function calls that provide the function with arguments (or parameters) whose types must match the function's signature; if they don't, C++ will attempt an automatic type cast, which may yield correct results, incorrect results, or a compilation error. A function call can appear anywhere a value of the same type as the function's return value is expected.

EXERCISES

9.1 What happens if we try to pass the wrong types of arguments to a function?

9.2 Is it possible to have functions with these signatures in the same program?

```
int myFunc( int )
float myFunc( float )
```

9.3 Is it possible to have functions with these signatures in the same program?

```
int myFunc( int )
float myFunc( int )
```

9.4 What is the difference between a function's return type and its signature?

9.5 Upgrade the divination game from Chapter 7 to make the computer generate the number the player must guess at random.

9.6 Write a menu-driven dice-rolling program to assist in role-playing character creation. The program must ask the user which type of dice to roll (2-, 4-, 6-, 8-, 10-, 12-, 20-, 30-, and 100-sided dice must be supported) and how many of them to roll at the same time. The program must then print the sum of the dice. Make the program run in a loop, and offer "Quit" as an extra menu entry.

10 Programmer-Defined Functions

In This Chapter

- Function Structure
- Function Prototypes
- Local Variables
- Dividing Programs into Functions

 All Listing code in this chapter can be found on the companion CD-ROM

This chapter explains how programmers can define their own functions to introduce an additional level of structure to their software. For now, all of your functions will reside in a single source file, along with the main program; you will begin using multiple source files in Chapter 12.

FUNCTION STRUCTURE

All user-defined functions are built according to the same general template, which you have already been using for `main()` functions since the beginning of this book. A function definition's components are:

The function's return type. In the case of `main()`, the return type is always `int`.

Its name. Of course, `main()`'s is always main, but for other functions any legal identifier will be satisfactory.

A list of formal parameters enclosed within parentheses. Each formal parameter needs a type and a name of its own. So far, the `main()` functions have had empty parameter lists, but you will learn how to pass parameters to `main()` directly from the command line in Part IV.

A function body. A block of code that must be terminated by a return statement.

As mentioned previously, the return type, the name, and the types of the parameters define a function's signature.

Example 10.1 outlined in Listing 10.1 shows a small program made up of a `main()` function and a short `average()` function that calculates the average of three numbers.

LISTING 10.1

```
/**********************************
  Learn C++ by Making Games
  Example 10.1: User-defined function
**********************************/

#include <iostream>
using namespace std;

// The following function calculates the
// average of its three parameters
double average( double a, double b, double c )
{
    return( ( a + b + c ) / 3.0 );
}

int main()
{
    // Read three numbers from the keyboard
    cout << "Please type in three numbers: " << endl;
    double n1, n2, n3;
    cin >> n1 >> n2 >> n3;

    // Calculate and print the average of the three
    cout << "Their average is: " << average( n1, n2, n3 )
         << endl;

    // And we're done!
    return 0;
}
```

In Example 10.1, you begin by defining the average() function, which takes three parameters of type double and returns a value also of type double. The return statement is a special keyword that takes as its argument a single value of the same type as the function; in this case, you are returning the result of a double-precision floating-point operation. (The parentheses surrounding this floating-point expression are not strictly required, but they make the code easier to read.)

Then, in the main program, you call the average() function, passing the values of the three variables n1, n2, and n3 to average() as its arguments. When the program's flow of execution enters average(), the values of the arguments are *copied* into the formal parameters a, b, and c, in the order in which they are passed to the function. Figure 10.1 shows what happens if you call average() when n1 is equal to 12, n2 is 4, and n3 is 7.

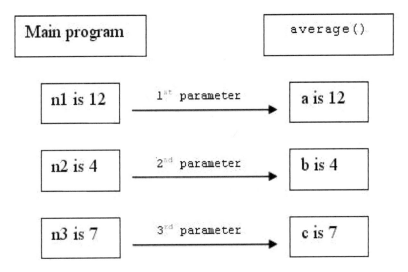

FIGURE 10.1 Formal parameters receiving their values.

Parameters are always copied in order, even if the types of the formal parameters and the arguments do not match. If a function expects a double followed by an int and receives an int followed by a double, C++ will not reorder the parameters; instead it will copy the function's first argument (the int) into its first formal parameter (the double) and truncate the second argument (the double) to make it fit into the second formal parameter (the int). Make sure to pass parameters in the correct order!

Parameter Scope

The names of the function's three formal parameters, a, b, and c, are local to the function; they are placeholders for the arguments passed to the function by its caller, and exist within its block and nowhere else. Therefore, the formal parameter names are said to have *local scope*.

This means that if main() or any other function in the program contains variables or parameters named a, b, or c, the two are entirely different variables with no connection to each other whatsoever. Therefore, any manipulation you perform on a parameter within the function has no impact on any variable of the same name that is declared anywhere else, *even if that other variable's value is passed to the function as a parameter.* Example 10.2 shown in Listing 10.2 and Figure 10.2 show what happens in this peculiar case.

LISTING 10.2

```
/ ***********************************
  Learn C++ by Making Games
  Example 10.2: Local Scope
  ********************************** /

#include <iostream>
using namespace std;

// This function adds 10 to its argument
// but does NOT propagate the changes
// back to its caller:
void adder( int theVar )
{
  theVar += 10;
  cout << "Inside adder, theVar is now " << theVar << endl;
  return;
}

int main()
{
  // We create a variable that has the same name
  // as the adder() function's parameter
  int theVar = 3;
  cout << "In Main, theVar is " << theVar << endl;

  // Now, call adder and see what happens
  adder( theVar );
  cout << "When we return from adder, theVar is "
      << theVar << endl;

  // And we're done!
```

```
    return 0;
}
```

The adder() *function in Example 10.2 returns no value; its type is therefore defined as* void *and the* return *statement at the end of the function receives no argument.*

Passing Parameters by Value

In Example 10.2, you have a variable called theVar in the main() function, and a formal parameter also called theVar in the adder() function. You even pass the main function's theVar to the function as an argument, so that when adder() begins its execution, its own theVar has received the value of the main function's variable of the same name.

Then, within adder(), you change the value of theVar and print the new value, which is now 13. However, the change has no effect on the variable that has been passed as an argument, so when you return to the main function its own theVar is unchanged; its value is still 3, as it has always been.

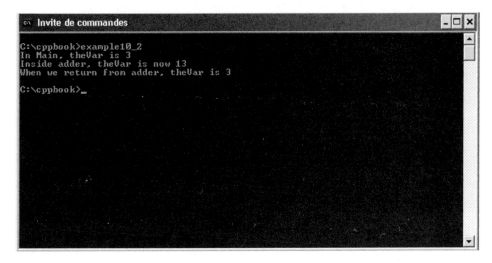

FIGURE 10.2   Changing a parameter has no effect outside the function.

This behavior defines what is called *passing a parameter by value*: The function receives its own copy of the value given as a parameter and can do whatever it wants to this local copy without changing the original. Among other things, passing parameters by value allows you to send constants and literals as arguments to functions: Since the function will store a local copy in what amounts to a local variable, it will not try to change the original constant or literal, which would be illegal. Example 10.3 detailed in Listing 10.3 and Figure 10.3 show what happens when we pass constants and literals as parameters-by-value.

LISTING 10.3

```
/*************************************
 Learn C++ by Making Games
 Example 10.3: Parameters by value
 *************************************/

#include <iostream>
using namespace std;

// This function adds 10 to its argument
// but does NOT propagate the changes
// back to its caller:
void adder( int theVar )
{
  theVar += 10;
  cout << "Inside adder, theVar is now " << theVar << endl;
  return;
}

int main()
{
  // This time, let's call adder with a constant
  const int theVar = 3;
  cout << "We will pass a constant of value 3 to adder.\n";
  adder( theVar );
  cout << "When we return from adder, the constant is still "
      << theVar << endl;

  // Now, let's try with a literal
  cout << "Let's call adder with the literal 16" << endl;
  adder( 16 );

  // And we're done!
  return 0;
}
```

You will learn about other ways to pass parameters in Chapter 11 and in Part V.

Function Termination

As soon as the flow of execution within a function reaches a `return` statement, the function terminates and control returns to the function's caller. This means that the

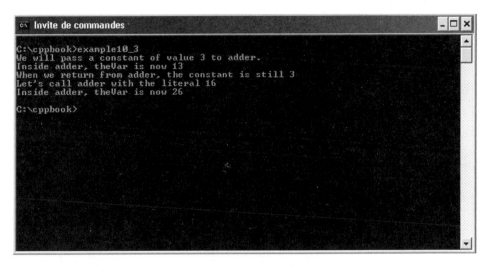

FIGURE 10.3 Passing constants and literals as parameters by value.

cout statement in the code snippet in Listing 10.4 will never be executed; most compilers will detect situations like this and raise a warning.

LISTING 10.4 Warning.

```
int totalPrice( int unitPrice, int units )
{
  return( unitPrice * units );
  cout << "Total price is " << unitPrice * units;
}
```

However, note that code that appears after a return statement in a function definition can be executed *if the return statement is not executed*. The snippet in Listing 10.5 shows a common case where programmers can use this rule to their advantage to force early termination if the function's arguments are invalid.

LISTING 10.5 Early termination.

```
void welcome( string name )
{
  if( name == "" )
    return;

  cout << "Welcome, " << name << endl;
  return;
}
```

The welcome() function prints a polite message if it receives a valid name, but if it receives an empty string instead, it just returns early and no output is produced.

FUNCTION PROTOTYPES

Just as variables and constants must be declared before they can be used, C++ functions must be declared before they are called for the first time. So far, you have ensured that your programs follow this rule by writing all of the subsidiary functions in full before writing the main() program. However, if you have many functions that call other functions, finding the right ordering can become problematic. Furthermore, it would seem to make sense to group together functions that perform related duties (for example, all of the mathematical operations, or all of the menu manipulations) to make the code easier to read, but the obligation to declare functions before they are called could make this more difficult. Finally, what if two functions need to call *each other*? In this case, there is *no* ordering that will work.

Fortunately, C++ provides a convenient way to work around these problems: function *prototypes*.

A function prototype is a one-line statement that declares a function's signature to the compiler. In essence, the prototype tells the compiler that a full function definition that matches the signature will be forthcoming eventually, and it is therefore safe to accept calls to this function even if it hasn't been defined yet. Example 10.4 shown in Listing 10.6 is a rewrite of Example 10.1 with a function prototype added.

LISTING 10.6

```
/********************************
   Learn C++ by Making Games
   Example 10.4: Function prototypes
 ********************************/

#include <iostream>
using namespace std;

// A prototype for the average() function
double average( double, double, double );

// The main program
int main()
{
  // Read three numbers from the keyboard
  cout << "Please type in three numbers: " << endl;
  double n1, n2, n3;
  cin >> n1 >> n2 >> n3;
```

```
    // Calculate and print the average of the three
    cout << "Their average is: " << average( n1, n2, n3 )
        << endl;

    // And we're done!
    return 0;
}

// The following function calculates the
// average of its three parameters
// Note that the function definition appears after
// the main program thanks to the prototype
double average( double a, double b, double c )
{
    return( ( a + b + c ) / 3.0 );
}
```

The prototype looks very much like the first line of the function definition, with two differences:

- Since it is an independent statement, it ends with a semicolon.
- The formal parameters are listed in type only; they have no name. (It is possible to give names to formal parameters in prototypes if you want, but the compiler will ignore them. They do not even need to match the names you will give the parameters in the actual function definition.)

It is usually good practice to write prototypes for all of your functions at the top of the source file, grouping them by functionality or by category to make the code easier to read.

LOCAL VARIABLES

Any variable or constant that is defined within a function's block is a *local variable* that has scope restricted to the function's body. Everything that has been said about parameters also applies to local variables: other variables of the same name defined in other functions are completely unrelated, the local variables go out of scope when the function terminates, and so forth.

Example 10.5 modifies the averaging function to include a local variable as shown in Listing 10.7.

LISTING 10.7

```
/****************************************
Learn C++ by Making Games
```

```
Example 10.5: Local Variables
***********************************/

#include <iostream>
using namespace std;

// A prototype for the average() function
double average( double, double, double );

// The main program
int main()
{
  // Read three numbers from the keyboard
  cout << "Please type in three numbers: " << endl;
  double n1, n2, n3;
  cin >> n1 >> n2 >> n3;

  // Calculate and print the average of the three
  cout << "Their average is: " << average( n1, n2, n3 )
       << endl;

  // And we're done!
  return 0;
}


// The following function calculates the
// average of its three parameters
// Note that the function definition appears after
// the main program thanks to the prototype
double average( double a, double b, double c )
{
  double theAverage = ( a + b + c ) / 3.0;
  return( theAverage );
}
```

DIVIDING PROGRAMS INTO FUNCTIONS

The purpose of the functional abstraction is to split programs into atomic chunks
that can be developed independently and solve problems piecemeal. In this section,
you will demonstrate functions' power by rewriting the single-pile NIM game from
Chapter 8 with a number of functions. This will be (by far) the most involved example yet, so you may want to spend some time analyzing the source code once you
are done with the text.

NOTE

The full source code for this version of the NIM game can be found on the companion CD-ROM, as Example 10.6.

ON THE CD First, you must ask yourself what independent operations are included in the NIM game:

- You ask the user who should play first.
- You let the user enter his moves.
- You play the computer's own moves.
- You check whether the game is over.
- You run the core game loop.
- You print out a welcoming message.
- You tell the user how many sticks are left in the pile.
- You tell the user who has won the game.

Each of these operations is a good candidate for a function. (The core game loop will be left in the main() function.) Some of which will be covered now; you can examine the rest directly in the source code.

The Welcome Message

A function that merely prints a message that never changes, requires no parameters, and does not need to return anything to the caller. Therefore, a void function with an empty parameter list will be satisfactory. Such functions are simply designed to isolate blocks of code and split a program into easily understood chunks. Their primary purpose is therefore one of clarity and modularity.

Listing 10.8 is the code for the welcome message function.

LISTING 10.8 welcomeMessage().

```
// welcomeMessage() - Say Hi to the player
void welcomeMessage()
{
  cout << "Welcome to the Game of Single-Pile Nim!" << endl;
  cout << "----------------------------------------" << endl
       << endl;
  return;
}
```

The Winner Congratulation Message

This time, you are still only giving the user feedback, so a void function is still appropriate. However, since there are two possible messages to print out (one if the player has won, one if he has lost to the computer), you will need a parameter to choose between the alternatives. Fortunately, the main program already contains a Boolean variable that holds the identity of the current player; whoever has just played when the game concludes is the winner, so you can pass this variable as a parameter.

The congratulations message function looks similar to Listing 10.9.

LISTING 10.9 congratulateWinner().

```
// congratulateWinner() - Tell the player who won
void congratulateWinner( bool theWinner )
{
  // If so, who has just taken the last stick?
  if( HUMAN_PLAYER == theWinner )
  {
    cout << "You win. Congratulations!" << endl;
  }
  else
  {
    cout << "I win! Better luck next time..." << endl;
  }
  return;
}
```

The isGameOver() Predicate

Next, you move to a function that returns a value. This simple function looks at the number of sticks left in the pile and returns true if it is zero (which means the game is over). Listing 10.10 outlines this function.

LISTING 10.10 isGameOver().

```
// isGameOver() - Have we reached endgame conditions?
// if there are no sticks left, yes
bool isGameOver( int pileSize )
{
  return( 0 == pileSize );
}
```

Boolean functions are often called *predicates*, and many programmers distinguish them from other functions by giving them names that begin with the word "is." This way, if-else statements that depend on the predicates' truth-values read more or less like natural English. For example:

```
if( isTheNumberPrime( theNumber ) )
  // do something useful
```

The Computer's Moves

The last function that will be discussed in this chapter is the one that calculates the computer's moves. The computer's optimal strategy has been discussed and you have written the code to implement it in Chapter 8. To transform this code into a function, you must make it return an `int` (the number of sticks the computer wants to remove) and accept another `int` (the number of sticks left in the pile) as an argument. As you can see by comparing the following function with the piece of code that performs the same job in Project 8.1, the modifications are minimal. Listing 10.11 details these modifications.

LISTING 10.11   `getComputerPlayerMove()`.

```
// getComputerPlayerMove() - Let the machine play
int getComputerPlayerMove( int pileSize )
{
  // A little piece of artificial intelligence :)
  // based on the mathematical analysis of the
  // game that we discussed in the chapter

  // Ideally, we'd like to leave a multiple of 5
  // sticks in the pile after the computer's turn
  int idealMove = ( pileSize % 5 );
  int currentPlayerMove;

  // If that's impossible, the position is lost,
  // so any move is as good or as bad as another
  if( 0 == idealMove )
    currentPlayerMove = 1;
  else
    currentPlayerMove = idealMove;

  // Announce the computer's move to the player
  cout << "I am taking " << currentPlayerMove
       << " sticks from the pile." << endl;

  return currentPlayerMove;
}
```

The Core Game Loop

Now that you have extracted the game's operations into functions, all you need to do is rewrite the core game loop located in the `main()` function so it includes calls to all of these helper functions. Listing 10.12 is what the `main()` function now looks like as a result of the entire process.

LISTING 10.12   main() rewrite.

```cpp
int main()
{
  // Start by saying hello to the player
  welcomeMessage();

  // Now, let's ask the human player who goes first
  bool currentPlayer = pickFirstPlayer();

  // Now that we know who plays first, we can start
  // the game by initializing the heap of sticks
  int nimSticks = 22;

  // CORE GAME LOOP: as long as there are sticks left,
  // we'll need to get moves from the opponents
  while( !isGameOver( nimSticks) )
  {
    // Show the status of the game
    gameStatus( nimSticks );

    // Let's get a move from the current player
    int currentPlayerMove;
    if( currentPlayer == HUMAN_PLAYER )
      currentPlayerMove = getHumanPlayerMove( nimSticks );
    else
      currentPlayerMove = getComputerPlayerMove( nimSticks );

    // Now that we know how many sticks the current
    // player wants to take, we remove them from the
    // pile
    nimSticks -= currentPlayerMove;

    // Do we have a winner?
    if( isGameOver( nimSticks ) )
      congratulateWinner( currentPlayer );

    // If there are sticks left in the pile, it is
    // now the other player's turn
    else
      currentPlayer = !currentPlayer;
  }

  // And we're done!
  return 0;
}
```

As you can see, the main function has shrunk in size by more than 50%; in fact, if you removed all the comments, it would hold in less than 20 lines of code. It is also far easier to understand than the giant `main()` from Project 8.1.

Final Comments

The full source code for Example 10.6 includes prototypes for all functions. You have also made the constants global since they are used in many functions. (This is a common programming idiom: generally speaking, constants will be made as global as possible so they don't have to be passed as parameters all the time. Global variables, on the other hand, are somewhat less common.)

SUMMARY

A C++ function is a block of code that has its own name, can accept parameters, and can return a value. Functions must be declared before they can be called; either the function must be written in full before any calls to it are made in the code, or a prototype that declares the function's signature to the compiler must be written first.

When a function is called and its parameters are passed by value, a local copy of the arguments will be made. Any manipulation performed on these local copies will not be reflected on the outside.

Like any C++ block, a function defines a scope, so it is possible to define variables that are local to a single function and unrelated to any other variable of the same name anywhere else in the program. The function's parameters are also local in scope.

The purpose of functions is to split code into easily understood blocks that solve atomic problems.

EXERCISES

10.1 What is wrong with this piece of code?

```
bool isNumberOdd( int num );
{
  return( ( num % 2 ) == 1 );
}
```

10.2 What is the difference between a function's signature and its prototype?

10.3 What is the purpose of the return statement?

10.4 What is a C++ predicate?

10.5 What should you do if you want to write a function that returns no value?

10.6 Rewrite Example 7.5 using a function addition to `main()`.

10.7 Rewrite Example 7.4 using at least two functions in addition to `main()`. Use prototypes.

10.8 Rewrite Example 5.1 using at least two functions in addition to `main()`. Use prototypes.

11 More about Function Parameters

In This Chapter

- Default Parameters
- Passing Parameters by Reference
- const Parameters
- Overloading Functions

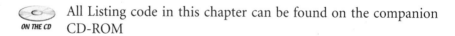 All Listing code in this chapter can be found on the companion CD-ROM

Every function you have seen so far has accepted a fixed number of parameters and left them all unchanged. This chapter broadens your options by introducing default values for parameters, which allows argument lists of variable lengths, and passing arguments by reference so the function can modify them.

You will also learn two related techniques: declaring parameters as constant, and overloading a function name by defining two or more functions with the same name but different signatures.

At the end of this chapter, you will know how to exploit the majority of C++'s features related to functions and parameter passing.

DEFAULT PARAMETERS

It is possible to declare parameters with *default values* that the function will use unless the default is overridden explicitly in the function call. For example, assume that a role-playing game features shops where adventurers can buy potions, and that the game requires a function that calculates the total price of an arbitrary number of potions sold at the same unit price, and is able to add sales tax to the total. One way to do it would be to pass the tax rate as an argument to the function, just like the unit price and the number of potions the character is buying; Example 11.1 outlined in Listing 11.1 shows one way this could be done.

LISTING 11.1

```
/**************************************
 Learn C++ by Making Games
 Example 11.1: Tax rate calculation
**************************************/

#include <iostream>
using namespace std;

// The tax rate function
double potionPriceCalculator( int potions, double unitPrice,
                              double taxRate )
{
  return( potions * unitPrice * ( 1.0 + taxRate ) );
}

int main()
{
  cout << "Total Price is "
       << potionPriceCalculator( 10, 5.25, 0.07 ) << endl;
  return 0;
}
```

Now, assume that a majority of the realm's shops apply the same tax rate, but a handful of potion peddlers sell their wares in the castles of particularly greedy local nobles who occasionally impose an additional tax on top of the king's own. In this case, you might want to avoid passing the standard tax rate as a parameter many times and only send specific data to the function when the situation calls for a tax rate out of the ordinary. The function could then define a *default value* for the tax rate, to be used in cases where calls to the function specify nothing at all; if a function call does specify a tax rate, the default will be overridden. Example 11.2 detailed in Listing 11.2 shows a version of the potionPriceCalculator() function that

has been enhanced with a default tax rate, and two calls to the function, one that relies on the default and one that overrides it.

LISTING 11.2

```
/************************************
 Learn C++ by Making Games
 Example 11.2: Default argument
************************************/

#include <iostream>
using namespace std;

// The tax rate function
double potionPriceCalculator( int potions,
                              double unitPrice,
                              double taxRate = 0.07 )
{
  return( potions * unitPrice * ( 1.0 + taxRate ) );
}

int main()
{
  // First, a call that relies on the default
  cout << potionPriceCalculator( 10, 5.25 ) << endl;

  // Then, a call that overrides the default
  cout << potionPriceCalculator( 10, 5.25, 0.11 ) << endl;

  return 0;
}
```

In Example 11.2, the default value is declared in the function's header; it looks
like an assignment statement. The main program shows two calls to potionPrice-
Calculator():

- The first call only sends two arguments to the function instead of the three it
  expects, but since a default value for the taxRate parameter has been declared,
  C++ automatically uses the default value of 7 percent instead of generating an
  error.
- The second call sends all three of the expected arguments, so C++ ignores the
  default value for the taxRate parameter and uses the value provided by the
  function call, which is 11 percent.

Default Argument Rules

In any function definition, the parameters that receive default values must all appear at the right end of the parameter list. Anything else will cause a compiler error as Listing 11.3.

LISTING 11.3 Compiler error.

```
int improper( int a, int b = 0, int c, int d = 0 );     // Error!
```

Furthermore, if the function receives fewer arguments than it expects, C++ will use default values starting with the rightmost parameter. Therefore, if you want to override the very last parameter's default value, you will have to specify values for all the parameters—even if you are satisfied with their defaults.

These rules may seem arbitrary, but without them many function calls that rely on default values could not be resolved unambiguously. Listing 11.4 shows an example of an ambiguous function definition.

LISTING 11.4 Ambiguous function.

```
int ambiguous( int a, int b, int c = 1, int d = 0 );
```

If the code contains a call to ambiguous(1, 2, 3), how should the compiler translate it? Is the programmer trying to override the third parameter and use the fourth's default value, or trying to override the fourth parameter and use the third's default? Should the compiler use the default value for c and rewrite the call as ambiguous(1, 2, 1, 3), or should it use the default value for d and rewrite the call as ambiguous(1, 2, 3, 0)? The rules say that the correct interpretation is the latter; if the programmer wanted to override d, he would have to write the call as ambiguous(1, 2, 1, 3) explicitly.

Finally, note that if a prototype is declared for a function, the values of the default parameters should be set in the prototype or in the function declaration itself, *but not in both*; many compilers will generate an error otherwise. (Some compilers demand that the default value be declared in the prototype.) The snippet in Listing 11.5 shows how to combine prototypes and default parameters properly.

LISTING 11.5 Prototype and default parameters.

```
// Prototype
int theFunction( int theStandardArg, int theDefaultArg = 5 );

// Declaration
int theFunction( int theStandardArg, int theDefaultArg )
{
  // do something useful
}
```

PASSING PARAMETERS BY REFERENCE

All the parameters you have seen so far have been passed by value, which means that a local copy of the argument is made for the function's benefit, and any change to the value is not propagated back to the caller.

A different scheme called *passing parameters by reference* exists for cases where the changes *should* be propagated back to the caller. In a parameter-by-reference situation, C++ sends the function a memory address where to fetch the argument and where to store the results of any manipulation performed on it, instead of giving it a copy to manipulate locally. In other words, the parameter name becomes an alias for the variable the caller passes to the function as its argument.

To declare a parameter as a reference, simply insert an ampersand (&) between the parameter's type and its name as outlined in Listing 11.6.

LISTING 11.6   Parameter as a reference.

```
int funcWithReference( int & argByReference )
{
  // do something useful
}
```

Spacing is immaterial; the ampersand can be located next to the type (`int&` `argName`), next to the name (`int &argName`), or separated from both by blank spaces (`int & argName`). This book will use the latter convention.

In a prototype without argument names, the ampersand follows the type:

```
int funcPrototypeWithReference( int & );
```

Calls to functions with by-reference parameters are identical to calls to functions with by-value parameters, except that the call may not pass a literal as an argument into the by-reference parameter; since the function must be able to change the value of the argument "in place," only a variable will do. (Some compilers will accept constants but will raise warnings and make local copies as if they had been passed by value; others will generate errors.)

Example 11.3 in Listing 11.7 demonstrates how to write a simple function that swaps the values of two variables and how to call it, and Figure 11.1 shows the result of its execution.

LISTING 11.7

```
/*************************************
  Learn C++ by Making Games
  Example 11.3 - Reference parameters
```

```
                **************************************/

#include <iostream>
using namespace std;

// Function swap(): take two parameters and exchange
// their values "in place"
// Note that the two parameters are declared as
// references
void swap( string & player1, string & player2 )
{
  string temp = player1;
  player1 = player2;
  player2 = temp;
  return;
}


int main()
{
  // First, let's get some data
  cout << "Type the names of the two players:" << endl;
  string pl1, pl2;
  cin >> pl1 >> pl2;

  // And show the results of the manipulation to the user
  cout << "Before the function call: " << pl1 << " " << pl2
       << endl;

  swap( pl1, pl2 );   // Remember: only variables can be
                      // passed by reference

  cout << "After the function call: " << pl1 << " " << pl2
       << endl;

  return 0;
}
```

Value and reference parameters can be mixed and matched in any combination, but the ampersand character must appear in the declaration of *each* reference parameter.

No Defaults

Of course, since by-reference parameters are linked to variables on the caller's side, they cannot receive default values: What would the "default variable" be?

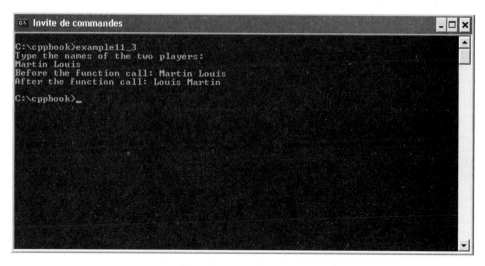

FIGURE 11.1   Exchanging the values of two reference parameters.

const **PARAMETERS**

It is possible to declare a function parameter to be const. This does not mean that the function will only accept constants as arguments for this parameter, but it "promises" the compiler that the function will not try to modify the parameter in any way, shape, or form, even if the parameter is by-value and the function has its own local copy. The compiler will generate an error if the code attempts to make modifications to the const parameter anyway.

At first glance, const parameters may seem strange, but they have two major uses:

- A const reference parameter can accept a constant, and not just a variable. Some compilers will even accept a literal.
- Passing a const reference is much faster and consumes much less memory than passing a large data structure (like the arrays and objects we will be studying in Parts IV and VI) by value, and just like passing by value, it ensures that the code will not propagate any unwanted changes to the data structure back to the caller.

You will be seeing const reference parameters often in later parts of this book. For now, Example 11.4 includes a function that accepts a const reference parameter and shows several calls using different constructs as arguments, shown in Listing 11.8.

LISTING 11.8

```
/*****************************************
 Learn C++ by Making Games
 Example 11.4 - Const Reference parameter
 *****************************************/

#include <iostream>
using namespace std;

// Function show(): take a string parameter and
// show it; don't try to change it or the
// compiler will raise an error because the
// parameter has been declared const

void show( const string & message )
{
  cout << "Show: " << message << endl;
}


int main()
{
  // Send show() a variable
  string myMessage = "Hello!";
  show( myMessage );

  // Send show() a constant
  const string myConstantMessage = "Passing a constant";
  show( myConstantMessage );

  // Send show() a literal; this may not compile
  // on every system!
  show( "Trying to show a literal" );

  return 0;
}
```

OVERLOADING FUNCTIONS

As long as two functions' signatures differ in more than their return types, C++ is able to distinguish between them. This means that an arbitrary number of functions can share the same *name*, as long as the number and/or the types of their *arguments* are not identical. In this case, the function name is said to be *overloaded*.

Example 11.5 outlined in Listing 11.9 declares three versions of the swap() function: one for double-precision floating-point numbers, one for strings, and one for integers. When a call to swap() is made, which version of the function to call is determined by looking at the types of the arguments. Figure 11.2 shows the results of Example 11.5's execution.

LISTING 11.9

```
/************************************
 Learn C++ by Making Games
 Example 11.5 - Overloaded functions
 ************************************/

#include <iostream>
using namespace std;

// Function swap(): take two parameters and exchange
// their values "in place"
// Note that there are 3 versions of this function,
// all with the same name and different parameter types
void swap( string & s1, string & s2 )
{
  string temp = s1;
  s1 = s2;
  s2 = temp;

  cout << "String swap: " << s1 << " " << s2 << endl;
  return;
}

void swap( double & d1, double & d2 )
{
  double temp = d1;
  d1 = d2;
  d2 = temp;

  cout << "Double swap: " << d1 << " " << d2 << endl;
  return;
}

void swap( int & i1, int & i2 )
{
  int temp = i1;
  i1 = i2;
  i2 = temp;

  cout << "Integer swap: " << i1 << " " << i2 << endl;
  return;
}
```

```cpp
int main()
{
  // First, let's get some data
  cout << "Please type two words: " << endl;
  string pl1, pl2;
  cin >> pl1 >> pl2;

  cout << "Now, type two floating-point numbers: " << endl;
  double d1, d2;
  cin >> d1 >> d2;

  cout << "Finally, two integers: " << endl;
  int i1, i2;
  cin >> i1 >> i2;

  // And now, swap the variables; C++ will pick the
  // right version to call based on parameter types
  swap( pl1, pl2 );
  swap( d1, d2 );
  swap( i1, i2 );

  return 0;
}
```

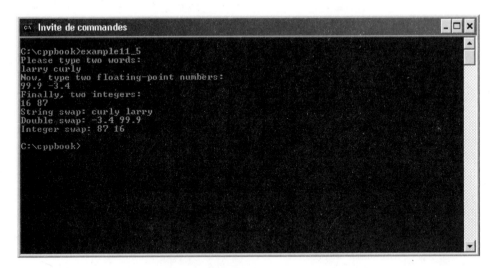

FIGURE 11.2 Execution of a program with overloaded functions.

SUMMARY

This chapter showed you how to enhance function writing with default arguments (which are automatically used when the caller supplies fewer than the expected number of arguments), reference parameters (which are aliases for the variables being passed as arguments), and const parameters (which provide additional safeguards against errors and will save us execution time and memory later).

You also saw how to overload functions so that multiple functions that perform the same job on arguments of different types can share a name.

EXERCISES

11.1 What is the difference between passing parameters by value and passing them by reference?

11.2 How many default parameters can a function have?

11.3 Is it possible to have two functions with the same name, the same argument types, and different return types?

11.4 Can you pass a constant to a function as a by-reference parameter?

11.5 Can you pass a literal to a function as a parameter?

11.6 How does the compiler decide which of a group of overloaded functions to call in any given case?

11.7 Write a function that reads the names of four players from the keyboard and returns them all to the caller. (Hint: Use by-reference parameters.)

11.8 Modify Example 11.2 to support an additional case: Suppose the king, in an effort to curb public health care expenditures in the realm, has decided that certain types of Potions of Healing would be tax exempt from now on. The potionPriceCalculator() function should now accept an additional Boolean parameter that states whether tax should be applied to any given calculation; this parameter has a default value of true.

12 Structured Programming

In This Chapter

- Header Files
- Handling Multiple Source Files
- The extern Keyword and Global Variables
- Inline Functions

 All Listing code in this chapter can be found on the companion CD-ROM

This short chapter will explain how to organize programs into multiple *source files* and user-defined *header files*.

C++ allows programmers to create their own header files, split source code into an arbitrary number of files for convenience, and refer to constants, variables, and code declared in one file from anywhere else in a program. This flexibility greatly simplifies teamwork, as each programmer can work on a different source file and link it into the main program when the work is finished. It also helps *modularize* code by grouping together related functions and data, which is an excellent way to manage moderately complicated projects.

At the same time, you will learn about *inline functions*, which are C++ constructs that allow small and frequently used pieces of code to be abstracted from the rest of the program, as if they were full-fledged functions, without incurring the performance cost of an actual function call.

HEADER FILES

In addition to the standard headers you have been using since the beginning of the book, it is possible for programmers to create their own header files. A programmer-defined header file differs from a normal source file in two ways:

- Its filename ends with the .h extension instead of .cpp.
- It must be included into each file that refers to any of the code or data in the header file; to include a header file called myheader.h, you would need the statement

```
#include "myheader.h".
```

Note the two differences between the preceding `#include` statement and the ones you have been using up to this point: the .h extension is listed explicitly, and the filename is enclosed within double quotes. The double quotes tell the compiler that the file is not stored with the standard headers, but in a user-defined location, probably in the same directory where the source file that is including the header is located; see your compiler's documentation for details on how to set up other kinds of include paths.

Technically, any legal C++ construct can appear in a header file, including entire functions (even `main()`). However, as a matter of style and convenience, programmers restrict the content of their header files to function prototypes, constant declarations, type declarations, and the occasional global variable.

Headers and Structured Programming

Example 12.1 is a rewrite of Example 10.6 (the NIM game split into many functions) that consists of two files; the header Example12_1.h and the source file Example12_1.cpp.

NOTE

To save space, only small portions of the .cpp file are printed here; you can examine both files in their entirety by fetching them from the companion CD-ROM.

ON THE CD

First, let's look at the header file detailed in Listing 12.1.

LISTING 12.1

```
/************************************
Learn C++ by Making Games
Example 12.1 - NIM with functions
Header File
************************************/

#ifndef EXAMPLE12_1_H
#define EXAMPLE12_1_h

// Let's define constants to identify the sides
const bool HUMAN_PLAYER = true;
const bool COMPUTER_PLAYER = false;

// Function Prototypes - Messages to the player
void welcomeMessage();
void congratulateWinner( bool theWinner );
void gameStatus( int pileSize );

// Function Prototypes - User Interface
// Decide who gets to play first
bool pickFirstPlayer();

// Function Prototypes - Moves
int getHumanPlayerMove( int pileSize );
int getComputerPlayerMove( int pileSize );

// Function Prototypes - Predicates
bool isGameOver( int pileSize );

#endif
```

You will deal with the preprocessor directives wrapping the declarations shortly. For now, as you can see, you have moved all of the function prototypes and constant declarations from the original game into the header file. These constitute the program's *interface*, which is the information a programmer would need to know to understand how the program works. For example, a programmer tasked with writing the main program would need to know the signatures of all the functions the main program must call to provide them with the right arguments and accept the correct return values. However, he would not need to know how each of these functions provides the intended services—from his perspective, each function would be like a black box that accepts input and provides output. This type of behavior, where each function can be treated as an independent service provider as far as other code segments are concerned, is at the core of the programming paradigm known as *structured programming*.

Now, you will follow that up with a quick look at the top of the Example12_1.cpp source file shown in Listing 12.2.

LISTING 12.2 CPP.

```
/**********************************
Learn C++ by Making Games
Example 12.1 - NIM with functions
Source file
**********************************/

#include <iostream>
#include "example12_1.h"
using namespace std;

// The main NIM Program
int main()
{
  // Start by saying hello to the player
  welcomeMessage();

  // Now, let's ask the human player who goes first
  bool currentPlayer = pickFirstPlayer();

  // ETC.: The rest of the main function is unchanged

  return 0;
}
```

The main source file no longer contains any prototypes and constant declarations; they have all been replaced by the #include "example12_1.h" statement. Once the header file has been included, the source file can behave as if every single declaration in the header file had been written directly into the source file—as indeed, from the compiler's perspective, they have been.

Avoiding Conflicting Declarations

Now, you will learn the reason why the header file's contents are wrapped in the heretofore-unseen preprocessor directives #ifndef and #endif.

The key to the answer lies in the fact that C++ does not allow multiple declarations of the same construct. If you write the same function prototype twice, or declare the same variable multiple times, the compiler will generate an error as shown in Listing 12.3.

LISTING 12.3 Multiple declaration error.

```
int myVar = 5;
int myVar = 10; // ERROR
```

However, it is quite possible for a program to consist of multiple source and header files. Several of these source files may need to include the same header (for example, because they all need access to the same helper function), or even for one header to include another. In such cases, it is very easy to run into situations where the same header will end up being included more than once into the same source file, which would normally generate a cascade of multiple declaration errors.

The #ifndef directive solves this problem by forcing *conditional inclusion* of the header's contents. #ifndef behaves very much like an if statement in the program, except that it governs code *compilation* instead of runtime execution. What this means is that its block, which ends with an #endif directive, is to be "executed" (that is, compiled) only if the argument provided to #ifndef (in this case, EXAMPLE12_1_H) is an *undefined value* at this point in the compilation process. It is common practice to use the header file's own name, with dots replaced by underscores, as the value to test in the directive, because it is easy to ensure that this value is uniquely associated with the right header file. (If you wanted the block to be compiled only if the value was defined, you would need an #ifdef directive instead.)

Now, the first time the preprocessor encounters the #ifndef directive during the process of compiling a source file, the EXAMPLE12_1_H value is undefined, so the block of code that ends in the #endif directive will be dealt with and passed along to the compiler. The first item in this block is a directive that #defines the value, so that the next time (and every other time after that) the header is included into the same source file, the #ifndef condition will fail and the preprocessor will ignore the entire block. The rest of the block is normal C++ code and is passed to the compiler, untouched by the preprocessor.

As a result of this trick, the declarations will be included into a given source file only once. (The process automatically starts anew with all values undefined when the compiler moves on to the next source file.)

HANDLING MULTIPLE SOURCE FILES

Nothing prevents a programmer from splitting a program into as many header and source files as he or she wants.

For example, all of the input-output functionality could be extracted into its own header/source file pair, all the math functionality into another, and the main() program be left alone in its own source file. This is a very common way to organize code in structured programming, and even more so in object-oriented programming (which you will study in Part VI). You will see many examples later in this chapter and as you progress throughout the book; just make sure to #include the proper headers into the proper source files, and consult your compiler's documentation to learn about any special configurations or command-line switches that it may require to create executable files out of more than one .cpp file.

THE extern KEYWORD AND GLOBAL VARIABLES

Referring to the same global variable in multiple source files requires two additional steps:

- One of the source files must declare the variable as a global in the usual manner; that is, outside of any function boundary.
- All other source files must declare the variable as extern to tell the compiler that they want to refer to the global that has been created elsewhere instead of creating a new variable of their own. Without the extern qualifier, the compiler will create a new variable of the same name for each source file, and give all of them *file scope*.

Since C++ allows a variable to be declared as extern and then created in the normal manner within a single file, the easiest way to satisfy the requirements is to:

- Put the extern declaration into a header that will be included in all source files that need access to the global.
- Then, create the global variable in any of the source files, usually the one that contains the main() function.

Example 12.2 detailed in Listing 12.4 shows a test case where two source files share a global thanks to a header file.

LISTING 12.4   Global sharing.

```
/*************************************
Learn C++ by Making Games
Example 12.2.h - Sharing a global
*************************************/

#ifndef EXAMPLE12_2_H
#define EXAMPLE12_2_h

// Declare the global for all to see
extern int i;
```

```cpp
// Some function prototype
void funct();

#endif

/************************************
 Learn C++ by Making Games
 Example 12.2a - Sharing a global
************************************/

#include <iostream>

// Gain access to the global
#include "example12_2.h"
using namespace std;


void funct()
{
  // make some changes to the global declared in the
  // other source file, to which we have gained
  // access thanks to the header
  i = 10;
  cout << "in funct " << i << endl;

  return;
}

/************************************
 Learn C++ by Making Games
 Example 12.2b - Sharing a global
************************************/

#include <iostream>

// Include the header to access the global
// and the helper functions
#include "example12_2.h"
using namespace std;

// Create the global here
int i;

int main()
{
  // Make some changes to the global
  // and show its value to the user
  i = 5;
```

```
cout << "in main " << i << endl;

// Call the helper function that will
// modify the global
funct();
cout << "after funct " << i << endl;

return 0;
}
```

INLINE FUNCTIONS

In every program, there are small tasks that must be performed repeatedly, often in many different areas of the source code. Normally, these tasks would be prime candidates for extraction into functions. But what if the job is very small (a handful of additions, for example) and the function must be called an enormous number of times—like 10,000 or 100,000 times per frame of animation in a game that runs at 60 frames per second? Many such tasks exist in real life; rendering one of the thousands of polygons that make up a scene in a 3D game certainly qualifies, for example.

In cases like this, the overhead associated with calling the function, passing parameters, and retrieving return values will overwhelm the amount of processing time actually spent in the function's body, and the entire process will become extremely inefficient. One solution would be to write the code in longhand every time some part of the source code needs to perform the job, but that would not be very satisfactory. A better alternative is to write the function as usual, but to declare it as *inline*, as in the snippet shown in Listing 12.5.

LISTING 12.5 Inline.

```
inline int twoTimesSquare( int theArg )
{
    return( 2 * theArg * theArg );
}
```

The `inline` keyword is a *hint* to the compiler, telling it that it should perform argument type checks at compile time but then expand the call to the inline function (e.g., replace it with the function's body), before producing object code. In some cases, using an inline function instead of a regular function can speed code execution by 50 percent or more.

However, remember that `inline` is a hint. Some functions cannot be `inline`'d at all because they are too large, contain loops that run an indefinite number of times, or call themselves recursively. (Not every compiler has the same rules regarding this process.)

Also, liberal use of inline functions tends to cause code to bloat; if a large program includes several hundred calls to the same inline function, each of which is replaced by 10 lines of source code at compile time, the program will instantly gain thousands of lines' worth of "hidden" code. If memory usage is more of an issue than execution speed—for example, when writing a card game to run on a low-end cell phone—inlining may be the wrong strategy.

Macros

C++ has also inherited from C a *macro language* that can be used to perform work similar to that of inline functions, among many other things.

Macros are created with `#define` preprocessor directives; the `#define` constants you discussed in Part I are a very small subset of the macro language, which is so powerful that programmers can even use it to create their own programming languages and write macro programs that will be translated into C++ by the preprocessor before they are compiled.

Unfortunately, C++ macros are also quite unwieldy, require obfuscated syntax, and, since they belong to the preprocessing stage of compilation, provide no type checking of any kind. Since `const` constants and inline functions have taken over most of the common tasks that were once delegated to macros, and since their more advanced applications tend to be the domain of very senior programmers, there will not be any further discussion on macros in this book.

SUMMARY

Large C++ projects are easier to manage when they are split into multiple files, especially when they involve multiple programmers.

A program can contain an arbitrary number of programmer-defined header files (extension .h), which typically contain function prototypes, type definitions, constants, and extern variable definitions, and an arbitrary number of source files (extension .cpp), which contain everything else.

Small tasks that must be performed repeatedly can sometimes be implemented as inline functions. The compiler will attempt to replace calls to inline functions with the functions' bodies, but may not be able to do it because not every C++ construct can be inlined. Inline functions tend to run faster, but consume more memory space than normal functions.

EXERCISES

12.1 Is an inline function guaranteed to be faster than an identical non-inline function?

12.2 Why do programmers wrap the contents of header files with `#ifndef` / `#endif` pairs?

12.3 What are the differences between the `#include` statements for standard built-in headers and programmer-defined headers?

12.4 Can header files contain entire functions?

12.5 What is the meaning of the `extern` keyword?

12.6 Modify your solution to Exercise 11.2 to extract all function prototypes and constants into a header file.

12.7 Modify your solution to Exercise 10.2 to extract all function prototypes and constants into a header file. Write the full definition of each function into a separate source file.

13

A Game of Blackjack

In This Chapter

- The Game of Blackjack
- Game Architecture
- Core Game Loop
- The Player's Hand
- The Dealer's Hand
- Dealing Cards

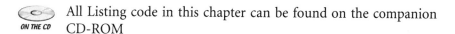 All Listing code in this chapter can be found on the companion
ON THE CD CD-ROM

This chapter concludes Part III with a classic card game of chance: Blackjack. This game is an excellent way to illustrate how to translate a game concept into code and how to divide a problem into a number of functions.

 Much of the game's code will be commented upon in the chapter; to see the entire files, check out Project13_1.h and Project13_1.cpp on the companion CD-ROM.

ON THE CD

THE GAME OF BLACKJACK

In this project, you will implement a simplified version of Blackjack, a classic card game. This version of Blackjack follows these rules:

- A single player plays against the dealer.
- The deck contains an infinite supply of cards.
- The goal of the game is to assemble a hand whose value is as close to 21 as possible, without going over. Whoever gets closest to 21 without going over wins the hand.
- Aces are worth either 1 point or 11 points, at the player's choice. Face cards are worth 10 points. All other cards are worth a number of points equal to their numerical value. Suits are irrelevant.
- The player gets at least two cards. After that, he can either ask to be "hit" with another card or decide to stay with his current hand. The player receives as many cards as he wants, until he is ready to stay or his hand's total value reaches 21 or more.
- The dealer is forced to stay on any hand worth 17 or more, and to hit on 16 and under.

Advanced features of the game, such as wagering, doubling bets, splitting hands, and playing with limited decks, are left to the reader as extra projects.

GAME ARCHITECTURE

To run a game of Blackjack, a program needs three major modules and a set of subsidiary functions. The major modules are:

- A core game loop that runs the game.
- A module that builds the human player's hand.
- A module that builds the dealer's hand.

The helper functions consist of drawing cards from a deck and giving output feedback to the user.

It would have been possible to place each of these modules into its own source file, but since they are all relatively small, it has been decided to put them all in the same file.

Header File

Every time you add a function to the project, you insert its prototype in the project's header file. You also declare all constants in the header. At the end of the project, the header file looks similar to Listing 13.1.

LISTING 13.1   Project13_1.h.

```
/**********************************
Learn C++ by Making Games
Project 13.1 - Simple Blackjack game
Header file
**********************************/

#ifndef PROJECT13_1_H
#define PROJECT13_1_H

// Constants defining the sides
const bool PLAYER_SIDE = true;
const bool HOUSE_SIDE = false;

// Functions shared by both sides
int drawOneCard();
int addCardToHand( int theHand, int theCard,
bool & handContainsAce11 );
int drawAndAddCardToHand( int theHand, bool & hasBigAce );

// Output functions, sending messages to the user
void announceCard( int theCard );
void announceHand( int theHand );
void announceResult( bool side, int theHand );
void whoWins( int playerHand, int houseHand );

// Functions involved in building the player's hand
bool isPlayerHolding( int theHand );
int buildPlayerHand();

// Functions involved in building the house's hand
int buildHouseHand( int theHand, bool & hasBigAce );
int drawOpenHouseCard( bool & hasBigAce );

#endif
```

Note that several functions have Boolean parameters that are passed by reference, and several by-value parameters. You will see why the reference parameter is important shortly.

CORE GAME LOOP

A hand of Blackjack is played in three steps:

1. First, the dealer unveils a card for himself, the "open card" or "face card." This card's value will influence the player's strategy and help him decide when to stay.
2. Then, cards are dealt to the player one at a time, until the player stays, reaches 21, or busts.
3. Then, if the player has not busted, the dealer deals cards for himself until his hand's value reaches 17 or more.

Whomever has the hand whose value is closest to 21 without busting wins. In your project, the game consists of a single hand; extending it to multiple hands is trivial. The core game loop is implemented in the main() function shown in Listing 13.2.

LISTING 13.2   Core main() function.

```
// The main program
int main()
{
  // Welcome message and initializations
  srand( time( 0 ) );
  cout << endl << endl;
  cout << "Welcome to the game of Blackjack!" << endl;
  cout << "--------------------------------" << endl << endl;

  // Show the house's open card
  bool houseHasBigAce = false;
  int houseHand = drawOpenHouseCard( houseHasBigAce );

  // Then, build the player's hand
  int playerHand = buildPlayerHand();
  announceResult( PLAYER_SIDE, playerHand );

  // Unless the player has busted, build the house's hand
  if( playerHand <= 21 )
  {
    houseHand = buildHouseHand( houseHand, houseHasBigAce );
    announceResult( HOUSE_SIDE, houseHand );
  }

  // Inform the player of the final result
  whoWins( playerHand, houseHand );

  return 0;
}
```

The houseHasBigAce flag is set to true whenever the house's hand includes an ace that is deemed to be worth 11 points. The reason why you need this flag is that it is possible to retroactively change an ace's value in the middle of a hand if needed. For example, suppose that the house's first two cards are an ace and a five. The hand's value is 16, so according to the rules the house is forced to draw. If the dealer draws a nine, the hand's value increases to 25—a bust. However, by changing the ace's value to 1, which can only be done if you know that the hand contains a "big ace," you can reduce the hand's new value to 15 and give the house another chance. As you look at the code, you will see that a similar mechanism is implemented on the player's side as well, so that we automatically avoid busts on both sides if there is a "big ace" available.

Also note that `houseHasBigAce` is a reference parameter, as demonstrated in the prototypes listed in the header file. When the helper function that draws cards generates an ace that can legally be worth 11 points, it assigns the value 11 to the ace automatically and sets the flag so the ace's value can be reduced later.

THE PLAYER'S HAND

When building the player's hand, two operations are crucial: adding a card to the hand, and asking the player whether to hold or hit again. The process begins with the dealer giving the player the minimum of two cards; then you alternate between polling the player and dealing cards until the player holds, busts, or gets a hand worth 21 points. The `buildPlayerHand()` function controls the entire process shown in Listing 13.3.

LISTING 13.3   `buildPlayerHand()`.

```
// buildPlayerHand: Draw cards for the player until the
// player holds or busts
int buildPlayerHand()
{
  // start with an empty hand
  int theHand = 0;
  bool hasBigAce = false;

  cout << endl
      << "The dealer will now deal cards to the player..."
      << endl;

  // Give the player two cards to begin...
  for( int i = 0; i < 2; i++ )
  {
    theHand = drawAndAddCardToHand( theHand, hasBigAce );
  }
```

```
// Then add one card at a time until the player holds or busts
bool playerHolds = false;
while( theHand < 21 && !playerHolds )
{
    playerHolds = isPlayerHolding( theHand );
    if ( !playerHolds )
    {
        theHand = drawAndAddCardToHand( theHand, hasBigAce );
    }
}

return theHand;
}
```

The function that determines whether the player holds is a simple input function the likes of which you have seen many times before as detailed in Listing 13.4.

LISTING 13.4 isPlayerHolding().

```
// isPlayerHolding: Ask the player whether to hold or
// draw another card, based on his hand's current value
bool isPlayerHolding( int theHand )
{
    cout << "Do you wish to hold on " << theHand
         << "? Type [Y]es or [N]o." << endl;

    // Ask for answers until one is entered...
    char answer;
    do
    {
        cin >> answer;
        answer = toupper( answer );
    } while( answer != 'Y' && answer != 'N' );

    // Player holds on 'Y'es
    return( 'Y' == answer );
}
```

THE DEALER'S HAND

On the dealer's side, hand building is split into two steps: drawing the open card before the player gets involved, and then completing the hand afterward. The functions that implement this behavior, and the rules of the game, are straightforward as you can see from Listing 13.5.

LISTING 13.5   drawOpenHouseCard().

```
// drawOpenHouseCard: Draw a face card for the house
// before the player builds his hand.
int drawOpenHouseCard( bool & hasBigAce )
{
  cout << "The dealer will draw an open card for the house..."
      << endl;
  return( drawAndAddCardToHand( 0, hasBigAce ) );
}


// buildHouseHand: Starting with a face card that has
// already been selected, draw cards until the house
// has at least 17
int buildHouseHand( int theHand, bool & hasBigAce )
{
  while( theHand < 17 )
  {
    cout << "The house draws on " << theHand
        << " and receives... " << endl;
    theHand = drawAndAddCardToHand( theHand, hasBigAce );
  }
  return theHand;
}
```

DEALING CARDS

Both the player and the dealer need cards to be added to their hands. Therefore, you have extracted the card-dealing process into a set of functions that serve both sides.

The function that is directly called by the dealer module and by the player module is drawAndAddCardToHand(), which executes the process in four steps:

1. Create a new card.
2. Announce its value.
3. Add the card to the hand and calculate the hand's new value.
4. Announce the hand's new value.

These steps are outlined in Listing 13.6.

LISTING 13.6   drawAndAddCardToHand().

```
// drawAndAddCardToHand: deal a card to the current side
int drawAndAddCardToHand( int theHand, bool & hasBigAce )
{
  int theCard = drawOneCard();
```

```
    announceCard( theCard );
    theHand = addCardToHand( theHand, theCard, hasBigAce );
    announceHand( theHand );
    return theHand;
}
```

In Blackjack, only the value of a card matters; the suit is irrelevant. Since you have simplified the process by assuming an unlimited supply of cards, you can just generate new cards at random whenever one is needed (with a 1 being an ace and a 13 being a king). Listing 13.7 provides some clarification.

LISTING 13.7 drawOneCard().

```
// drawOneCard: Pick a card at random; we assume an infinite
// supply of cards
int drawOneCard()
{
    return( rand() % 13 + 1 );
}
```

The tricky part happens when a card is added to a hand.

The function addCardToHand() accepts three parameters: the hand's current value before adding the card, the card's value, and a reference parameter that identifies the presence of a "big ace."

First, you add the new card's value to the hand. If the new card is an ace and can legally become a big one, you make it a big ace automatically. Then, once the card's value has been added to the hand, you check whether the hand is a bust; if so, you look for a big ace to downgrade to a small ace of value 1, to avoid the bust. Listing 13.8 clarifies this.

LISTING 13.8 addCardToHand().

```
// addCardToHand: Add the new card to the side's hand. If the
// new card makes the hand's total value higher than 21, see if
// the hand doesn't contain an ace whose value we can lower from
// 11 to 1.
int addCardToHand( int theHand, int theCard,
                   bool & handContainsAce11 )
{
    // Add the nominal value; face cards are all worth 10 points
    if( theCard > 10 )
      theHand += 10;

    // Aces are worth 11 if that is possible without busting,
    // 1 otherwise
    else if( 1 == theCard && theHand <= 10 )
    {
```

```
    theHand += 11;
    handContainsAce11 = true;
  }
  // In all other cases, the card's face value is added
  else
    theHand += theCard;

  // If the new hand value is over 21, try to shrink it
  if( theHand > 21 && handContainsAce11 )
  {
    theHand -= 10;
    handContainsAce11 = false;
  }

  return theHand;
}
```

Note that the function accepts the hand's initial value as an input parameter and returns the hand's new value as the function's output value. It would have been perfectly acceptable to make the hand's value a reference parameter instead. (In fact, some programmers would have made the hand's value a reference *and* returned it from the function.)

SUMMARY

With multiple functions, reference parameters, prototypes, and header files, it is possible to create projects of moderate size that are easy to organize and understand.

However, Blackjack is a very special case among card games, because with the exception of the "big aces" that we discussed earlier, the identities of individual cards are unimportant once they have been added to the hand; only the hand's aggregate value matters. In a more traditional game like Rummy, Poker, or even Crazy Eights, it is crucial to know the identity of each card in a player's hand at all times. This cannot be done easily with the simple variables you have been using since the beginning of this book—in Part IV, you will add data structures to your arsenal, thus introducing a great deal of additional flexibility into our programming.

EXERCISES

13.1 Add some random functions to the game to allow the dealer to gamble with a hand of 17 or higher. For example, if the dealer ends up with a hand of 18 then he has a 20% chance of pressing his luck by drawing another card.

13.2 For additional fun, assign an increasing percentage as the dealer's hand gets close to 21. In other words, once the dealer's hand passes 17 then assign a different chance for each value up to 20. The chances of the dealer going for another card at 20 is a significantly lower then if the dealer had 18 for example.

OTHER PROJECT IDEAS

Expand the Blackjack program in any one or more of the following ways:

- Play any number of hands, keeping statistics on the number of wins, losses, draws, and Blackjacks on each side.
- Allow the player to bet on each hand and keep a running total of his bankroll. Play until a set number of hands has been played, the player has lost all of his initial bankroll, or he has broken the bank by winning more than an arbitrary limit.
- Announce the suits of cards in addition to their values.
- Allow the player to double his bet after receiving his first two cards.

(Advanced) Study the arrays in Part IV of the book and rewrite the Blackjack game in such a way that it uses a single deck of 52 cards for each hand. Make sure there are no duplicates among the cards drawn by the dealer.

Part
IV
Elementary Data Structures

After working through Part III and the Blackjack project, you should feel comfortable with using functions to attempt to apply some structure to your programs.

Part of the process of organizing your programs to flow more smoothly is to work at streamlining how the data is represented for the application. This might include the need to store collections of elements.

When working with most games, it is clear fairly early in the development of the game, that a need for a custom data type of some kind is essential to finishing the game. The standard `float`, `char`, `int`, and `double` data types are fine, but it would be nice to create your own data type that is composed of the atomic types.

At the end of this part of the book, you will be able to leverage elementary data structures to develop a more complex game: Battleship. Have fun!

14 Single-Dimension Arrays, Searches, and Sorts

In This Chapter

- Searching and Sorting
- Sorting
- Working with String Data
- Finding Tokens in the String

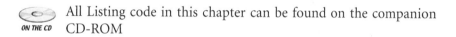 All Listing code in this chapter can be found on the companion CD-ROM

Inevitably, it will be necessary to store or manipulate a collection or group of objects within your program. C++ provides this storage mechanism known as an *array*. An array can have as many elements as you wish; however, all of these elements must be of the same data type. For example, you cannot have a single array containing a mixture of `int` and `char` elements.

An array can be defined as:

```
Datatype arrayname[size]
```

Datatype: The type of element stored in the array. This can be `int`, `float`, `char`, or any other legal C++ data type.

Arrayname: The variable identifier assigned to this array.

Size: The number of elements to store in the array.

After defining the array you wish to use, the compiler will automatically set aside enough memory to hold all of the elements. The number of brackets used also defines what is known as the *dimension* or *subscript* of the array.

For some examples on using arrays, look at the code snippet outlined in Listing 14.1.

LISTING 14.1   Some basic array declarations.

```
//the following is a 52 element array of ints
//it has one pair of brackets, so it's a single dimension
int cards[52];

//the following is a 10 element array of floats
//it has one pair of brackets around the 10, so it's
//a single dimension
float grades[10];

//the following is a 20 element array used to store a name
//it has one pair of brackets around the 20, so you can
//also say it has one subscript
char employee[20];
```

Array elements are always created sequentially in memory, which makes it easier to manipulate as you will see in the section on Pointers. You will also learn more about the subscript in Chapter 15.

You must use an integer value to access each element in the array known as the *index*. In the C++ language, arrays are zero-based, meaning the first element in the array is located at index "*0*." In the cards array that you defined in Listing 14.1 for example, cards[0] is the first array element, cards[1] the second element, and so on.

Listing 14.2 provides some additional clarification.

LISTING 14.2   Accessing the index—Example 14_1.cpp.

```
//include our necessary headers
#include <iostream>
using namespace std;
int main(int argc, char* argv[])
{
  int cards[52];

  //just loop through the cards and initialize them all to 3
  for(int i = 0; i < 52; i++)
  {
    cards[i] = 3;
```

```
    }

    //now just print out the first card
    cerr << "card 1 is: " << cards[0] << endl;

    //print out the second card
    cerr << "card 2 is: " << cards[1] << endl;

    return 0;

}
```

Listing 14.2 defines an array of integers with enough room to hold *52* elements.
All you are doing in the For loop is setting every element within the array to the value of three. Finally, you are printing out the value of the first card in the array contained in cards[0].

Out of Bounds

For C++ beginners, one common mistake is accessing an element that is outside of the array declaration. This is also known as "*out of bounds*" accessing.

Suppose, for example, that you have the cards array of *52* elements defined with the first card at cards[0] and the last card in the deck at cards[51]. You are still new to using arrays in C++, so you might forget that the first element of every array is at index zero. In other words, during the program you might accidentally try to access the final element at cards[52] instead of the correct cards[51].

What Happens?

The integer data type is four bytes in size. When you define the cards[52] array, the compiler sets aside enough room for *52* integers of four bytes in size. If you try to access an element outside the declared size of the array, the program will attempt to access the memory location four bytes after the area in memory that was set aside for the array. If you are lucky, this causes an immediate program crash, which instantly signals that there is an illegal access instruction. However if you are unlucky, this access can overwrite other data in the program, which may create strange results later in the execution of the code, making it much more difficult to trace.

In a real-world example, this is similar to asking directions at a gas station. Usually, the attendant will tell you to head four blocks in one direction, before making a turn, and then move in another direction toward your final destination. After you leave the station, you might be unsure which block the attendant meant as the first one in his instructions. If you go one block past the turning point described by the attendant, you might be lucky and discover that it is a building or parking lot or other such obvious clue that you started at the wrong block. If you are unlucky, however, it is another road, and so it is not immediately obvious that you are on the wrong street until much later.

Initializing Arrays

The C++ language provides a way to initialize each element of an array of simple data types when you declare it in a program. Listing 14.3 details how this is done.

LISTING 14.3   Initializing the array.

```
//After the array variable name, we can put an = sign and a list of
//values
//defining each element
int someArray[5] = { 0, 1, 2, 3, 4 };
```

In Listing 14.3, you declared an integer array of five elements, initializing `someArray[0]` to zero, `someArray[1]` to one, and so on. For a graphical representation of this array, Figure 14.1 provides some clarification.

FIGURE 14.1   `someArray` representation in memory.

You also have the ability to allow the compiler to create the proper size of an array given an initialization list. Listing 14.4 demonstrates this automatic array sizing.

LISTING 14.4   Automatic array sizing.

```
//instead of declaring how many elements are in our array,
//we can leave it
//blank and let the compiler do the work for us
int someArray[] = { 0, 1, 2, 3, 4 };
```

In Listing 14.4, you created the same sized array that was defined in Listing 14.3. This is an easier (and potentially safer) way to define and initialize an array. It is illegal to use an initialization list that contains more elements than you have defined, but it is perfectly legal to use a shorter list. Listing 14.5 provides some clarification.

LISTING 14.5   Array initialization.

```
//This declaration will be marked illegal since we are trying to
//initialize an
```

```
//array larger than what was declared
int someArray[5] = { 0, 1, 2, 3, 4, 5, 6 };

//However, we can use an initialization list shorter than the size
//of the array
//so someArray[0] will be 0, and someArray[1] will be 1.
int someArray[5] = { 0, 1 };
```

SEARCHING AND SORTING

A common task for using any array is to search for a desired element of a specific value. This is known as *searching*. There are various methods and algorithms for creating and designing the optimal sorting/searching algorithm for arrays, but you will only focus on a few of them here.

The brute force method of searching through an array is to iterate through each element in the array until you find the desired one. Listing 14.6 demonstrates this method.

LISTING 14.6   Brute force searching—EXAMPLE 14_2.CPP.

```cpp
#include <iostream>

int main(int argc, char* argv[])
{

  int cards[5] = { 1, 3, 5, 7, 9 };
  int position;

  //we only want to find the index of the "5" card
  for(int i = 0; i < 5; i++)
  {
    if(cards[i] == 5)
    {
      position = i;
      break;
    }
  }

  cout << "Our 5 card is at index " << position << endl;

  return 0;
}
```

This example shows how you first declare an array large enough to hold five cards. The For loop then iterates through each element of this array until the position of the number-five card is found. This position in the array is then saved, and the loop is exited. The program then prints out the array index of the desired card.

With this small example, it is a trivial matter to use this method of searching for finding what is needed in small arrays. Rarely do games ever store information of so few elements in arrays. What if the array contains 1,000, or 100,000 items?

SORTING

To minimize the time spent searching for a particular item within an array, you also have the option of sorting your array elements. Depending on the array size and makeup of the elements, this can save you quite a bit of time in a critical area of your game. There are several ways to sort your array, but luckily, the C++ standard library can be your savior. The language provides a generic sorting algorithm known as qsort.

The qsort function in C++ provides a generic function that allows you to sort nearly anything you want to. All you need to do is provide the actual sorting logic in a separate function, which is then used by the qsort method each time an object requires a comparison with another. Listing 14.7 provides an example of using qsort.

LISTING 14.7   Using qsort—Example 14_3.cpp.

```cpp
#include <iostream>

int main(int argc, char* argv[])
{
    int cards[10] = { 1, 3, 2, 10, 20, 40, 99, 5, 7, 9 };
    int position;
    int bruteforce_calcs = 0;
    int qsort_calcs = 0;

    //we only want to find the position of the "5" card
    for(int i = 0; i < 10; i++)
    {
        bruteforce_calcs++;
        if(cards[i] == 5)
        {
            position = i;
            break;
        }
    }

    //call the default qsort function that comes with
```

```
//the standard
//param 1 - pointer to your array
//param 2 - number of items in the array
//param 3 - size of each item
//param 4 - comparison function
qsort((void*)cards, 10, sizeof(cards[0]), sortCards);

//we only want to find the position of the "5" card
for(int i = 0; i < 10; i++)
{
  qsort_calcs++;
  if(cards[i] == 5)
  {
    position = i;
    break;
  }
}

cout << "Our 5 card is at position " << position << endl;
cout << "It took " << bruteforce_calcs << " bruteforce steps" <<
  endl;
cout << "It took " << qsort_calcs << " qsort steps" << endl;

return 0;
}
```

While not a genuine algorithm test, Listing 14.7 tries to get the point across. You first declare a cards array containing 10 elements. A brute force method (without sorting) of finding the index of the card number five is performed with the number of loop iterations recorded in the bruteforce_calcs variable. You are then passing the cards array into the qsort function, which sorts the array from the lowest element to the highest. Finally, the array is analyzed again to see how many iterations it takes to find the five card, with the result stored in the qsort_calcs variable. These two variables are then displayed to the console.

The actual sorting function used in the call to qsort is actually defined by you since the computer has no idea how you might want to sort your array. This gives you the flexibility of sorting arrays of string data, and sorting from either the lowest value to the highest, or the highest value to the lowest. Listing 14.8 provides the sortCards function used by Listing 14.7.

LISTING 14.8   sortCards function.

```
int sortCards( const void *a, const void *b)
{
    int objA = *((int*)a); //cast the void* a into an int
    int objB = *((int*)b); //cast the void* b into an int
```

```
    if( objA < objB )      //if a is less than b return -1
       return -1;
    if( objA == objB )     //if a equals b then return 0
       return 0;

                           //otherwise, a is larger than b so
    return 1;              //return 1
}
```

Every sort function you wish to use with qsort is always declared as a function with two void parameters returning an int value.

TIP

WORKING WITH STRING DATA

Although you have been working with several examples of printing text messages back to the console, you have not quite had the official overview of working with string data in C++. With the introduction to single dimensional arrays still fresh in your mind, it will be easier to understand string data. It is a "special" type of single dimension array that contains a list of char elements terminated with a NULL ('\0') character. You can declare and initialize string data the same as any other array as shown in Listing 14.9.

LISTING 14.9   Initializing string data.

```
char welcome[] = { 'H', 'e', 'l', 'l', 'o', ' ', 'N' , 'u' , 'm' ,
                   'b', 'e', 'r', 'v', '6', '\0' };
```

This type of initialization is not without problems, as it has a high potential for an error or typo to be made. Listing 14.10 provides another way this could be written.

LISTING 14.10   More initialization.

```
char welcome[] = "Hello Number 6";
```

There are two key differences you might have noticed:

- You do not have a list of single-quoted characters within a set of braces; the version in Listing 14.10 is a simple double-quoted string.
- You do not need to add the terminating NULL character in the method shown in Listing 14.10.

When you declare a string, it is important as with every other array that you choose a size that is needed. The length of the string data is enough room to contain it and the trailing NULL character. For example, the "Hello Number 6" string is *15* bytes since the letters are all one byte each, including the two spaces and the trailing NULL character.

String Functions

Included with the default C++ libraries are several useful functions to manipulate string data.

Copying Strings

One of the most heavily used string functions is strcpy, which is responsible for copying the contents of one string into another along with the trailing NULL character. Listing 14.11 provides a small sample.

LISTING 14.11 strcpy—Example 14_4.cpp.

```cpp
#include <iostream>
#include <string.h>

using namespace std;

int main(int argc, char* argv[])
{
  char string1[] = "Stovokor";
  char string2[80];

  strcpy( string2, string1 );

  cout << "string1 := " << string1 << endl;
  cout << "string2 := " << string2 << endl;

  return 0;
}
```

Listing 14.11 is a straightforward example of using strcpy to copy the contents of string1 into string2. One word of caution when using this function is that you have to ensure the destination string is large enough to contain the source string; otherwise, this could lead to the source string overwriting past the boundaries of the destination.

Comparing String Data

In most programs, a test performed quite often is to determine if a given string data is equal to another string. For example, a common occurrence in games today is a console that can appear in the game for the player to input various commands.

Most often, developers use this console to enter instructions to test various aspects of the game; such as to ensure the player's position is being properly updated within the game world. In such systems, there is usually an underlying codebase that compares the string entered by the player to a known list of other strings, which then instruct the game on what action to take. In the default C++ library, you have access to the strcmp function, which is responsible for performing lexicographical analysis of the given strings. In other words, the function begins by comparing the first character of each given string. If they are the same character (i.e., equal), the function continues to the next character in each string to perform the same test. This process continues until the end of the source string is reached and/or the characters differ. Listing 14.12 provides an example of using strcmp.

LISTING 14.12   strcmp.

```
#include <iostream>
#include <string.h>
using namespace std;
int main(int argc, char* argv[])
{
  char string1[] = "Stovokor";
  char input[80];
  do {
    cout << "Where do Klingons battle in the afterlife?: ";
    cin >> input;
  }while( strcmp(string1, input) != 0);
  cerr << "That's correct! You are with honor! " << endl;
  return 0;
}
```

Listing 14.12 simply presents a prompt for entering data. Once you enter some text, the program then uses this input text and compares it to string1. If the two strings match, the program exits the do-while loop and the code then displays a congratulations message. Otherwise, the program loops to allow you to try again.

Determining Length of Strings

Another useful function made available to you via the default C++ libraries is strlen. This function will calculate the length of the string in question including the terminating NULL character. This is commonly used in games and applications to validate the given input from the player; such as a character creation dialog in which the player must enter a name for his Avatar. To prevent the player from entering a name with too many (or too little) characters, the underlying code can use the strlen function to determine the given input is valid and legal. Listing 14.13 provides an example of using strlen.

LISTING 14.13   `strlen-Example14_5.cpp.`

```
#include <iostream>
#include <string.h>
using namespace std;

int main(int argc, char* argv[])
{
  char string1[] = "Stovokor";
  int length = 0;
  length = strlen( string1 );

  cout << "string1 := " << string1 << " with length := " << length
       << endl;

  return 0;
}
```

There is nothing mysterious here. The example in Listing 14.13 simply calculates the length of the given string and displays it back on the console.

FINDING TOKENS IN THE STRING

A common requirement for most games is the ability to parse given data into actions that can be resolved by your game. For example, your game might allow a console that accepts string commands from the player. One method to parsing this string data is to use a function like strtok, which is provided by the standard C++ library.

This is a handy string manipulation function that allows you to scan an input string for token delimiters. Listing 14.14 provides a sample function using strtok.

LISTING 14.14   Using strtok-Example14_6.cpp.

```
#include <iostream>
#include <string.h>

using namespace std;

int main ()
{
  char str[] ="My favorite NES code is UU-DD-LR-LR-BA-START.";
  char *pch;
  cout << "Splitting string \" << str << " in tokens:\n";
  pch = strtok (str," ");
  while (pch != NULL)
  {
```

```
        cout << pch << endl;
        pch = strtok (NULL, " ,.-");
    }

    return 0;
}
```

In Listing 14.14, you are taking the input string contained in str and are using strtok to parse this string separating each individual word. If the specified delimiter is found in the input string, its position is marked by a NULL character, with the previous characters returning from the function. The function then enters a small while loop, which continues to go through the given input string from the current NULL value until the next delimiter is found.

SUMMARY

In this chapter, you learned about arrays and how to use them in your programs. You also were introduced to the concepts of sorting your array elements to attempt quicker searches for specific elements. You were also introduced to the string, which is a special case of the single dimension array. The standard C++ libraries also include several string manipulation functions that can benefit you greatly. In the next chapter, you will delve deeper into the subject of arrays by learning how to create and manipulate multidimensional arrays.

EXERCISES

14.1 What are the first and last elements of MyArray[42]?

14.2 How many characters are stored in the string "Gaming is Fun!"?

14.3 What is the last character in the string "I love to program in C++"?

14.4 Create a string reversal function. Have the function reverse the input string.

15 Multidimensional Arrays

In This Chapter

■ Working with a Multidimensional Array

 All Listing code in this chapter can be found on the companion CD-ROM

In Chapter 14, you learned the basics behind arrays and how to manipulate array elements. The focus of the chapter was on single arrays, which are also known as "single dimension" arrays, since they only have one subscript. In this chapter, you will learn about working with arrays of more than one subscript, also known as *multidimensional* arrays. If a one-dimensional array has only one subscript, then a two-dimensional array has two subscripts; a three-dimensional array has three subscripts, and so forth.

 Arrays can have any number of dimensions, although it is unlikely in a game situation that you will require more than two or three.

A good example of a two dimensional array is a chessboard as shown in Figure 15.1. In a standard board there are eight horizontal lines (known as "rows") and eight vertical lines (known as "columns").

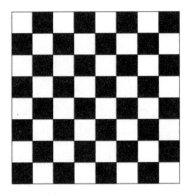

FIGURE 15.1   Chessboard example of a multidimensional array.

Listing 15.1 demonstrates a two dimensional array declaration that you could use for a chessboard.

LISTING 15.1   Chessboard declaration.

```
//the following declaration instructs the compiler to allocate
//enough space to hold
//8 rows and 8 columns of int elements
//since there are two pairs of brackets involved we can say
//that it has 2 dimensions or 2 subscripts
int chessboard[8][8];
```

Initializing Multidimensional Arrays

Very similar to their one-dimensional brethren, multidimensional arrays contain garbage values when first declared. To properly initialize them, you can use a similar declaration method that you employed for single dimension arrays; using a list of characters. Listing 15.2 provides some clarification on handling initialization.

LISTING 15.2   Multidimensional initialization.

```
//think of a Tic-tac-toe board containing 'X' and 'O' values
//you just need an initialization list similar to one dimensional
//arrays
char TicTacToeBoard[3][3] = { {'O', 'X', 'O' },
                             {'X', 'O', 'X'},
                             {'O', 'X', 'O'}};
```

If any array elements are left out of your initialization list, they are set to zero.

From Listing 15.2 the compiler will ignore the inner braces of the initialization list, but they provide you with more readability and make it easier to visualize the assignments.

Therefore, Listing 15.3 is a rewrite of the initialization code presented in Listing 15.2.

LISTING 15.3 Another way to initialize.

```
char TicTacToeBoard[3][3] = { 'O', 'X', 'O',
                              'X', 'O', 'X',
                              'O', 'X', 'O' };
```

WORKING WITH A MULTIDIMENSIONAL ARRAY

When you are working with an array of a single dimension, as shown in Chapter 14, you normally only require a single For loop to process each element in the array. When you work with multidimensional arrays, the rule of thumb is the requirement of a For loop per subscript of the array.

In other words, if you have an array with two subscripts, it will require two For loops to process each row and column entry of this array. Listing 15.4 clarifies in detail how to work with a two-dimensional array, which is a common task in many games.

LISTING 15.4

```
//Example 15.1
#include <iostream>

using namespace std;

int main(int argc, char* argv[])
{

   //first initialize the 2 dimensional array using a list
   int myArray[3][3] = { { 0, 1, 2}, { 4, 5, 2 }, { 5, 3, 8 } };

   //since we are working with a two dimensional array, we will need
   //two for loops;
   //one to iterate through the rows and another inner loop to
   //iterate through the columns
   //of the matrix formed by the array
   for(int i = 0; i < 3; i++)
```

```
      {
        for( int j = 0; j < 3; j++ )
        {
          cout << "myArray[" << i << "][" << j << "] := ";
          cout << myArray[i][j] << endl;
        }
      }

      return 0;
    }
```

In Listing 15.4, you first declared the multidimensional array and used an initialization list to assign the elements in the array. Then it was time to detail how to display each element in the array. You created two For loops; one to represent the particular "row," and one to represent the particular "column" of the array. The inner For loop started from the first element and proceeded through each until the end of the row was reached. Once that finished, the outer loop counter (the "row") would increment. This continues until each element in the array is printed out to the console as shown in Figure 15.2.

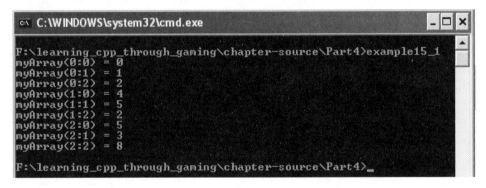

FIGURE 15.2 Example 15.1 output.

SUMMARY

In this chapter, you learned more about multidimensional arrays. These arrays are very useful in some game situations. They allow you to create arrays of arrays, which is helpful when representing any kind of "grid" such as a chessboard, tic-tac-toe board, and so forth.

In the next chapter, you will learn about array parameters, which is the process of passing arrays into functions.

EXERCISES

15.1 How do you declare a multidimensional array?

15.2 How do you declare an array with two dimensions?

15.3 Create a program to initialize the array `myBigArray[10][10]`.

16 Array Parameters

In This Chapter

- Single Dimension Arrays
- Multidimensional Arrays

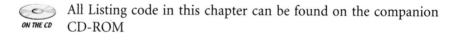 All Listing code in this chapter can be found on the companion CD-ROM

A s you proceed to learn more about the usefulness of arrays, you will probably wish to begin using them as parameters of functions. Back in Chapter 14, during the section on qsort you learned that you pass the array that you need to sort into the qsort function along with the other parameter information.

SINGLE DIMENSION ARRAYS

In the C++ language, it is perfectly legal to pass arrays into any function, the same way you use any other valid data type as a parameter. The only difference when working with arrays is that you only pass the memory address of the array into the function, rather than defining every element in the array. Because you are only using the memory address of the first element in the array as the parameter, the function body itself does not know the bounds of the array; you are responsible for providing that necessary information. Listing 16.1 provides an example of using an array of int elements as a parameter to a function.

LISTING 16.1

```cpp
//include our necessary headers
#include <iostream>

using namespace std;

int doSum(int myArray[], int number_of_elements)
{
  int total = 0;
  for(int i = 0; i < number_of_elements; i++)
  {
    total = total + myArray[i];
  }
  return total;
}

//in some program we have a list of values in an int array which
//need to be added together

int main(int argc, char* argv[])
{

  int values[10] = { 2, 3, 5, 4, 1, 2, 4, 8, 9, 8 };
int sum_total = 0;

  //call the doSum function using the array of ints as
  //well as the size of the array to provide a boundary
  //for the function
  sum_total = doSum( values, 10 );


  //now just print out the total number of cards
  cout << "card sum is: " << sum_total << endl;


  return 0;

}
```

MULTIDIMENSIONAL ARRAYS

When working with more than one dimension as a parameter for a function, some of the same guidelines apply. You still should include a range parameter of the size of your array, but declaring the array as a parameter is slightly different from the single-dimension argument. For a multidimensional array, you only need to include the size of all the dimensions past the first one. To see this demonstrated, look at Listing 16.2.

LISTING 16.2

```
//include our necessary headers
#include <iostream>

using namespace std;

void printMatrix(float mat[][4], int number_of_rows)
{
  for(int i = 0; i < number_of_rows; i++)
  {
    cout << "| ";
    for(int j = 0; j < 4; j++)
    {
      cout << mat[i][j] << " ";

    }
    cout << "|" << endl;
  }

}

//in some program we have a list of values in a float array which
//need to be added together

int main(int argc, char* argv[])
{

  float matrix[4][4] = { {1.0f, 0.0f, 0.0f, 0.0f },
                         {0.0f, 1.0f, 0.0f, 0.0f },
                         {0.0f, 0.0f, 1.0f, 0.0f },
                         {0.0f, 0.0f, 0.0f, 1.0f } };

  //call the printMatrix function using the array of floats as
  //well as the size of each row in the matrix to provide a
  //boundary for the function
  printMatrix( matrix, 4 );
```

```
    return 0;

}
```

If you execute the Example16_2 source code, you will see some output similar to Figure 16.1.

FIGURE 16.1 Example16_2 output.

SUMMARY

In this chapter you received an introduction to passing around arrays from one function to another, which just involves passing the address of the array instead of the entire memory chunk occupied by the array. You learned how to handle and manipulate both single- and two-dimensional arrays. In the next chapter, you will be introduced to the principles of recursion to solve some algorithms.

EXERCISES

16.1 Create a function to initialize an array of int elements.
16.2 Create a function to initialize a two-dimensional array declared as myArray[4][2].
16.3 Create a function to add up every item within a given single-dimension array.

17 Recursion

In This Chapter

■ Recursion

 All Listing code in this chapter can be found on the companion
CD-ROM

RECURSION

In the broad sense of the word, *recursion* can be thought of as a technique of repeating a process to actually solve the same process. For most computing languages,
this involves a two-step approach:

1. Defining a base case; in other words, a specific case of the problem in which
   the solution is reached.
2. Defining a rule (or set of rules) to break down complex cases into simpler
   ones.

A recursive function can be either direct or indirect. A function is *directly* recursive if it calls itself during the execution of the function. It is known as *indirect* recursion when a function calls another function, which in turn executes the first function.
In other words, function A calls function B, which in turn executes function A.

TIP

It is important to remember that when a recursive function calls itself, a new copy or instance of the function is generated in memory. Therefore, the local variables of the newly created function cannot reference the local variables of the original version of the function.

While it sounds a bit confusing for those who have never seen recursion, it can be a handy way of solving certain types of problems.

For example, assume you have a number series that you wish to solve within a program as shown in Listing 17.1.

LISTING 17.1   Series.

```
1, 1, 2, 3, 5, 8, 13, 21 …
```

Each number after the second one is the sum of the two numbers before it. In mathematics and computer science, this particular number series is famously known as the Fibonacci sequence.

To determine a particular result of the series, you should first examine the approach used for each calculation.

If the first two numbers in the sequence are *1* and each subsequent number is the sum of the previous two numbers, this means that the ninth number is the sum of the eighth and seventh numbers in the series. In other words while n > 2, the nth number equals the sum of n − *1* and n − *2*.

To demonstrate this sequence in a program, first look at Listing 17.2.

LISTING 17.2

```cpp
#include <iostream>

using namespace std;

int fib( int n )
{
  if(n < 3)
    return 1;
  else
    return( fib(n − 2) + fib( n − 1 ) );
}

int main(int argc, char* argv[])
{
  int n, result;
  cout << "Enter the position in the sequence to find: ";
  cin >> n;
  result = fib( n );
```

```
    cout << result << " is the " << n << "th Fibonacci sequence
      number" << endl;
    return 0;
}
```

In the first part of Listing 17.2, you are merely querying the user to input which value you wish to generate of the Fibonacci sequence. After the player inputs the desired number via the keyboard, the program then calls the recursive `fib()` function using the value the player entered. The `fib()` function will continue to recursively call itself until the stop condition is reached; when the current value in the function is less than three. It then returns to the previous executed instance of the `fib()` function, which in turn returns to its previous `fib()` function, and so forth, all the way up the chain until the program arrives at the original call to the `fib()` function.

The result is then displayed to the player. Figure 17.1 provides a snapshot of the output of this example.

```
C:\WINDOWS\system32\cmd.exe                              _ □ ✕

F:\learning_cpp_through_gaming\chapter-source\Part4>Example17_1
Enter the position in the sequence to find: 10
55 is the 10th Fibonacci sequence number

F:\learning_cpp_through_gaming\chapter-source\Part4>_
```

FIGURE 17.1   Example17_1.cpp output.

 Recursive programming is a tricky subject of any language, not just C++. It is presented here because it can be useful to see and understand the theory behind how it works.

Recursion Dangers

When you become used to working with recursion, you might be tempted to use that approach for nearly every problem you encounter. Although for some problems this is an acceptable choice for the algorithm you use, it can be the wrong choice for others, capable of leading to disastrous results. As previously mentioned, every time the recursive function is executed, a copy of itself is created in memory. This is known as *overhead*, because the program will create a new copy of this function in memory, which involves creating new copies of any local variables, and so forth.

Generally speaking, using an iterative approach to solving your problem is preferred to using recursion.

SUMMARY

In this chapter, we discussed the concept of recursion, which can be a popular and potentially useful tool for approaching certain types of problems. Although they can be the ideal solution in some cases, there is an overhead attached to using this type of problem solving. Being aware of this overhead will only help determine if the use of recursion is warranted for the given problem. In the next chapter, you will learn more about the use of structures.

EXERCISES

17.1 Take another look at Example 17.1 in this chapter, and more specifically the Fibonacci function. Add some cout statements to this function to see for yourself how new versions are being called and how they are returning when the function hits the stop condition.

17.2 Create a recursive function to calculate the factorial of a given integer.

17.3 Create another function to calculate the factorial of a given integer without using recursion.

18 Structures and Unions

In This Chapter

■ Structures
■ Unions

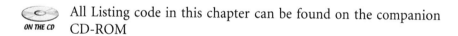

ON THE CD All Listing code in this chapter can be found on the companion CD-ROM

In the first few chapters, you learned about the various atomic or simple data types of the C++ language: int, float, double, and char.

These simple data types might be perfectly acceptable for small programs you may need to create; however, the need for more is required when working with larger pieces of software such as a game. As your game takes shape, and your problems become larger and more complex, you need to have some other way to represent data.

STRUCTURES

Structures are just such a tool. They provide you with a way to use your atomic data types within a common container (or grouping if you will) to provide another way to represent and define data. The `struct` keyword is used to specify and declare a structure within the C++ language.

```
struct <your_type_name>
{
  <data members>
};
```

For some clarification, Listing 18.1 provides some examples of `struct` declarations.

LISTING 18.1   `struct` declarations.

```
//a simple structure containing three floats
struct sVector3
{
  float x;
  float y;
  float z;
};

//a simple structure containing some elements relevant to
//a person
struct tPerson
{
  char name[256];
  int age;
  char bloodtype[1];
};

//Once a struct is declared, it is a legal datatype to use
//within another struct
struct sAsteroid
{
  sVector3 position;
  sVector3 rotation;
};
```

TIP

While you do not need to follow them, a common standard for naming the `struct` *is to precede the type name with an "s" or "t."*

For example you may be designing a space exploration game. The purpose of the game is to gather as many rare elements from different planets within various sectors of the galaxy and bring them back to home base to be refined for wealth. While you can define a list of elements using the atomic data types, this can lead to trouble later in the program. What if you decide to change an attribute or property of the specific element? What if you want to add a new element to the system? It can also become difficult to manage the world data for the game.

One way to approach this type of problem is to use a structure to define the elements the player must search for throughout the game world. You can use a basic approach to create something as shown in Listing 18.2.

LISTING 18.2   struct Element.

```
struct sElement
{
  char description[80];
  float refined_value;
};
```

Once you have declared a struct variable, you can use it in any program the same way you can use any other legal C++ data type. Listing 18.3 provides a small code snippet outlining how to define a struct in a program.

LISTING 18.3   Defining a struct.

```
struct sElement
{
  char description[80];
  float refined_value;
};

//the sElement data type is now valid and can be used throughout
//your
//program such as:

//a matrix representing the galaxy
int galaxy[10][10];

//the player can only hold 10 elements at a time
sElement manifest[10];
```

Accessing Elements in a struct

When you are accessing a component of a struct variable, you only need to use the period (.) character to signal that you are referring to a specific member element of the struct.

In other words, the dot (.) character is inserted between the object name and the member variable name. For another small sample program to demonstrate the struct, please inspect Listing 18.4.

LISTING 18.4

```cpp
#include <iostream>

using namespace std;

//let us use the element structure we have seen
struct sElement
{
  char description[80];
  float refined_value;
};

int main(int argc, char* argv[])
{

  sElement elements[2]; //define an array of two sElement items

  strcpy(elements[0].description, "dilithium crystal");
  elements[0].refined_value = 1000.0f;

  strcpy(elements[1].description, "solonoid crystal");
  elements[1].refined_value = 10.0f;

  for(int i = 0; i < 2; i++)
  {
    cout << "element[" << i << "] has: ";
    cout << elements[i].description << " and is worth ";
    cout << elements[i].refined_value << " on the open market.";
    cout << endl << endl;
  }

  return 0;
}
```

In the example code shown in Listing 18.4, you can see that you have defined a struct with the variable name sElement, which functions as a container for the element member variables. You then are declaring a small array that holds two sElement items. After using the dot notation to assign values to each of the member variables of the struct, you then print out the contents of the data structure to the screen. The output from Listing 18.4 is shown in Figure 18.1, which gives you a better picture of what is happening.

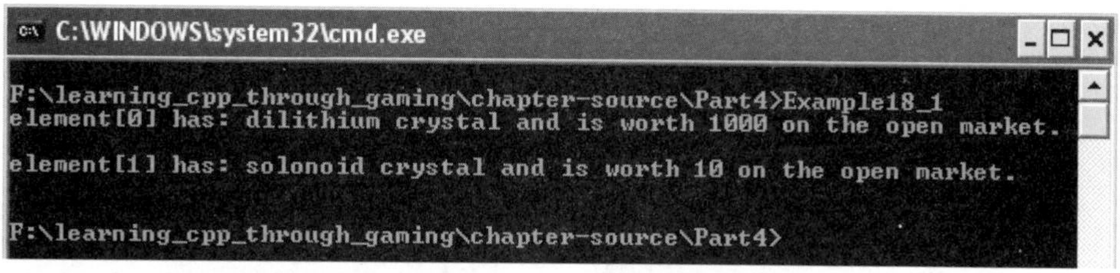

FIGURE 18.1   Example 18_1.cpp output.

UNIONS

Although similar in nature to structures, unions function differently in that members defined within a union all occupy the same physical location in memory. In other words, the struct allows you to declare a collection of data variables, also known as data member variables, which allows you to store data into each variable. A union, on the other hand, can contain a number of data types, but only has one to define the union at any given time.

Listing 18.5 provides some clarification to this explanation on using unions.

LISTING 18.5

```
#include <iostream>

using namespace std;

//let us use the element structure we have seen
//but declare it as a union
union sElement
{
  char description[80];
  float refined_value;
};

int main(int argc, char* argv[])
{

  sElement dilithium;

  strcpy(dilithium.description, "dilithium crystal");
  dilithium.refined_value = 1000.0f;

  cout << dilithium.description << " is worth ";
  cout << dilithium.refined_value << " on the open market.";
  cout << endl << endl;
```

```
        return 0;
    }
```

The output of Example 18.2 is shown in Figure 18.2.

FIGURE 18.2 Output of Example 18.2.

As you can see, you should not confuse the union with the struct. A union should be used where it does not matter what the size of a variable is at a given location, or when variables sharing the same memory location is not a concern.

Unions should also be avoided when working with a section of memory that is accessed regularly in a high-performance application such as a game.

SUMMARY

In this chapter, you learned more about using structures in your programs, which represents a way to create a custom data type that can contains values composed of simple data types. You learned how to work with struct data, and how to access each member variable of a struct. You were also introduced to a similar type, the union, which functions similar in nature to a struct; however, only one data member of the union occupies the defined memory location at one time. In the next chapter, you will focus on working on the project for this part of the book, which is a Battleship game that uses the concepts introduced so far in the book.

EXERCISE

18.1 What is the dot operator and what does it do?

19 Battleship

In This Chapter

- The Game of Battleship
- Game Architecture

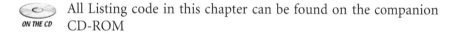 All Listing code in this chapter can be found on the companion CD-ROM

Part IV of this book has been all about the definition and use of simple data structures to accomplish a task along with creating your own custom data type to define some particular data. This chapter focuses on the application of these data structures to create a small game of Battleship.

Much of the game's code will be commented upon in the chapter; to see the entire files, check out Project19_1.h and Project19_1.cpp on the companion CD-ROM.

THE GAME OF BATTLESHIP

In this project, you will implement a simple game of Battleship, a classic board game that illustrates what you have learned so far in this book. This version of Battleship follows these rules:

- The goal of the game is to sink your opponent's fleet before he sinks yours.
- The board is randomly generated for the players. You will not be able to position your fleet.
- The board is five rows by five columns.
- Each player takes turns firing at the other player's fleet until the winning condition is reached (either the enemy sinks your fleet or you sink theirs).

GAME ARCHITECTURE

To run a game of Battleship, your program will need several modules and subsidiary functions. The major modules needed are:

- A core main loop that runs the actual game.
- A module that processes player1's firing commands.
- A module that processes player2's firing commands.
- A module that analyzes player1's and player2's shots to determine if the opposing player's fleet has been sunk; ergo the end of game.

It would have been possible to split this project into several modules. However, the project is relatively small so it is kept in one source and header file.

Header File

As with the Blackjack game covered in Part III, every time a new function is added to the main source file, you should add a corresponding function declaration in the header file.

Core Game Loop

A round of the Battleship game involves several steps:

1. First, player1's view of the game is displayed on the console with a rough representation of the game board. All the player will be able to see is his own ships, and any sectors containing known hits of player2's fleet.

2. Player1 will input his firing commands. This input is simply which row and column number the player wishes to target.
3. The weapons are launched, and Player1 receives either a "hit!" or "miss" message.
4. It is then player2's turn, in which the listed steps are repeated.
5. At the end of each round, after both players have taken their turns, the game will check if any side has achieved victory. If so, the game ends with a congratulations message to the winning player.

SUMMARY

In this project for Part IV, you were able to directly implement your knowledge of elementary data structures to create a small fun game of Battleship. Take some time to go through the source code of the project to understand how things are working together to create the final game. Above all, do not be afraid to experiment with your own modifications to the game!

In the next part of the book, you will be introduced to the use of pointers, which is a critical and valuable tool in your C++ education.

EXERCISES

19.1 Add some additional logic to the small Battleship game to only show one board at a time depending on who's currently taking their turn. In other words, only display player 1's board when it is player 1's turn.

19.2 For some additional fun allow each player to name the ships in their respective fleets. This could also be extended to also modify any messages to the player which would then use the affected ship name.

Part V | Pointers

After working with single- and multidimensional arrays, you now have the beginnings of a system to track data that can exist in a game. You can create arrays of various types to track different inventory systems, or perhaps to store map locations of monsters and other objects. The one difficulty is that you could potentially have several large arrays that you may be using in functions or as globally declared chunks of memory.

In this part of the book, you will learn part of the very core of the C++ language: pointers. Pointers allow you to work with giant sections of data, without the need to pass these large blocks of memory around. This pointer can be manipulated several ways and is capable of directly modifying the data being pointed to, when necessary. You will also learn about creating function pointers and working with references.

At the end of this part of the book, you will take the Battleship project used in Part IV, and will create a way to dynamically alter the game. Best of luck, and have fun!

20

Introduction to Pointers

In This Chapter

- Learning about Memory
- Using a Pointer to Store the Address
- Void Pointers

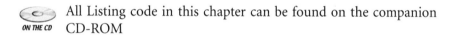 All Listing code in this chapter can be found on the companion CD-ROM

Now that you have covered some basic data structures such as arrays in Part IV, Part V begins by covering the concept of *pointers*. Pointers are an incredibly powerful tool in the C++ language and are extremely versatile in their usage.

Pointers can be thought of as an object in memory that references (or "points to") another location of data in memory (known as the *address*). This can make your program much more efficient and easier to work with. Instead of manipulating a large block of memory containing important game data, for example, you only need to pass around a pointer to the address of this memory block. If this at first sounds confusing, do not worry. There are enough samples in this chapter to help you understand this fundamental concept of the C++ language.

LEARNING ABOUT MEMORY

To understand more about pointers and how they function, you should have a basic understanding of how the memory in your computer is organized. Computer memory is divided into memory locations that are sequentially numbered (Figure 20.1).

FIGURE 20.1 Memory architecture.

Retrieving a Variable's Memory Address

Luckily, the operating system and underlying computer shield the very low-level basics of memory management. You do not need to know where in memory a variable you declare in your program is stored, since the underlying operating system handles that for you. There are instances, though, where you need to know this memory address of the variable. The unary address-of operator (&) is provided by the C++ language for this purpose. For further details, look at Listing 20.1 to see this operator in action.

LISTING 20.1 Address-Of Operator (&).

```cpp
#include <iostream>

using namespace std;

int main(int argc, char* argv[] )
{
  int value1 = 5;
  cout << "value1 := " << value1 << " and it's address is at: " <<
    &value1 << endl;

  return 0;
}
```

When you declare a variable in your program, the compiler does the work of determining how much memory space to allow based on the data type of the variable. The compiler also takes care of allocating this memory and automatically assigning an address for it. Refer back to Chapter 2 and your compiler documentation for determining how much room each data type is assigned. Running Listing 20.1 will produce the output similar to Figure 20.1.

USING A POINTER TO STORE THE ADDRESS

You can also use a pointer to store the memory address location of a particular variable. Remember that every variable has a particular address assigned by the compiler. This address is of a given size assigned by the compiler depending on the data type. When you declare a pointer variable of a specific data type, the compiler will set aside enough memory to hold an address. Therefore, a pointer can also be thought of as another data type.

No matter the data type, every pointer is the same size in memory. Refer to your specific compiler documentation, but usually this is four bytes in size on a 32-bit processor, and eight bytes on a 64-bit processor.

Listing 20.2 provides some additional clarification on this discussion.

LISTING 20.2   NULL pointer.

```
int original_value;
int *pValue = 0; //NULL pointer assignment
double* pShaman; //uh-oh..this is a wild pointer!
```

When you initialize a pointer to zero, as you did with the pValue variable in Listing 20.2, you are creating a NULL pointer. In other words, it is not pointing at anything.
    If you do not assign anything to a pointer upon declaration, it can be pointing to anything, including complete garbage. This is also known as a "wild" pointer.

For a pointer to hold the address of a variable, you need to remember to assign the memory address to it. Listing 20.3 provides some more details.

LISTING 20.3   Pointer initialization.

```
int original_value = 3;
int *pValue = 0;
pValue = &original_value;
```

Listing 20.3 details how you assigned the address of a variable to a pointer using the address-of operator (&). Determining the value of the address assigned to the pointer is also known as pointer *indirection*. In other words, you are manipulating the value of original_value by the pValue pointer rather than modifying original_value itself.

When you are using indirection to determine the value of an address pointed to with a pointer, you need to use the (*) operator, which is also known as the *dereferencing* operator.

In other words, when you dereference a pointer, you are retrieving the value of the address stored at the pointer. For an example to underscore this discussion, examine Listing 20.4.

LISTING 20.4 Pointer dereferencing—Example20_2.cpp.

```cpp
#include <iostream>

using namespace std;

int main(int argc, char* argv[])
{
  int original_value = 3;
  int *pValue = 0;
  pValue = &original_value;
  original_value = 10;
  cout << "original_value has value := " << *pValue << endl;
  return 0;
}
```

After running Listing 20.4, you may be surprised to see the results shown in Figure 20.2.

FIGURE 20.2 Example20_2.cpp output.

You might have noticed that the dereferencing operator (*) is the same as the multiplication operator. You do not need to worry, as the compiler will know which one to execute depending on the context of your call.

Void **POINTERS**

In the C++ language, the void data type represents the absence of any type. Therefore, void pointers are pointers that point to a value with no type. The benefit of the void pointer is that it can be used as a chameleonic pointer, being able to point to an int, an array of doubles, or even a char string. In short, void pointers are considered generic because they can point to anything. While this might sound highly useful, there is a catch. Since the data type is unknown, the compiler does not know how to dereference the pointer. To manipulate the data being pointed to, you always must first cast the pointer to a known data type to be properly dereferenced. Listing 20.5 provides an example of using the void pointer.

LISTING 20.5   Void pointers—Example20_3.cpp.

```cpp
#include <iostream>

using namespace std;

void countdown(void* data, int size)
{
  switch(size)
  {
    case sizeof(char) : (*((char*)data))--; break;
    case sizeof(double) : (*((double*)data))--; break;
  }
}

int main(int argc, char* argv[])
{
  char a = 'Z';
  double b = 1602.0;
  countdown(&a,sizeof(a));
  countdown(&b,sizeof(b));
  cout << a << ", " << b << endl;
  return 0;
}
```

As you can see in Listing 20.5, you are starting out with some known variable data types. You are then passing their address as a void pointer into the countdown function. Within this function, the size of the parameter is calculated, which allows the function to determine which data type to cast with. Figure 20.3 displays the output from Listing 20.5.

FIGURE 20.3   Example20_3.cpp output.

SUMMARY

This chapter provided an introduction to the sometimes complex world of pointers in the C++ language. You learned how to create and define a pointer, and how to use them within a program.

In the next chapter, you will learn more about pointer arithmetic, which is a way of using some basic addition and subtraction measures to manipulate pointer variables.

EXERCISES

20.1 What is a pointer?

20.2 Why is a pointer important?

20.3 What is the difference between an address stored in a pointer, and the value of that address?

21 Pointer Arithmetic

In This Chapter

 All Listing code in this chapter can be found on the companion CD-ROM

In Chapter 20 you were introduced to pointers and how they are used to reference an address in memory. In this chapter, you will learn more about the concept of pointer "arithmetic," and how your program can benefit from manipulating pointers to big blocks of memory, rather than working directly with the big blocks of memory.

Mathematically wise, there are several useful aspects of working with pointers to reference memory addresses. Pointers can be added and subtracted from one another, while another popular technique is to use pointer arithmetic to find out how many elements separate two chosen locations in an array. Using addition and subtraction with pointers varies slightly in that it does depend on the size of the data type being pointed to.

If you recall from Chapter 2, you learned that each data type can vary in how large a size in memory it occupies. To refresh your memory, a char takes up one byte, a short takes two bytes, and an int occupies four bytes. Listing 21.1 defines some pointers to these data types for our discussion.

LISTING 21.1 Some pointer declarations.

```
char* pChar;
int* pInt;
short* pShort;
```

For the sake of argument, you can also make the assumption that these three pointers point to memory location *300*, *1300*, and *2300*, respectively.

With pointer arithmetic, you are allowed to use the postfix (++) operator, which will increment each of these pointers by one. However, by one what?

When using pointer arithmetic, the pointer will increase or decrease the same number of bytes as the data type being pointed to. Therefore, in this case, the three new memory locations being pointed to by the char, short, and int pointers are *301*, *1302*, and *2304*, respectively.

Figure 21.1 might help shed some light on using arithmetic.

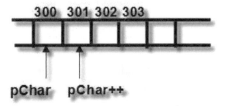

FIGURE 21.1 Some pointer arithmetic.

SUMMARY

In this chapter, you learned more about pointer arithmetic, which is a useful way of manipulating a pointer to modify array data. You can add and subtract two pointers, and use them to discover the difference between two chosen locations in a given array.

In the next chapter, you will study a comparison between pointers and arrays when using them as parameters for functions.

EXERCISES

21.1 What is pointer arithmetic?

21.2 Which mathematic functions can our pointer use to manipulate memory?

22   Using Pointers and Arrays

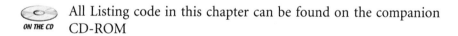 All Listing code in this chapter can be found on the companion
CD-ROM

ON THE CD

With the basic introduction to pointers covered in Chapter 20, you are
ready to start experimenting with one of the most powerful features of
the C++ language: pointers.

POINTERS IN FUNCTIONS

When you wish to pass pointers into functions, there is no great mystery in creating
the necessary function prototype. The desired parameter is just defined as a pointer.
Listing 22.1 provides some clarification on how to pass pointers into functions.

LISTING 22.1 Pointers into functions.

```
#include <iostream.h>

using namespace std;

//function prototype
void printMessage(char* strMessage);

int main(int argc, char* argv[])
{
  printMessage("Hello Hockey Fans.");

  return 0;
}

void printMessage(char* strMessage)
{
  cout << strMessage << endl;
}
```

As you can see from Listing 22.1, you are declaring a function prototype using a pointer to an array of char elements. Within this function, you are displaying the char elements to the screen.

POINTERS AND ARRAYS

As you learn more about pointers and arrays, you can start to appreciate the amount of connection and interweaving that exists between the two. Consider a simple C-style string declaration such as Listing 22.2.

LISTING 22.2 Simple string.

```
#include <iostream>

using namespace std;

int main(int argc, char* argv[])
{
  char best_ever[] = "UltimaIV"; /** create a char array large
enough */

  return 0;
}
```

In Listing 22.2 you are declaring a NULL terminated char array containing the text "UltimaIV". Using what you have learned about arrays from Chapter 14, you already know that they are stored sequentially in memory and that the char data type uses one byte of memory. Therefore, you can represent the best_ever string from Listing 22.2 as Table 22.1.

TABLE 22.1   Representation of "UltimaIV" in Memory

Variable Name	Variable Type	Memory Address	Data
best_ever	char	105	'U'
	char	106	'l'
	char	107	't'
	char	108	'l'
	char	109	'm'
	char	110	'a'
	char	111	'l'
	char	112	'V'
	char	113	'\0'

Taking what you have learned about passing pointers into a function, the C++ language also allows you to pass arrays into functions. Since arrays are sequentially ordered in the computer's memory, this amounts to only needing to pass the first element of the array as a pointer.

Listing 22.3 may provide further clarification about this.

LISTING 22.3   Arrays as parameters.

```
#include <iostream>

using namespace std;

void printMessage(char* strMessage);

//note that the following declaration is also valid
//void printMessage( char[] strMessage );

int main(int argc, char* argv[])
{
  char best_ever[] = "UltimaIV";
```

```
            //currently, the best_ever char array
            //has 9 elements including the terminating
            //NULL character

            //The first element of the array is by
            //default pointed to by the name of
            //the array itself
            printMessage( best_ever );

            return 0;
        }

        void printMessage(char* strMessage)
        {
          cout << strMessage << endl;
        }
```

In Listing 22.3, you took the declared char element array containing the string data "UltimaIV" and sent this array to the printMessage function. Although it is not obvious, in the C++ language when you declare an array of string data, the name of the array becomes the actual pointer to the array data. Thus, when you pass the best_ever char array into the printMessage function, the function will internally receive a char pointer to the first element of the array. When this char pointer is processed, the program has enough internal logic to keep processing every byte of data until the terminating NULL byte is handled.

SUMMARY

In this chapter, you were introduced to a comparison of sorts between using a pointer for a function parameter versus using an array for the same purpose. In the next chapter, you will learn much more about function pointers, which allow you to manipulate actual pointers to functions.

EXERCISES

22.1 Create a small program that uses a pointer to display the elements of an array.

22.2 Create a function that accepts two arrays and proceeds to swap their elements with each other.

23

Function Pointers

In This Chapter

■ The Case Against Function Pointers

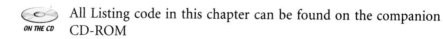 All Listing code in this chapter can be found on the companion
CD-ROM

Throughout the discussion concerning pointers in the previous chapters, you learned that they are used to contain a memory address that can be distributed throughout your program in a small, efficient manner.

If you recall in Chapter 22, an array name is automatically a constant pointer to the first element in the array. Similarly, a function name is a constant pointer to the function itself. Therefore, it is possible to declare a pointer variable that points to a function, and to call that same function using the pointer. In some situations, this can be an elegant approach to a particular problem. Depending on the user's input, for example, with function pointers you could determine at runtime what function to call.

The only difference from regular pointers is how to determine the type of the object being pointed to. If a pointer to an int data type points to an integer variable, what does a function pointer point to?

A pointer to a function must point to a function of the same return type and match the function signature. Listing 23.1 provides some clarification on a function pointer declaration.

LISTING 23.1   Function pointer.

```
Data_Type (* Function_Name)( parameter list to function )
bool (* loadVideoCard)( int width, int height, int depth );
```

In Listing 23.1 `Function_Name` is declared as a pointer. It is critical to surround the name with the parentheses, remembering that brackets have a higher precedence than the (*) operator. If you forgot to use the parentheses to define your function pointer, the compiler will assume that the function name uses the parameter list and returns a pointer.

To outline this difference, look at Listing 23.2.

LISTING 23.2   Parentheses.

```
bool * function ( int, int );
bool (* function)(int, int );
```

Seeing them declared together, it is easier to understand why the parentheses are needed.

For a longer example of where function pointers might be used, please examine Listing 23.3, which demonstrates one way to use them.

LISTING 23.3

```
#include <iostream>

using namespace std;

int add( int& opA, int& opB )
{
   return( opA + opB ) ;
}

int sub( int& opA, int& opB)
{
   return( opA - opB );
}

int product( int& opA, int& opB)
{
   return( opA * opB );
}
```

```
int main(int argc, char* argv[])
{

  int x = 0;
  int y = 0;
  cout << "enter two numbers: " ;
  cin >> x;
  cin >> y;

  int (* pMathFunc)( int&, int &);
  int sel;
  cout << "(1) add (2) subtract (3) multiply: ";
  cin >> sel;

  switch( sel )
  {
    case 1: pMathFunc = add;      /** set pMathFunc to add function
    ptr */
    break;
    case 2: pMathFunc = sub;      /** set pMathFunc to sub function
    ptr */
    break;
    case 3: pMathFunc = product; /** set pMathFunc to product ptr */
    break;
  }

  /** now that our function pointer has been set, we can have one
  * common access method which will work across all 3 math functions
  */
  cout << "The result of the desired operation is := "
    << pMathFunc( x, y ) << endl;
  return 0;
}
```

As you can see from Listing 23.3, the program first asks you to input which math function you wish to execute. Then, you enter two values to operate the desired operation on. Using function pointers, the program is then able to simply use a `switch` statement to determine which math function is desired. In the final batch of statements, you are just calling the function pointer to handle the desired operation. For a sample output of Listing 23.3, inspect Figure 23.1.

THE CASE AGAINST FUNCTION POINTERS

Although you learned how to use function pointers in this chapter, they are generally very dangerous to use, and for the most part should be avoided unless determined as

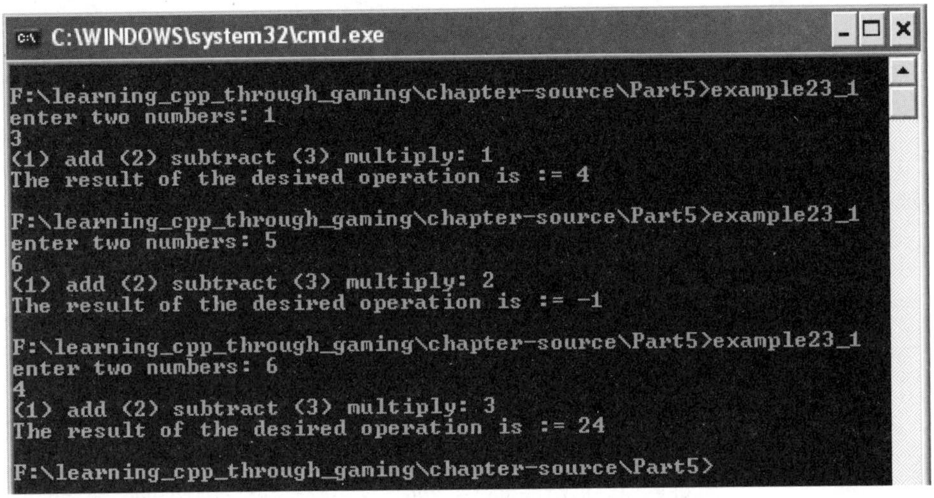

FIGURE 23.1 Example23_1.cpp output.

absolutely necessary by your code. They were popular during the days of the C programming language, but with the power and flexibility that object-oriented programming gives you with C++, they are no longer needed.

You will learn more about this in Part VI of this book.

SUMMARY

Although a somewhat advanced topic in the C++ language, the use of function pointers can be beneficial when used properly. This practice can be extremely dangerous, however, as you can accidentally call the function when you only meant to assign it to its pointer. In the next chapter, you will learn more about the differences and similarities when working with pointers and references.

EXERCISES

23.1 Show the declaration for a pointer to a function returning an int value and accepts two floats as parameters.

23.2 Explain where you would not use function pointers. Explain where you would.

24

Pointers versus References

In This Chapter

- Pointers versus References

All Listing code in this chapter can be found on the companion
CD-ROM

As you have learned through this book so far, and specifically in this chapter
on pointers, there is very little difference between using a pointer and using
references. As your journey in the C++ language matures, you will "know"
when to use pointers and when to use references, but for now, it would be nice to
have some signposts to help foster the experience.

If you recall, an indirect reference is an object that can be used to indirectly
refer to another object. While a pointer uses the (*) operator, remember that the
references use the unary (&) operator.

For example, you can look at Listing 24.1 for a regular declaration.

LISTING 24.1   A regular declaration.

```
int x = 4;
```

With the information you have learned on pointers, you can manipulate Listing 24.1 to produce Listing 24.2.

LISTING 24.2   Pointer initialization from an address.

```
int x = 4;
int *px = &x;
```

This declares px as a pointer to an int, which is set to the address of x. You could also write the code as shown in Listing 24.3.

LISTING 24.3   Pointer and reference initialization.

```
int x = 4;
int *px = &x;
int &rx = x;
```

This declaration is specifying that a reference of type int is set to the value of x.

Although there are always exceptions to the rule, most C++ developers tend to favor working with references rather than manipulating pointers. References give the code a cleaner "feel" and are easier to use. References cannot be reassigned, though, once declared. If you need to point to one object, then later must switch to another, you must use a pointer. References also cannot be NULL, so if there is any chance that the data you wish to reference can be NULL, it is probably better to use a pointer.

Although you will learn about it more in Part VI of this book, you are able to create and destroy your own memory on the heap using the new operator. As you will learn, the new operator returns a pointer to the block of allocated memory. Since there is a possibility (however small) that an allocation can fail, you should not create a reference until you first ensure the memory returned is not NULL. Listing 24.4 has an example of this.

LISTING 24.4   Reference checking.

```
int* pInt = new int;
if( pInt != NULL)
int &rInt = *pInt;
```

In the few lines of code in Listing 24.4, you are declaring a pointer to an int and attempting to initialize it with the memory returned by the new operator. The address in pInt is then tested to ensure it is not NULL. If it passes this test, then the pInt pointer is dereferenced. The net result of dereferencing an int variable is an int object. rInt is then initialized to refer to that object. In other words, rInt becomes a working alias to the int returned by the new operator.

SUMMARY

An important lesson in the C++ language is to learn the difference between working with an object by a pointer, and working with the object by a reference. In the next chapter, you will modify the Battleship game created in Part IV to allow the player to resize the game board.

EXERCISES

24.1 What is the difference between a pointer and a reference?

24.2 When must you use a pointer rather than a reference?

24.3 Create a small program that declares a `char` array, a reference to this `char` array, and a pointer to the `char` array. Use the pointer and the reference to manipulate the values stored in the `char` array.

25

A Game of Variable-Sized Battleship

In This Chapter

- Adding Variable Size
- Processing the Command Line
- Modifying Game Board Access

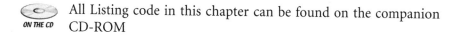 All Listing code in this chapter can be found on the companion CD-ROM

P art V of this book concludes with a small modification to the Battleship game used in Part IV to demonstrate the implementation of the material on pointers that we've covered.

 Much of the source code will be commented on during this chapter. To follow along, browse through the same source code on the companion CD-ROM. Project25_1.h and Project25_1.cpp.

ADDING VARIABLE SIZE

Based on your foundation in working with pointers, you can now modify the Battleship game from Part IV to allow a variable-sized game board. For a high-level view of the modification, when the player launches the game, he will be able to specify the dimensions of the board as a command-line argument. Once the game loads up, it will use these parameters to create the board for the game. This will mean a few new functions:

- A function to process the command line. This will involve reading the command line of the application and determining what size the player has specified. If there are no command-line arguments or they are outside a range of acceptable boundaries, then have some default board sizes ready.
- The game board itself will need to be created during the game since it will vary in size, rather than be a select size as it is now. This may also impact the functions you have created to access the game board.

PROCESSING THE COMMAND LINE

A common task for many applications and some games is to scan the command line for a given set of arguments. For the project, there will not be any fancy algorithm to allow users to input any command-line option in any order they wish. While this can be added later, for now it is more important to process things in a certain order.

Since the goal of this phase of the Battleship project is to allow the player to specify any size for a board, this is the only argument you need to look for when parsing the command line. Although a quick and dirty introduction to command-line parsing, the only thing you need to remember is that when you launch your application, the operating system will also pass any argument (aka parameter) you type after the executable name of your application. In the C/C++ language, the argc and argv parameters to the main function contain any command-line arguments. Argc is an integer containing the number of parameters to your function, while the argv array is an array of string pointers to the command-line data itself. Listing 25.1 is an example of this.

LISTING 25.1   Using argc and argv.

```
#include <iostream.h>
using namespace std;
int main(int argc, char* argv[])
{
```

```
        cout << "argc = " << argc << endl;
        /** just loop through each string in the argv string array */
        for(int i = 0; i < argc; i++)
        cout << "argv[" << i << "] = " << argv[i] << endl;
        return 0;
    }
```

So, when you execute your application, any text you separate with a space be-comes a "parameter" in the eyes of your function. If you also notice, the argv[0] el-ement is the actual name of the program itself.

For the purposes of the project, you will only provide very limited command-line support. The accompanying source code outlines the steps taken to parse the command line, but it is nothing fancy. You are just using a brute-force approach to test if the text of a given parameter is anything you need to worry about for the game.

MODIFYING GAME BOARD ACCESS

You will need to slightly alter how the board is generated and accessed. You will therefore need to create the board with a pointer.

You will also be using the given size parameter you just finished examining to determine how much memory to allocate for your game board.

For this project, however, you are restricted to using a square size, meaning you will not be able to allow a 1×5 or 2×6 game board. You will always have either a 5×5, 10×10, or 20×20 array (or whatever you specify the size).

While not critical, it may be prudent to restrict the size to something manage-able and a bit easier for you to find the enemy ships. You do not want to suddenly find yourself in a four-hour showdown because you decided to make a 100×100 game grid!

The accompanying source code outlines the steps taken to convert the board into a resizable array.

SUMMARY

In this chapter, you focused on using the concepts you have learned through the book so far, to apply them to a small modification of the Battleship game used in Part IV. Although you are encouraged to experiment, the plan of action for the modifications was to allow the user to specify the size of the game board via the command line. This also necessitated the altering of how the game board is accessed since it becomes a pointer instead of a declared array of a given size. Feel free to play with the code and make any fun changes wherever you decide. Take as much time as you need to experiment with a new algorithm or function to modify the game.

This concludes Part V of the book. In the next part of your introduction to the C++ language, you will learn more about object-oriented programming theory and techniques that mesh seamlessly with the C++ language.

EXERCISES

25.1 For some additional challenge, modify the project to allow the player to create a game board of any size, not necessarily square. For example, the player could specify they wish to play the game using a 10 x 20 grid.

Part VI

Concepts of Object-Oriented Programming

The concepts covered in Part V helped to establish how to manipulate blocks of memory referenced by the pointer to their address. Until now, you have been covering the C++ language in a very procedural fashion. The code instructions are executed from start to finish until the program's end.

In Part VI, you begin to focus on the underlying power and flexibility the C++ language offers; object-oriented programming (OOP). The concepts you will be covering form the cornerstones and foundation of OOP using the C++ language. You will learn more about creating your own objects and defining how they behave and interact with other objects in the system. You will learn more about creating a "family tree" of your objects that also introduces you to creating abstract interfaces that are used to provide a "bottom layer."

This will then culminate in some modifications to the Battleship project from Part V to re-engineer the game in a more object-oriented friendly way. Happy hunting, Captain!

26 Concepts of Object-Oriented Programming

In This Chapter

- Classes
- Encapsulation
- Abstraction
- Inheritance
- Polymorphism
- Composition
- Class Declaration and Implementation
- Your First Class
- Object Scope

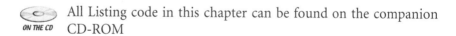 All Listing code in this chapter can be found on the companion CD-ROM

So far, you have been covering the C++ language in more or less a procedural fashion. Your programs run through each instruction, and then terminate when finished.

In today's ever-growing software with millions of lines of code, a procedural approach does not always suffice. Software is now developed in teams, with members being added (or leaving) throughout the development lifecycle. Thus, it can be difficult to train new members on how the software is structured and functions. Companies are also relying more on the ability to reuse the internal modules developed by their programmers, rather than start from scratch with each new project.

Applications today also are run in graphical user environments such as the Windows®, Linux/Unix, or MacOS operating systems. In these environments, programs are event-driven, meaning that your software responds to events generated by your user, rather than running in a procedural fashion from beginning to end.

Every time you press a key on the keyboard, for example, or move the mouse around, it is sending an *event message* to your application. Through this message-sending mechanism, the application then distributes the work depending on the received message. By this event handling system, you can therefore potentially run many more programs than in a procedural environment, as each program will not completely take control of the host operating system.

CLASSES

Within the C++ language, *classes* are the blueprint representation of objects. They typically contain many different variables and data members to define what the class does.

Another example of a class is to think of an everyday object such as an airplane. An airplane has certain specific properties such as how much cargo it can carry, how many people, how many engines, the number of wings, and so forth. Not only does the airplane have a set of properties, it can perform actions as well. The plane can lower or retract its landing gears, accelerate on the runway, and come to rest at the terminal.

Having all of your functions and properties of an object defined in one place forms a core of the C++ language and OO design in general. Everything related to the object is in one place. It is easier to find if you have any bugs, and it is easier to pass around your game system. Other parts of the program that use a class can do so without caring about the internal implementation of the object. These other objects calling your class only need to know how to use the object.

ENCAPSULATION

When you use the term *encapsulation* in the English language, you are usually referring to an enclosed object that can contain other smaller objects. For example, a car is an outer shell containing people and various mechanical components.

This definition is more or less the same in C++. A class can be thought of as a capsule as well, since it contains data members and member functions. In OOP, the use of encapsulation allows you to hide information in a lower level object of your system from higher level implementations. For example, if you were to create an object responsible for managing basic bank account transactions or processes, then other objects that use this one need not concern themselves with how a specific transaction is performed. It is quite similar when you physically go to a bank teller to withdraw or deposit monies. You do not care how the bank tellers internally process your request; you only need to inform them where to put what money. The rest is handled by the tellers. In effect, encapsulation can also be loosely thought of as a type of "black box" in your system.

ABSTRACTION

Another powerful feature of the C++ language and a cornerstone of OOP is the ability to determine the required data members and/or functions of an object. This is known as *abstraction*. It is a common practice in most software designs to define a clear distinction between the abstract properties of an object, and more functional or concrete details of its implementation. In this way, you can then define methods for public consumption. That is, what other objects will see of your object, while the implementation of these public facing methods is handled internally by the object itself.

INHERITANCE

As in the world of biology, objects can inherit properties from other objects to create new ones or to define new behaviors. In other words, one generation of objects can take properties or methods from a previous generation.

The main benefit of inheritance is that it can give you a way to extend an existing object to create a new one that does not modify the parent.

For example, in a real-world situation, consider the inheritance involved in something like an automobile design. You can possibly design an automobile with an inheritance tree that details how an object is created from atomic components. For example, you may have a standard car that is delivered to your customer. However, for the sake of this example, the same plant that produces this standard car also produces a very high-end sports car that can travel at mach speeds. Theoretically then, this sports car could inherit some of the basic properties of the standard car, while defining its own new ones. It would probably use a different engine, for example.

POLYMORPHISM

Polymorphism is another feature of the C++ language that makes OOP fun. *Polymorphism* is the ability to define methods in each inherited object using the same name but will function differently depending on the object executing the function.

For example, consider a situation in which you have several different objects all deriving from one common base class (which you will learn more about throughout this book). In a real-world situation, consider the polymorphic properties of your common everyday automobile. Once you learn how to drive a car, you can virtually hop behind the wheel of dozens of different vehicles. You can drive two-door sports cars, or four-door minivans. The car is a polymorphic object, so no matter which car you drive, you can pretty much jump into any other car and drive it just the same. In a 1969 Gremlin if you press the brake pedal the result is the same as pressing the brake pedal of a 2008 Chevy; the automobile stops.

Objects versus Classes

In some cases, the term *object* is used interchangeably with the concept of classes. However, you should recognize a clear distinction immediately. A class defines an idea, whereas an object is a concrete instance of that idea. In other words, you do not control or manipulate the concept of an airplane, but you do pilot a specific instance of an airplane such as a Cessna or a 747.

As you continue through the book, this distinction will make itself clearer.

Data and Function Members

As you create and design each class or object in any of your programs, you eventually must settle on a list of behaviors or properties each object should possess. Integral to each object then are member functions and data; properties that usually define the purpose of the class.

Member functions of the class usually operate on the internal data members themselves. For example, if you were using an Airplane object, it would probably have some data members defining the plane's cargo manifest. A logical member function of the airplane, therefore, is a function that would add new cargo to the manifest, and one to remove it.

COMPOSITION

Classes can be structured in a number of different ways; however, they must all follow the same structure constraints. They are defined using the keyword `class` and contain a body that declares any functions or variables that are a part of the class. Listing 26.1 details a `class` skeleton.

LISTING 26.1 The `class` Skeleton.

```
//This is our first C++ class.
class Person
{
```

```
<access qualifiers>

<data member variables>

<member functions>

};
```

You will learn much more about classes as you progress through this chapter and the rest of this book.

CLASS DECLARATION AND IMPLEMENTATION

Until now, your projects and other sample code that has been worked throughout this book has been condensed into one .h header file containing your function declarations, and one .cpp source file containing the necessary code.

When beginning to work with the C++ language, there are some basic common practices that C++ developers employ to provide easier readability and better project management. One of these practices is to separate your C++ object; the class declaration is located in a .h header file, while the implementation of the object is located in a .cpp file.

YOUR FIRST CLASS

Earlier in this chapter, you learned about basic class composition. It is now time to see a class in action to provide some foundation for the rest of your C++ use.

You start by declaring a class within its own .h header file. You begin by using the keyword class, then specifying a name to refer to this class with. Finally, you surround the class with curly braces and the semicolon. Listing 26.2 provides an example.

LISTING 26.2   First class.

```
class Airplane
{
   //empty for now!
};
```

When you want to create an instance of this class, you simply treat it the same as every other valid data type you are using in C++. Listing 26.3 provides some further clarification.

LISTING 26.3   Instantiating the `airplane`.

```
//declare an int
int number;

//declare an Airplane
Airplane Cessna;
```

Adding Data Members

Once you have created your class definition, you can add data members. Remember, these are properties that define what the class has. For example, an airplane contains a number of wings, wheels, and whether it is powered by a jet engine or propeller. Listing 26.4 provides more detail.

LISTING 26.4   `Airplane`.

```
class Airplane
{
public: //ignore this keyword for now
  int wings;
  int wheels;
  bool jet;
};
```

When you want to access the data members of your object, you must use the dot (.) operator. Listing 26.5 provides some examples.

LISTING 26.5   Accessing `airplane` members.

```
//declare an Airplane
Airplane Cessna;
Cessna.wings = 5;    //don't you have a 5-winged Cessna?
Cessna.wheels = 3; //3 wheels
Cessna.jet = false;    //it's a prop plane
```

Adding Member Functions

Adding member functions to your class is similar to adding the data members. You declare the function as you have already learned throughout this book. Listing 26.6 provides some additional detail.

LISTING 26.6   Adding member functions.

```
class Airplane
{
public: //ignore this keyword for now
  int wings;
```

```
    int wheels;
    bool jet;

    void startPropellers();
    void stopPropellers();
};
```

To execute these member functions of a class, again you use the dot (.) operator in the same way you did with accessing data members. Listing 26.7 shows you another example.

LISTING 26.7   Accessing member functions.

```
//declare an Airplane
Airplane Cessna;
Cessna.wings = 5;    //don't you have a 5-winged Cessna?
Cessna.wheels = 3; //3 wheels
Cessna.jet = false;    //it's a prop plane

//is ready to take off, so start the propellers
Cessna.startPropellers();
```

In most C++ naming conventions of source code you might find on the Internet, member data variables usually have a leading underscore (_) character or the letter "m" followed by an underscore to signal that they are member variables.

OBJECT SCOPE

When you are providing the implementation (code) for your class, you have to provide the compiler with the *scope* of the function. Similar to the scope rules you covered earlier, all this means is that you need to inform the compiler where a function belongs. Listing 26.8 might provide a better explanation.

LISTING 26.8   Object scope during implementation.

```
class Airplane
{
public: //ignore this keyword for now
    int wings;
    int wheels;
    bool jet;

    void startPropellers();
    void stopPropellers();
```

```
};

void Airplane::startPropellers()
{
  //do work for starting the propeller
  //such as firing ignition, or whatever
}

void Airplane::stopPropellers()
{
  //do work for stopping the propellers
  //reduce power to them or whatever
}
```

Notice that when you define the implementation of a member function, you just need to insert the name of the class in front of the function signature (but after the return data type). In other words, think of it as defining which object owns which member functions.

SUMMARY

Although this was a fairly abstract chapter, you have covered many of the main "talking points" of object-oriented programming (OOP). As you start to work through these concepts throughout the rest of this book, these concepts will become clearer.

You were also introduced to the basic layout of a class definition. You worked through adding some simple data members, some member functions, and how to properly access them. In the next chapter, you will learn more about controlling the access to your object.

EXERCISES

26.1 Define a Cat class.
26.2 Add some properties to the Cat class to keep track of age, weight, and how many bowls of cat food per day he eats.
26.3 What is encapsulation?
26.4 What is abstraction?

27 Accessing the Object

In This Chapter

- C++ Modules and OOP
- The `friend` Function

 All Listing code in this chapter can be found on the companion CD-ROM

In Chapter 26, you covered some basic object-oriented programming defini-tions and the basics behind providing a class definition. In this chapter, you will learn how objects (and data) are accessed from within the object and from the outside world of the system.

C++ MODULLES AND OOP

When working with C++ modules and OOP in general, there are plenty of design cases when you wish to restrict access to your objects. In other words, you wish to protect the internal data contained within each object from the other objects in the system to avoid any accidental data loss or modification. In this chapter, you focus on how to restrict this access.

The C++ language gives you three access qualifiers to work with: `public`, `protected`, and `private`.

If a data member or function of a class is marked using the `public` qualifier, this allows the other objects in the program to directly access it. Listing 27.1 provides some additional clarification.

LISTING 27.1   `public` Access.

```
#include <iostream>
using namespace std;

//This snippet demonstrates the "public" qualifier
class Tank
{
public:
  int wheels;
};

int main(int argc, char* argv[])
{

  Tank sherman;
  sherman.wheels = 12;

  cout << "Tank has " << sherman.wheels << " wheels! " << endl;

  return 0;
}
```

As you can see from Listing 27.1, the `wheels` data member of the `Tank` class is qualified with `public` access. Since it is marked with `public` access, you are then able to directly manipulate the `wheels` of the `sherman` instance of the `Tank` class from wherever you want in your program.

Notice how this is the same way you access members of a `struct`.

In most cases, this is perfectly acceptable and nothing to worry about. However, situations might arise in which you do not want this type of access allowed to the data member for fear of accidental corruption of the value. There is also the chance that in a future version of your program, this data member may not exist! This would entail hunting through the source code to correct the use of this variable in every module in which you reference it.

If a data member or function of a class is marked using the `protected` qualifier, this restricts access to only internal member functions. Listing 27.2 demonstrates the use of this qualifier, but leaves everything else from Listing 27.1 to show how the compiler will signal that this use is illegal.

LISTING 27.2   protected qualifier (with errors).

```
//This snippet demonstrates the "protected" qualifier
class Tanks
{
protected:
 int wheels;

};

int main(int argc, char* argv[])
{

  Tank sherman;
  sherman.wheels = 24; //this will not work!

  //accessing sherman.wheels directly will not work!
  cout << "Tank has " << sherman.wheels << " wheels. " << endl;

  return 0;
}
```

To correct this access problem, you must create what is known as *accessor* functions, also known as the more colloquial "*getter and setter*" functions. These small class utility functions are used to set and get the necessary value of the data member. For now, all your accessor functions should be qualified with public access. Listing 27.3 provides some additional clarification on accessors.

LISTING 27.3   Adding Accessors.

```
class Tank
{
protected:
  int wheels;
public:
  void setWheels( int newWheels ) { wheels = newWheels ; }
  int getWheels(){ return wheels; }
};

int main(int argc, char* argv[])
{
  Tank sherman;
  sherman.setWheels( 24 );

  cout << "Tank has " << sherman.getWheels() << " wheels. "
    << endl;
  return 0;
}
```

As you can see from Listing 27.3, to set or retrieve the number of wheels of the sherman instance of Tank, you have to use the setWheels() and getWheels() member functions. The output of Listing 27.3 is shown in Figure 27.1.

FIGURE 27.1   Example27_2.cpp output.

Similarly, if a data member or function of a class is marked using the private qualifier, this restricts access to the internal member functions only. For the case of the Tank class you are working with, perhaps when you set the number of wheels for the machine you also need to perform some internal action on the wheel components themselves to realign them properly. However, this action can only be performed internally when you are setting the number of wheels.

Listing 27.4 provides some additional clarification on the use of this qualifier.

LISTING 27.4   private qualifier.

```cpp
#include <iostream>
using namespace std;

//This snippet demonstrates the "private" qualifier
class Tank
{
private:
  int wheels;
protected:

public:
  void setWheels(int newWheels){ wheels = newWheels; }
  int getWheels(){ return wheels; }
};
int main(int argc, char* argv[])
{
  Tank sherman;
  sherman.setWheels( 24 );
  cout << "Tank has " << sherman.getWheels() << " wheels. "
    << endl;
  return 0;
}
```

Structures do not need the public *qualifier because all of their data members are* public *by default. Similarly, classes do not need to specify the* private *keyword, as their internal members are* private *by default.*

Spotting the subtle differences between the private and protected qualifiers will become clearer as you continue through this book and learn more about inheritance.

THE friend FUNCTION

Depending on the design of your library or family tree, there might be a definite need for one object to access member data of another object that has been secured with either the private or protected qualifier. The C++ language allows you to get around this through the use of marking the function in question as a *friend* function. Listing 27.5 provides some clarification on the use of a friend function.

LISTING 27.5   friend function.

```
#include <iostream.h>
using namespace std;
class Square
{
private:
  int width;
  int height;
public:
  Square(int x, int y)
  {
    width = x;
    height = y;
  }
  ~Square();

  int area()
  {
    return( width * height );
  }
  Square magnify(Square param)
  {
    Square temp;
    temp.width  = param.width * 10;
    temp.height = param.height * 10;
     return( temp );
  }
```

```
};
int main(int argc, char* argv[])
{
  Square sq1(5,10), sq2;
  sq2 = magnify(sq1);
  cout << "Area of the clone is := " << sq2.area() << endl;
  return 0;
}
```

Using friend Classes

You can mark functions as *friends* of one object to the other, and mark entire classes as friends of another class. Again, by granting objectB friend access to objectA, you are allowing objectB to directly access objectA's protected and private members. In Listing 27.6, you will add another object to the code you saw in Listing 27.5.

LISTING 27.6 friend class.

```
#include <iostream.h>
using namespace std;
class Square
{
private:
  int width;
  int height;
public:
  Square(int x, int y)
  {
    width = x;
    height = y;
  }
  ~Square();
  int area()
  {
    return( width * height );
  }

  friend Square magnify(Square param)
  {

    Square temp;
    temp.width = param.width*10;
    temp.height = param.height*10;
    return(temp);
  }
};

int main(int argc, char* argv[])
```

```
{
  Square sq1(5,10), sq2;

  sq2 = magnify(sq1);
  cout << "Area of the clone is := " << sq2.area() << endl;
  return 0;
}
```

The only other thing to keep in mind when using friend is that objects must be explicitly granted friend access. If ObjectA is a friend of ObjectB, for example, and you then derive ObjectC from ObjectB, this does not mean that ObjectA is also a friend of ObjectC.

C++ purists will only have bad things to say about the friend qualifier, since it provides a way for the code designer to "hack" relationships between certain specific objects. These are also usually the same people who frown on the use of "goto" statements within any program.

SUMMARY

In this chapter, you learned the different ways a C++ program can restrict data members or functions within objects. You saw the public, protected, and private access qualifiers and have some idea as to their purpose. You also were shown what a friend function is and how it operates. In the next chapter, you will learn more about the purpose behind constructors and destructors.

EXERCISES

27.1 What is the difference between private, public, and protected?
27.2 What does a friend function do?
27.3 What are getter and setter methods?

28 Object Construction and Destruction

In This Chapter

- Constructors
- Destructors

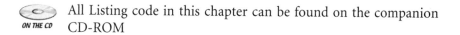 All Listing code in this chapter can be found on the companion CD-ROM

In the code samples you have gone through so far, you demonstrated how to initialize the data members of a class after it has been declared. This process of variable assignment is fine when you are only using one or two objects in a program, but what happens when you are working with objects numbering in the dozens or hundreds? Your program will quickly be littered with so much initialization code, it could become difficult to read anything else.

As part of the necessary underpinnings of OOP, the C++ language provides a way for you to automatically initialize any data member during object instantiation, and automatically clean up any data member when an object is removed from the system.

CONSTRUCTORS

A constructor function is a member function that has the same name as the class. For instance, if a class is named `Person`, the constructor member function is `Person()`.

The constructor can take as many parameters as you want for your object, but it may never have a return value, not even of type `void`.

When the constructor takes no arguments, it is known as the *default* constructor. In fact, whenever you define a new object, the compiler will automatically create a default constructor for that class. If you return to the `Airplane` object you created in Chapter 26, you can see how the default constructor functions as shown in Listing 28.1.

LISTING 28.1 Displays the `Airplane` object.

```
//This object defines
class Airplane
{
public:
  int wheels;

  void setWheels(int new_wheels);
};
```

Again, although you are not explicitly defining it here, the compiler has automatically created the default constructor for the object. It is empty and contains no instructions, but it is there. Listing 28.2 provides further illustration.

LISTING 28.2 Airplane default constructor.

```
int main(int argc, char* argv[])
{

  //When we declare an object, the program automatically calls the
  //default
  //constructor for that object
  Airplane Cessna;

  //note that this is identical to declaring Cessna as
  //Airplane Cessna();

  cout << "Our airplane has " << Cessna.wheels << " wheels"
    << endl;

  return 0;
}
```

In Listing 28.2, although you do not have a constructor defined for `Airplane`, the compiler will automatically call it when you declare the `Cessna` instance.

To further illustrate the default constructor, Listing 28.3 now proceeds to add the proper declaration to the `Airplane` class.

LISTING 28.3   Airplane default constructor.

```cpp
class Airplane
{
public:
  int wheels;

public:
  Airplane()
  {
    cout << "Airplane::Constructor()" << endl;
    wheels = 4;
  }

  void setWheels(int new_wheels)
  {
    wheels = new_wheels;
  }
};
```

In Listing 28.3, you defined a default constructor for `Airplane` that initialized the wheels variable to 4. If you run the same program from Listing 28.2, the output will now show that the `Cessna` instance of `Airplane` has four wheels as shown in Figure 28.1.

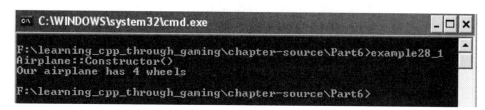

FIGURE 28.1   Example 28_1 output.

As mentioned, the constructor function can also take parameters. Listing 28.4 demonstrates how to create a constructor that allows you to initialize the `wheels` member variable upon object construction.

LISTING 28.4   Setting member variables.

```cpp
class Airplane
{
```

```
public:
  int wheels;

public:
  Airplane()
  {
    cout << "Airplane::Constructor()" << endl;
    wheels = 0;
  }

  Airplane( int new_wheels )
  {
    cout << "Airplane::Constructor(int)" << endl;
    wheels = new_wheels;
  }

  void setWheels(int new_wheels)
  {
    wheels = new_wheels;
  }

};
```

Listing 28.4 illustrates that you now have the ability to customize the wheels member variable upon declaring the object. Listing 28.5, the source for Example 28.2, provides some additional clarification.

LISTING 28.5 Example 28_2.cpp.

```
int main(int argc, char* argv[])
{

  //When we declare an object, the program automatically calls the
  //default
  //constructor for that object
  Airplane cessna(12);

  Airplane spitfire;

  //note that this is identical to declaring Cessna as
  //Airplane Cessna;
  //Cessna.setWheels(12);

  cout << "Cessna has " << cessna.wheels << " wheels."
    << endl;

  Cout << "spitfire has " << spitfire.wheels << " wheels."
    << endl;
```

```
    return 0;
  }
```

You should see the same output as shown in Figure 28.2.

```
F:\learning_cpp_through_gaming\chapter-source\Part6>example28_2
Airplane::Constructor(int)
Airplane::Constructor()
Cessna has 12 wheels.
Spitfire has 0 wheels.

F:\learning_cpp_through_gaming\chapter-source\Part6>_
```

FIGURE 28.2   Example 28_2.

> *While it can be tempting in some situations, try to avoid calling functions from a constructor that has the chance of failing. Operations such as loading or saving data should be performed from a member function once the object has finished instancing, not in the constructor method itself.*

DESTRUCTORS

Just as you have been learning about how an object can initialize member variables when it is instantiated on the memory heap, so too can it clean up any used internal memory when the object is removed.

Similar to the default constructor, when your object is defined the compiler will also create a default destructor. The destructor can never take any parameters, nor can it ever return anything. It is denoted by a squiggly (~) in front of the name. Listing 28.6 provides an example.

LISTING 28.6   Adding a destructor to `Airplane`.

```
class Airplane
{
public:
  int wheels;

public:
  Airplane()
  {
    cout << "Airplane::Constructor()" << endl;
```

```
        wheels = 0;
    }

    Airplane( int new_wheels )
    {
      cout << "Airplane::Constructor(int)" << endl;
      wheels = new_wheels;
    }

    //destructor
    ~Airplane()
    {
      cout << "Airplane::Destructor" << endl;
    }

    void setWheels(int new_wheels)
    {
      wheels = new_wheels;
    }
};

int main(int argc, char* argv[])
{
  Airplane cessna(12);
  int i = 0;
  do
  {
    static Airplane spitfire;

    i++;
  }while(i < 100);

  return 0;
}
```

The destructor is only called in two places: either the object is moving out of scope or it is explicitly called.

Listing 28.6 produces the output shown in Figure 28.3.

FIGURE 28.3 Example28_3.cpp output.

SUMMARY

In this chapter, you were introduced to the constructor and destructor member functions that are generated for every class you create. If you do not specify them in your class definition, the compiler will automatically generate the default constructor and default destructor member functions. In the next chapter, you will learn more about function overloading and how you can use it to decrease the amount of code you might need for an object.

EXERCISES

28.1 When is a constructor called?

28.2 When is a destructor called?

28.3 What types of operations should be avoided in a constructor?

29

Function Overloading

In This Chapter

■ Function Overloading

```
ON THE CD
```
All Listing code in this chapter can be found on the companion CD-ROM

In Part III, you learned all about functions and how to properly declare them. In this chapter, you will revisit functions somewhat and learn how to leverage the power and flexibility of the C++ language to extend their usefulness within an object.

As previously discussed, functions are declared as:

```
[return type] function_name( param1, param2, etc, …)
```

This might be fine for a majority of functions you need to create for a class. However, a design situation may arise in which the given parameters of a function change their type, but the function implementation can stay the same.

To illustrate this concept, consider a function defined to generate a random number between two values as shown in Listing 29.1.

LISTING 29.1 A `MathUnit`.

```
class MathUnit
{
  public:

    int generateRandomNumber( int min, int max )
    {

      int value = max - min;
      int num = value * rand() / RAND_MAX;
      return (num + min);

    }

};
```

As you can see, there is nothing mysterious going on here. You are defining a class called `MathUnit`, which creates a member function that generates a random number within the range of the given `min` and `max` boundaries.

Later in the design, you might wish to create a way for a random number to be generated between two float values. You do have the option of simply cutting and pasting the existing function, but then you will have two sections of code that require maintenance. Should you find a bug in this function, you will now have to correct it in two locations.

If you later decide to alter the design of the project to change things slightly to accommodate some different parameters, you might also potentially need to hunt through the program adjusting the old function name and parameters with the new one.

The C++ language has accounted for this type of eventuality in a program and provides you with a tidy way to re-use the same function name. Known as *overloading* the function, you are able to create the two different function bodies required, but maintain the same function name.

This is perfectly legal within C++, as long as you do not keep the parameters the same; this is the key. If you are working with different data types in the parameters to a function, the same function name can be used. Thus, the code in Listing 29.2 would be valid.

LISTING 29.2 Function overriding.

```
class MathUnit
{
public:

  int generateRandomNumber( int min, int max )
```

```
    {
      int value = max - min;
      int num = value * rand() / RAND_MAX;
      return (num + min);

    }

    float generateRandomNumber( float min, float max )
    {
      float value = max - min;
      float num = value * rand() / RAND_MAX;
      return (num + min);
    }
};
```

The compiler is smart enough to inspect the data types of the parameters and match them with the appropriate function implementation. In other words, when you call the generateRandomNumber function in the program, the compiler will analyze the signature of the data types of the min and max parameter values you specify and will execute the matching function body.

SUMMARY

In this chapter you learned about the design and method of overloading functions. It is a necessary piece of the overall OOP puzzle that will reveal itself as you progress through the rest of the material. The next chapter will involve the introduction of overloading the operators.

EXERCISES

29.1 What is function overloading?

29.2 Explain a situation in which function overloading is helpful/not helpful.

30 Overloading Operators

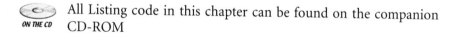 All Listing code in this chapter can be found on the companion CD-ROM

In Chapter 29, you were introduced to the concept of function overloading, which forms a base component of object-oriented programming. The next logical step in the language is to provide a mechanism for overloading the very operators you use. Known as operator overloading, this chapter focuses on how to extend the use of your standard operators to work with any custom objects you create. This can allow you to integrate your objects into existing software layers, while providing a way to create intuitive access to them.

THE Rectangle CLASS

To help you illustrate and work through this chapter, you will be building a Rectangle object that will also allow you to provide a logical implementation of operator overloading. As you might expect, a `Rectangle` is an object that uses a width and a height parameter to specify its dimensions.

For a basic class outline, this chapter will start with the following class declaration contained in Listing 30.1.

LISTING 30.1   `Rectangle`.

```cpp
#include <iostream>
using namespace std;

class Rectangle
{
public:
  Rectangle()
  {
    width = 0;
    height = 0;
  }

  ~Rectangle(){}

private:
  int width;  /** width of our rectangle */
  int height; /** height of our rectangle */
};

int main(int argc, char* argv[])
{
  Rectangle rcA;

  return 0;
}
```

So far, the class is fairly unusable. It does not do much of anything and the small test program at the end of Listing 30.1 just declares a variable of the `Rectangle` object before exiting.

In the default constructor, you are setting the `width` and `height` member variables to `0`.

Adding `Rectangle` Objects Together

There can be many situations in which adding two `Rectangles` together is desired. Perhaps you have one `Rectangle` representing a spaceship boundary, while another `Rectangle` object represents the current dimensions of an enemy ship. Addition is a simple enough task for a `Rectangle`, as you only need to evaluate the sum of the width components and the sum of the height components together. Listing 30.2

outlines the process of adding the necessary support for the (+) operator, which is normally the default operator used for adding or joining objects.

LISTING 30.2   Adding + operator.

```
#include <iostream>
using namespace std;

class Rectangle
{
public:
  Rectangle()
  {
    width = 0;
    height = 0;
  }

  Rectangle(int nx, int ny)
  { width = nx; height = ny; }

  ~Rectangle(){}

  Rectangle operator+ (const Rectangle& p1)
  {
    return Rectangle( width + p1.width, height + p1.height );
  }

  int getWidth(){ return width; }
  int getHeight(){ return height; }

private:
  int width;
  int height;
};

int main(int argc, char* argv[])
{
  Rectangle ptA(1, 2);       /** create a 1x2 rectangle */
  Rectangle ptB(3, 4);       /** create a 3x4 rectangle */
  Rectangle ptC = ptA + ptB; /** add them together */

  cout << "The sum of RectangleA and RectangleB is:= ("
      << ptC.getWidth() << ","
      << ptC.getHeight() << ")" << endl;

  return 0;
}
```

After executing Listing 30.2, you will see the console output shown in Figure 30.1.

FIGURE 30.1 Example30_1.cpp output.

SUBTRACTING RECTANGLES

Similar to the overloading of the (+) operator you just learned, it is with the same ease that you can overload the subtraction (-) operator. In the context of the Rectangle class, this just subtracts the width and height components as shown in Listing 30.3.

LISTING 30.3 Overloading Subtraction Operator.

```cpp
#include <iostream>
using namespace std;

class Rectangle
{
public:
  Rectangle()
  {
    width = 0;
    height = 0;
  }

  Rectangle(int nx, int ny)
  { width = nx; height = ny; }

  ~Rectangle(){}

  Rectangle operator+ (const Rectangle& p1)
  {
    return Rectangle( width + p1.width, height + p1.height );
  }

  Rectangle operator-(const Rectangle& p1)
  {
    return Rectangle( width - p1.width, height - p1.height );
```

```
        }

        int getWidth(){ return width; }
        int getHeight(){ return height; }

    private:
        int width;
        int height;
    };

    int main(int argc, char* argv[])
    {
        Rectangle ptA(1, 2);
        Rectangle ptB(3, 4);
        Rectangle ptC = ptA - ptB;

        cout << "The difference of RectangleA and RectangleB is:= ("
             << ptC.getWidth() << ","
             << ptC.getHeight() << ")" << endl;

        return 0;
    }
```

Upon execution of Listing 30.3, you will see the output shown in Figure 30.2.

FIGURE 30.2 Example30_2 output.

When working with operator overloading, a few guidelines need to be followed and/or rules that cannot be broken.

- Operators for built-in data types, such as the `int`, `float`, `double`, or `char` cannot be overloaded.
- You cannot create or define your own custom operators, so attempting to use something like `^^` to define an "exponential" operator is illegal.

The Assignment Operator

Although you will learn more about the Copy constructor in Chapter 31, you can learn to manipulate the assignment (=) operator, which is used whenever your object is assigned to another.

This situation is used constantly in many applications, not just games. Perhaps you wish to set the contents of one instance of the object with the values of another. Listing 30.4 outlines this.

LISTING 30.4 Assignments.

```cpp
#include <iostream>
class Book
{
public:
  Book(char*, char*);
private:
  char* title;  /** dynamic pointer to char array */
  char* author; /** dynamic pointer to char array */
public:
  Book& Book::operator=(const Book& b)
  {
    if (this != &p)     /** make sure it's not the same object */
    {
      delete [] author;/** delete author memory */
      delete [] title; /** delete title memory */

      author = new char[strlen( b.author) + 1]; /**create new
      author */

      title = new char[strlen( b.title ) + 1]; /** create new title*/

      strcpy(author, b.author ); /** copy author data */
      strcpy(title, b.title);    /** copy title data */
    }
    return *this;     /** return reference for multiple assignments
                          (such as a = b = c = d ) */

  }

};
int main(int argc, char* argv[])
{
  Book* pA = new Book( "Aardvark", "Be an Aardvark on pennies a
  day");
  Book* pB = new Book( "Speelburgh", "ET vs. Howard the Duck");
  pA = pB;
  return 0;
}
```

As you can see from Listing 30.4, the overloaded assignment operator of the Book class demonstrates how to perform a deep copy on the object. This implies that the object has copied its internal data to the other object, along with making sure the memory allocation has been properly transferred from one to the other. Again, you will learn more about this process in Chapter 31.

When working with this style of assignment and performing a shallow copy to transfer the appropriate data, it could create a memory leak in the object. This can occur when you free the allocated memory from one object, before any other objects of the same type have done the same. To protect your application from the memory leak issue, you can test the *this* pointer to ensure that you are not trying to assign the same object to itself.

SUMMARY

In this chapter, you were introduced to the concept of operator overloading, which allows you to provide additional functionality to your objects. Rather than having to create clunky methods, you can override the operators, which can be a much more intuitive way to manipulate your object. The addition, subtraction, and assignment operators were used in a couple of examples to ensure that you are ready to put them into your applications.

In the next chapter, you will learn about working with the copy constructor to manage the object.

EXERCISES

30.1 What is operator overloading?

30.2 What operators cannot be overloaded?

30.3 Finish the Rectangle class that was created in this chapter. Overload the * and / operators, and test to see if one Rectangle object is equivalent to another.

31

The Copy Constructor and This

In This Chapter

- copy Constructor
- The this Pointer

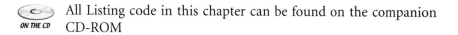

All Listing code in this chapter can be found on the companion CD-ROM

You have been steadily progressing through your introduction to working with objects and classes using the C++ language. In this chapter, you will learn more about the copy constructor and the this pointer, which are deeply embedded in any C++ application or game.

copy CONSTRUCTOR

As you saw in Chapter 28, whenever you provide a class definition the compiler will automatically generate a default constructor and destructor. Another default function created by the compiler is the copy constructor. This special function provides a way for you to use a reference to the same class to copy each member to create a new one. The version of the copy constructor that is created by default in the compiler performs a member-to-member copy from one object to the other. This is also known as *shallow* copying. While on the surface this may be reasonable for most classes, there might be times where you will need to provide your own implementation for the `copy` constructor to ensure proper data integrity.

To illustrate where you might want to provide your own implementation, look at Listing 31.1, which provides a class definition for a Monster entity.

LISTING 31.1   Monster entity.

```cpp
class Monster
{
public:
Monster(char* new_name, int new_hitpoints)
{
  hitpoints = new_hitpoints;
  name = new char[strlen(new_name) + 1];
  strcpy(name, new_name);
}

~Monster()
{
  delete[] name;
}

char* getName(){ return name; }

protected:

  char* name;

  int hitpoints;
};
int main(int argc, char* argv[])
{
  Monster orc("BloodThunder",220);
  cout << orc.getName() << endl;
  return 0;
}
```

In Listing 31.1, notice that the name field for the `Monster` class is a pointer to a dynamic array of `char` data types. The constructor method accepts a `char` array of the `monster` object's name, along with a number of hit points to initialize the object with. Within the constructor, you are dynamically allocating enough space to contain the new name, and then are performing a string copy to set its value. Since you are dynamically allocating memory with a call to `new`, you must pair it with a corresponding call to `delete`. The destructor method takes care of this memory cleanup.

Now suppose you have a case where you wish to copy the orc object from Listing 31.1 to another Monster. With the default copy constructor in place, the code in Listing 31.2 uses valid syntax, but will generate an error if executed.

LISTING 31.2   Using the default copy constructor (will crash).

```
int main()
{
 Monster orc("BloodThunder",220);
 cout << orc.getName() << endl;

 //Perhaps later in the code, BloodThunder develops
 //the ability to make himself boss
 Monster orc_boss( &orc );

 //The above creates a copy of the orc object using
 //the default copy constructor to perform a shallow
 //copy of each member

 return 0;
}
```

Although on the surface, Listing 31.2 appears to be valid and compiles, there is a problem when you try to execute the code. Within the default copy constructor, the member-wise copy of the hitpoints data member is properly copied. However, it also performs a copy of the address stored in the pointer name from the orc object to the orc_boss object. Both of these pointers now contain the same memory address. In other words, both of these name pointers now refer to the same block of memory on the free store. This is obviously dangerous and unwanted, since if you ever modify the name of orc_boss, it will also modify the name of the original orc object! Another danger is that one of these objects could go out of scope, which would automatically call the destructor to clean up the memory, which would deallocate name from both objects. If the other object then tries to access its own name, there will be bad problems.

The solution is to provide your own copy constructor that will probably transfer the contents of one Monster object to another one. This way, you can dynamically create a new block of memory in the free store to copy the name contents of the original Monster, rather than just a copy of the pointer. Listing 31.3 provides some clarification. Note that this listing also uses the new operator, which is discussed in further detail in Chapter 32.

LISTING 31.3   Example31_2.cpp.

```
class Monster
{
```

```cpp
public:
Monster(char* new_name, int new_hitpoints)
{
  hitpoints = new_hitpoints;

  //create an array of chars big enough to
  //contain the monster's name
 name = new char[strlen(new_name) + 1];

  strcpy(name, new_name);

}

~Monster(){ delete [] name; }

//This is the declaration and body of the copy constructor.
//Since you should never be modifying the original data, you
//can protect it by declaring it as a const reference.
Monster(const Monster &original)
{
  hitpoints = original.hitpoints;
 name = new char[strlen(original.name) + 1];
  strcpy(name,original.name);
}

char* getName(){ return name; }

int getHP(){ return hitpoints; }

protected:

  char* name;

  int hitpoints;

};

int main(int argc, char* argv[])
{
 Monster orc("BloodThunder",220);
 cout << orc.getName() << endl;

  int i = 0;
  do
  {
    //the following declaration uses the copy
    //constructor of the Monster class to create a
    //new orc_boss instance of Monster using the member data
```

```
      //of orc.
      static Monster orc_boss( orc );

      i++;
   }while( i < 10 );

   cout << orc_boss.getName() << endl;

   return 0;
}
```

This will function much better with the custom copy constructor you just created.

THE this POINTER

As you have learned so far, any class can define member functions that usually operate on internal data members. In the C++ language, along with the explicit parameters you define in these member functions, every function will also receive a special hidden pointer known as the this pointer. The this pointer addresses the object upon which the function was called. As you will see, there are some cases when it is absolutely necessary to use the this pointer to implement some internal function or behavior.

To understand more about the this pointer and why it exists, it is necessary to refresh your memory on how the members of a class are stored in memory. Every object in your application has its own set of internal data members, but they all share the same set of member functions. In other words, when the program is compiled and linked, there is only a single set of a class' member functions. Upon this revelation, your first natural question is, if each instance of a class shares the single set of member functions, how does the program "know" which data members of which object instance to modify? The answer is that the compiler will use the hidden this pointer to interpret which object's data members are being modified. For an example, look at Listing 31.4.

LISTING 31.4   In Need of this.

```
class Monster
{
public:
  ....
  void setMana(double val)
  {
    mana = val;
  }
private:
```

```
    ....
    double mana;
    ....
};

int main()
{

    Monster orcGrunt;        /** declare a Monster object */
    Monster orcMage;         /** declare another Monster */

    orcGrunt.setMana(10.0);  /** set the mana property of one */
    orcMage.setMana(400.0);  /** set the mana property of the other
*/

}
```

You can see from Listing 31.4 that you have two object instances of the Monster class. In the test program, you are using a "setter" member function of the Monster class to adjust the internal mana data member. How does the program "know" to set the mana of the orcGrunt instance to *10.0* and the mana value of the orcMage instance to *400.0*?

During the compilation stage of the program, the compiler will automatically insert the this pointer into the functions, which looks something similar to Listing 31.5.

LISTING 31.5   Inserting this.

```
    /** This function just demonstrates what the compiler is actually
doing
 * to the function you have created. It automatically inserts the this
 * pointer to each function */
    void Monster::setMana(Monster *this, double mana)
    {
      this->_mana = mana;
    }
```

The this pointer allows you to concatenate functions of an object together. Working with the Monster class used in the chapter so far, it would be handy to provide a member function to multiply the Monster's health and mana by a double value. Listing 31.6 details this addition to the Monster class.

LISTING 31.6   Monster class.

```
    class Monster
    {
```

```
public:

  Monster();
 ~Monster();

  void setHealth(double val)
  {
    health = val;
  }

  void setMana(double val)
  {
    mana = val;
  }

  void applyBurst(double val)
  {
    health *= val;
    mana *= val;

  }

private:
  double health;
  double mana;
};
```

To use this class you might create the code to look something like Listing 31.7.

LISTING 31.7   Using Monster.

```
Monster orcMage();
orcMage.setHealth( 40.0 );
orcMage.setMana( 100.0 );

//Perhaps the orcMage runs into a trap or gets hit with another
//magical spell
//that causes burst damage to the creature
orcMage.applyBurst( 0.75 );
```

However a more natural and elegant way of writing this could look like Listing 31.8.

LISTING 31.8   Concatenation.

```
orcMage.setHealth( 40.0 ).setMana( 100.0 ).applyBurst( 0.75 );
```

How is it possible to allow statements like Listing 31.8? The answer lies in the proper manipulation of the this pointer. Recall that the member access operators such as the dot (.) and arrow (->) are left associative. In other words, the expression in Listing 31.8 is evaluated from left to right as outlined in Listing 31.9.

LISTING 31.9   Concatenation—part 2.

```
( ( orcMage.setHealth( 40.0 ) ).setMana( 100.0 )).applyBurst( 0.75 );
```

With the current definition of the Monster class, however, Listing 31.9 would not be possible. The setMana() function is called upon the result of the setHP() function. However, for that to work, the setHealth() method must return a copy of the class rather than void. Similarly, the applyBurst() method is called upon the setMana() method. Since setMana() only returns void, this usage again will not work. To satisfy the usage of a statement similar to Listing 31.9, you would need to modify the member functions of the Monster class to use the this pointer along with returning a reference to the object. Listing 31.10 provides additional detail.

LISTING 31.10   Monster.

```cpp
class Monster
{

public:
 Monster();

  ~Monster();

  Monster& setHealth(double val)
  {
    health = val;
    return *this;
  }

  Monster& setMana(double val)
  {
   mana = val;
    return *this;
  }

  Monster& applyBurst(double val)
  {
```

```
    health *= val;
    mana *= val;

    return *this;
  }

private:
  double health;
  double mana;
  };
```

SUMMARY

Within the C++ language, the default copy constructor is a special member function that is generated by the compiler. You learned in this chapter that using the default function is not always desired and can lead to unwanted and unpredictable results. You then were introduced to defining your own copy constructor to handle special cases within your class. You also learned about the special this pointer, which is passed into every member function of an object. In the next chapter, you will learn more about dynamically manipulating blocks of memory to store your program data.

EXERCISES

31.1 What is the this pointer?
31.2 Briefly explain how the this pointer is used by every object in C++.

32

Dynamic Objects New and Delete

In This Chapter

- The new Operator
- The delete Operator
- Cleaning Up Dynamic Arrays
- Memory Leaks

All Listing code in this chapter can be found on the companion CD-ROM

THE new OPERATOR

During the runtime of your application, the program has access to a pool of memory known as the "memory heap" or "free store." To access additional memory for your application, the new operator assigns memory from the free store. You must then use the delete operator to properly clean up this created memory from the memory heap.

Dynamic memory and pointers mesh together, as when you declare a new block of memory on the heap, the program will return an address of this new location in memory. This address must be stored in a pointer.

However improbable, it is theoretically possible for the new operator to fail. The system might be out of available memory, for example. In system critical code, it is therefore necessary to perform the required error checking to ensure you are given a valid memory location.

Using new requests the system to allocate a block of space on the memory heap of the appropriate size for the object. For example, a declaration of new int will allocate four bytes of memory (on most operating systems) for the integer.

After the object has been dynamically allocated, it will need to be initialized; currently, it is just containing random bits. Listing 32.1 demonstrates how to request dynamic creation on the memory heap.

LISTING 32.1   Using new.

```
int *pInt = new int;        /** allocate memory for an integer */
*pInt = 10;                 /** assign the integer */

char *pChar = new char;     /** allocate memory for a char */
*pChar = 'W';               /** assign the char */
```

If you recall, the default C++ data types all contain a default constructor; thus, the following declarations in Listing 32.2 are all valid as well when allocating new objects on the heap.

LISTING 32.2   Using new and the default constructor.

```
int *pInt = new int( 10 );

char *pLetter = new char('W');
```

Dynamically Allocating Arrays

Arrays of the standard data types and custom created objects can all be dynamically created. The syntax is nearly identical, with the only exception being that you declare the dimension of the array using the [ ] brackets, which has been defined in the C++ language as the array operator. Listing 32.3 details a sample of allocating arrays on the heap.

LISTING 32.3   Allocating arrays.

```
//declare an array of integers with room for 20 elements
int *pInt = new int[ 20 ];
```

With what you have learned about pointers, you should also be careful during a dynamic array declaration. Listing 32.4 demonstrates some valid statements that compile properly but perform different actions.

LISTING 32.4   Dynamic allocation confusion.

```
/* request a memory block large enough to hold 50536 int elements
*/
int *pInt = new int[50536];
```

```
/* assign the int pointer a value of 50536 */
int *pInt = new int(50536);

/* request a memory block large enough to hold 1000 double elements
 */
double *pDouble = new double[1000];
/* assign the double pointer to a value of 1000 */
double *pDouble = new double( 1000 );
```

Can you spot the subtle difference in Listing 32.4? There is definitely a problem even though the code snippet would compile correctly and has valid syntax. When you define the array with the square brackets, you are requesting an array large enough to hold the specified number of elements, whereas when the round brackets are used, you are attempting to initialize the pointer to the value in the brackets.

As with other dynamically created objects, the array elements all contain garbage values. They should be initialized upon creation as shown in Listing 32.5.

LISTING 32.5   Array initialization—Example32_1.cpp.

```
int main(int argc, char* argv[])
{

    int *pInt = new int[200]; /** allocate memory for 200 integers */
    for(int i = 0; i < 200; i++)
    {
      pInt[i] = 0;
    }

    //Note that the following code will work as well using pointer
    //arithmetic
    for(int i = 0; i < 200; i++)
    {
      *pInt = 0;
      pInt++;
    }

    return 0;
}
```

THE delete OPERATOR

Now that you have the opportunity to allocate blocks of the memory heap for the application, you are also responsible for cleaning it up. Known as *deallocation*, it is an essential component of working with dynamic memory. For every object and/or data type created with the `new` operator, you just need to use the `delete` operator along with the variable name. Listing 32.6 provides some examples of using `delete`.

LISTING 32.6   Using `delete`—Example32_2.cpp.

```
int main(int argc, char* argv[])
{

    int *pInt = new int( 10 );          /** allocate memory for an
integer */

    char *pLetter = new char('W');      /** allocate memory for a char
*/

    //*snip*
    //do things with pInt and pLetter
    //*snip*

    delete pInt;                        /** clean up memory from the
integer */

    delete pLetter;                     /** clean up memory from the char
*/

    return 0;
}
```

CLEANING UP DYNAMIC ARRAYS

Much as you have learned how to deallocate and clean up memory used by objects, cleaning up the memory for dynamic arrays is just as simple. Using the `delete` operator, you simply need to add square brackets in between the `delete` statement and the variable name. Listing 32.7 provides a detailed look.

LISTING 32.7   Deallocating Dynamic Arrays—Example32_3.cpp.

```
int main(int argc, char* argv[])
{

    int *pInt = new int[50536];  /** allocate memory for 50536
integers */

    double *pDouble = new double[1000]; /** allocate 1000 doubles */

    float (*pFloat)[10][10];            /** declare multi-dimension array
*/
```

```
        pFloat = new float[10][10][10]; /** use it to allocate what we
need */

        //*snip*
        //Do something with the allocated arrays
        //*snip*

        delete [] pInt;      /** clean up allocated memory of the integers
*/

        delete [] pDouble;  /** clean up allocated memory of the doubles
*/

        delete [] pFloat;   /** clean up allocated multi-dimensional
array */
                            /** note: we clean it up the same as the
others*/

        return 0;
    }
```

When cleaning up an array, do not forget the square brackets. Otherwise, you are only removing the first element of the array, leaving the rest "dangling" in memory causing a memory leak.

MEMORY LEAKS

When working with dynamic memory, there is always a chance of memory leaks in the application. Allocated memory is not automatically returned to the free store. If a pointer variable is pointing to memory on the heap and the pointer suddenly leaves the scope, the allocated memory is not returned. A memory leak cannot be recovered until the program actually terminates. In other words, memory is leaking out of the computer altogether! In a worst case scenario, leaked memory can only be recovered by the machine if you physically reboot the computer—not a nice surprise for anyone trying your software! Listing 32.8 provides some sample code that leaks memory.

LISTING 32.8   Memory leaking.

```
int main(int argc, char* argv[])
{
  char* pBlock = new char[65536]; /** allocate 65536 bytes */
  char* pBlock2 = new char[1024]; /** allocate 1024 bytes */
```

```
delete pBlock2; /** uh-oh! We've only deleted the pointer of the
first
                    element! The other 1023 bytes are a-dangling! */
return 0;
}
```

Although it may be obvious by this time, Listing 32.8 demonstrates some common examples of leaking memory. The pBlock dynamic array of 65536 bytes is never cleaned up, and there is a typo in the delete of the pBlock2 array; the [] operator is missing!

SUMMARY

This chapter dealt with the explanation and clarification of the concepts behind dynamically manipulating objects within your program. Through the use of the new and delete keywords, you can create or destroy objects on the program's memory heap available during the runtime of the application. This can greatly impact (or hinder) your game's performance if used correctly. In the next chapter, you will learn more about object-oriented analysis techniques, which will hopefully help you spot any performance draining sections of code.

EXERCISES

32.1 What is a memory leak?

32.2 Create a program that leaks on purpose.

32.3 If the new allocation of memory should fail, is anything returned?

32.4 How does an object's constructor and destructor interact with the new and delete operators?

33 Inheritance and Hierarchies

In This Chapter

- Is-A and Has-A
- Inheritance
- Plymorphism
- Multiple Inheritance

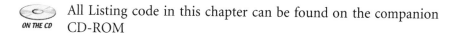 All Listing code in this chapter can be found on the companion CD-ROM

I n Chapter 26, you were briefly given an overview of OOP methodology and the popular "catchphrases" of the C++ language. In this chapter, you will learn more detail about the principles of inheritance, and using hierarchies to organize the objects in your game.

IS-A AND HAS-A

One of the first questions you should be asking when designing the classes you need and/or your family tree model is, what is this class doing and how is it composed?

The two prime questions C++ designers use to create their tree models, is "is-a?" or "has-a?" primarily to determine if the thing in question belongs to an existing object, or if a new one needs to be created.

Inherited classes should almost always answer "yes" to the is-a question, since it is derived from a base class but has a little extra functionality. In other cases, if the thing in question belongs as a member to an object, the "has-a" question would have a "yes" answer.

If this sounds a little confusing, do not worry. As you get used to seeing more OO diagrams and code, you will begin to learn what belongs in an existing object and what constitutes a brand new one.

INHERITANCE

A key principle of the C++ language and OO in general is the ability to use existing objects to create new ones. In other words, OO designers like to emulate the "real world" and try to build objects with relationships between them. This is where the access qualifiers come into play that you learned about in Chapter 27. The type of qualifier you use on an object directly affects how other objects can work with this one.

When you *derive* an object, you are using an existing object to create a new one. Listing 33.1 provides an example.

LISTING 33.1 Basic derivation.

```
/** This base object contains some useful function or ability that
* we want to expand upon via other classes
*/
class BaseObject
{
public:
  /** constructor */
  BaseObject();
  /** destructor */
  ~BaseObject();
 };

/** DerivedObject is deriving the base functionality from
 BaseObject
* but adding its own "twist" or useful features
*/
class DerivedObject : public BaseObject
{
public:
```

```
/** constructor */
DerivedObject();
/** destructor */
~DerivedObject();
};
```

In Listing 33.1, you are creating two objects. One is the `BaseObject` and the other is the `DerivedObject`, which is derived from `BaseObject`. You will notice that you specified the `public` qualifier before `BaseObject`. What does this mean?

When you create the `DerivedObject`, the qualifier next to the class you are deriving from specifies what kind of access the `DerivedObject` is receiving from the `BaseObject`.

In this case, since there is the `public` qualifier next to `BaseObject`, this signals the compiler that you wish to create a derived object known as `DerivedObject`, which receives all of the `public` data and member functions of `BaseObject`.

How do the `protected` and `private` qualifiers work then?

Listing 33.2 defines a class definition with each of the three qualifiers defined.

LISTING 33.2 BaseOne.

```
class BaseOne
{
public: //accessible by the world
  int a;//anyone can mod me!
  int b;//anyone can mod me!
protected: //protected means that it is only available to INHERITED
           //classes
    int c; //only classes that extend BaseOne can mod me
    int d; //only classes that extend BaseOne can mod me
  private: //private by default. Can never be passed on through
inheritance
    int e; //only this object can mod me
    int f; //only this object can mod me
  };
```

In other words, members that are `public` are accessible to every other object in the system. Members that are guarded by the `protected` qualifier are available only to the class and any derived classes. `Private` members are only available to the class.

Derived classes cannot alter anything about the base class. No matter what the base class contains, private members remain private, protected members retain protected status, and public members are left as public.

How derived objects receive base class members needs further explanation.

When a derived class inherits with the private qualifier in front of the base class (or when no qualifier is in front of the base class), all inherited protected and public members will appear in the new derived object as private members.

Whenever a derived class inherits with the protected keyword in front of the base class, all inherited protected and public members of the base class will appear in the new derived object as protected members.

Whenever a derived class inherits with the public keyword in front of the base class, the inherited protected members of the base class remain protected in the derived class. All inherited public members will remain public when they appear in the derived class.

POLYMORPHISM

One of the key principles that makes C++ a very object-oriented friendly language is the implementation of polymorphism. *Polymorphism* is translated from Greek to mean *many forms*. While this may sound like a "bad idea" when developing code, it is in fact a key tool for providing proper object-oriented support and design. You will learn more about implementing polymorphism in Chapter 34.

To understand more about polymorphism, it might help to provide a small tree (aka hierarchy) that can be used to illustrate the concept.

Figure 33.1 defines a small hierarchy with a base class Building, and several derived objects of Building.

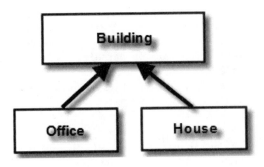

FIGURE 33.1 Building hierarchy.

As you can see, you have the root Building object, which provides you with a bottom layer set of basic Building functionality. From this object are two other objects derived from Building: Office and House. Although these are two different objects, they both share the basic properties of Building.

Looking at some code, you might structure a program similar to Listing 33.3.

LISTING 33.3   Building code.

```
//create an array of pointers to Building objects
Building * buildings[2];
Buildings[0] = &Office;
Buildings[1] = &House;
//in a for loop execute some base member of Building
for(int i = 0; i < 2; i++)
{
  Buildings[i]->someFunction();
}
```

This is an example of polymorphism, since the Buildings array is composed of classes derived from the Building base class. In other words, even though you have extended the Building class to create an Office or House definition, the fact that they are derived from the Building class allows you to manipulate the pointer to call a method of Building from the Office instance.

MULTIPLE INHERITANCE

The hierarchy and inheritance models you have learned so far are centered on a single inheritance concept. In other words, the objects in your hierarchy all only have one immediate parent they inherit from. In some cases, however, it is possible to create the black sheep of the family tree: multiple inheritance. As you might expect, *multiple inheritance* occurs when an object has not one, but two immediate parent objects.

For an example of multiple inheritance, consider an OO hierarchy in which you have a base class Animal, which provides some basic member functions for manipulating a creature. So, he may have member functions for setting his position or to calculate how fast he is moving, or even to perform basic actions such as eating. From the Animal base class, you could derive several other instances of Animal such as Cat or Mouse. These are all Animals, but have their own unique properties and behaviors.

Figure 33.2 provides a small inheritance diagram of Animal.

Now, for an example, what if you also had an object Endangered that abstracted some common properties of endangered animals? Theoretically, you might end up with a situation in which an object inherits from both the Animal object and the Endangered object.

Figure 33.3 provides some additional clarification.

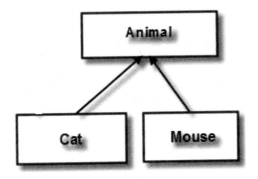

FIGURE 33.2   Animal tree.

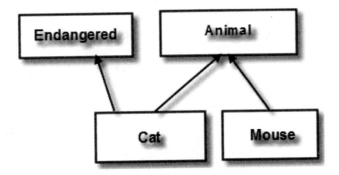

FIGURE 33.3   An example of multiple inheritance.

SUMMARY

In this chapter, you were given an explanation about the principles and foundations behind using inheritance in your application design. One of the tenants of the C++ language and OOP is to create a useful collection of classes that can easily be reused in other games. Most inheritance and hierarchy design principles favor the concept of reuse.

EXERCISES

33.1 What is polymorphism?

33.2 What is multiple inheritance?

33.3 What do the access qualifiers specify in inherited objects?

34   Virtual Functions

In This Chapter

■ Early and Late Function Binding
■ Abstract Base Classes

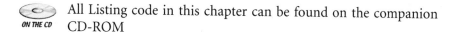 All Listing code in this chapter can be found on the companion CD-ROM

In Chapter 33, you received a thorough introduction to the possible hierarchy options available to you within the C++ language. Knowing which facet of inheritance to implement at which time involves key decisions that every object-oriented programmer must face. In this chapter, you will learn more about the considerations you will encounter when you combine the power of pointers with the possibilities of inheritance.

As you begin to learn and use the principles of inheritance you learned about in Chapter 33, you will begin to create an object hierarchy that in many ways resembles a family tree.

In other words, as you create and extend classes from their parent classes, you are creating a *family* of classes. The concept of family to describe the process of creating an object hierarchy is chosen on purpose, as you will realize when learning more about abstract base classes (ABCs) later in this chapter.

A true family structure is somehow connected or related by a single common base class. Although it is implied, this does not mean the classes are sequentially related, however. Your family tree can look any number of ways as you organize the layout of your tree to maximize the usefulness of your hierarchy. Figure 34.1 provides two different, but valid, organizations.

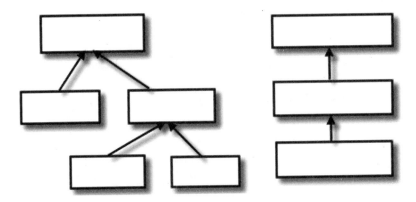

FIGURE 34.1 Different family organizations.

EARLY AND LATE FUNCTION BINDING

Early binding is a process by which it is determined which functions to call during the compilation of your code. While this sounds overly technical, it need not be; early binding has been used for every function you have created from this book so far. When you define a function call along with a function definition, this is early binding in action.

To discuss what late function binding is, and how it operates, involves the need to provide some code samples for clarification. As an example, consider a game situation in which you might create a base object known as Building. Listing 34.1 details this class.

LISTING 34.1 Building.

```
class Building
{
protected:
  char address[50];  /** store the location of our building */
  float sqfoot;      /** store the square footage of our building
*/

  public:
  /** constructor */
```

```
    Building(char a[], float sqft) : sqfoot(sqft)
    {
      strcpy( address, a );
    }
    ~Building();
    void PrintStats()
    {
      cout << "Building address: " << address << " of " << sqfoot
          << endl;
    }
};
```

This is a straightforward class definition and it should not surprise you in the least. The PrintStats member function is responsible for printing the stats of the building, which for now only include its address and square footage.

As you work on your object hierarchy and the game, you create several new classes that are derived directly from this one. Listing 34.2 provides an outline for the HauntedHouse object, which can be derived from the Building class.

LISTING 34.2   HauntedHouse.

```
/**
 * This object is an extension of the Building object, yet also has
some
 * properties of its own.
 */
class HauntedHouse : public Building
{
protected:
  int ghostcount; /** how many ghosts this building has */

public:
  HauntedHouse(char a[], float sqft, int g ) : Building(a, sqft)
  {
    ghostcount = g;
  }
  ~HauntedHouse();
  /**
   * Notice how this PrintStats function is identical in function
   * prototype to the same PrintStats function in the Building
   * Class
   */
  void PrintStats()
  {
    cout << "Building address: " << address << " of " << sqfoot
        << " and has " << ghostcount << " ghosts! Yow!" << endl;
  }
};
```

As you can see, both objects have a member function PrintStats, which accomplishes the same thing for each object. There is a problem, though. When you execute the PrintStats method in your program, which object's implementation will be used?

This problem is demonstrated in Listing 34.3 since in this case it may be easier to demonstrate what happens rather than providing a long discussion.

LISTING 34.3 A hierarchy that does not quite work—Example34_1.cpp.

```cpp
#include <iostream>
using namespace std;

class Building
{
protected:
  char address[50];
  float sqfoot;
public:
  Building(char a[], float sqft) : sqfoot(sqft)
  {
    strcpy( address, a );
  }

  ~Building(){}

  void PrintStats()
  {
    cout << "Building address: " << address << " of " << sqfoot
         << endl;
  }
};

class HauntedHouse : public Building
{
protected:
  int ghostcount;

public:
  HauntedHouse(char a[], float sqft, int g ) : Building(a, sqft)
  {
    ghostcount = g;
  }
  ~HauntedHouse(){}

  void PrintStats()
  {
    cout << "Building address: " << address << " of " << sqfoot
```

```
                    << " and has " << ghostcount << " ghosts! Yow!" << endl;
    }

};

int main( int argc, char* argv[] )
{

  /** declare an array of Building pointers able to hold 2 of them */
   Building* props[2];
  /** create a HauntedHouse object which can be stored in the props
   * array, since it's derived from Building */
  props[0] = &HauntedHouse("Elm Street", 470.2f, 300);
  /** create a normal Building object */
  props[1] = &Building("Duggan Drive", 200.5f);

  /** call the PrintStats member function from each class to
   demonstrate
  *   what happens
  */
  for(int i = 0; i < 2; i++)
  {
    props[i]->PrintStats();
  }

  delete props[0]; /** delete the HauntedHouse */
  delete props[1]; /** delete the Building */
  return 0;
}
```

As you can see from Listing 34.3, you are creating two objects in the free store: HauntedHouse and Building. Once created, you execute the PrintStats member function from each object and will see output similar to Figure 34.2.

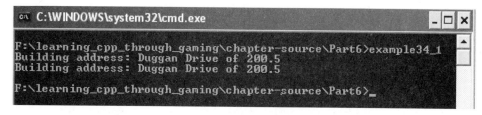

FIGURE 34.2   Example34_1.cpp output.

What happened?

As you can see, although you created a HauntedHouse object, it is using the PrintStats member function of the Building instead, which is not what was intended!

The culprit in this case is early binding. When Listing 34.3 is compiled, it must make a decision on how to handle the PrintStats member function. Since you are defining the props array using the base class Building, the compiler decides that the PrintStats member of the Building class should be used later. There needs to be a way to signal to the compiler that this binding should not occur early, but rather during the runtime of the application when the objects pointed to can decide which method to call.

This is what the virtual keyword allows you to do. By inserting the virtual keyword in the Building object right before the PrintStats member function, you are signaling to the compiler that you only want the base object's PrintStats member function called if the *this pointer is from the base object, Building. You can rewrite the Building class as shown in Listing 34.4.

LISTING 34.4   Building (fixed)—Example34_2.cpp.

```
class Building
{
protected:
  char address[50];
  float sqfoot;

public:
  Building(char a[], float sqft) : sqfoot(sqft)
  {
    strcpy( address, a );
  }

  virtual ~Building(){}

  virtual void PrintStats()
  {
    cout << "Building address: " << address << " of " << sqfoot
      << endl;
  }
};
```

If you make this fix in Listing 34.3 and run Example34_2, you will now see the number of ghosts living on Elm Street, as shown in Figure 34.3.

As you may notice from Listing 34.4, the destructor to the Building class is declared with the virtual keyword. You have just learned that when a class method for a derived object is declared using the virtual keyword, the *this pointer is evaluated during the runtime of the program to determine which appropriate member function to execute. The destructor functions the same way. To properly ensure the object is destroyed during cleanup (either explicitly or if the object leaves the current scope), the *this pointer will need to be evaluated to determine which object is leaving scope.

FIGURE 34.3   Example34_2 output.

ABSTRACT BASE CLASSES

When creating your object hierarchy or family tree, it is often the case where you decide on a high-level base object from which other objects derive. In most object-oriented designs, these high-level objects cannot be directly instantiated. In other words, the only way you can use member functions of these higher level objects is to use a derived object instead. These high-level objects are known as *abstract base classes* (also known as ABCs). They are abstract because they can never be instantiated directly, and form a base class for other objects in the hierarchy to depend on. Now that you understand what ABCs are, how do you tell the compiler?

The answer is to declare the member functions as *pure virtual* functions. This means that each member function is marked as virtual, and assigned to zero. By declaring a function this way, you are signaling to the compiler that this object cannot be instantiated explicitly by the program. Instead, the developer will need to create a derived object from the ABC. Listing 34.5 converts the Building object into an ABC.

LISTING 34.5   Building object as an ABC.

```
class Building
{
protected:
  char address[50];
  float sqfoot;

public:
  Building(char a[], float sqft) : sqfoot(sqft)
  {
    strcpy( address, a );
  }

  virtual ~Building();

  virtual void PrintStats() = 0;
```

```
};

//snip
//The Building object is now an ABC. You cannot declare it
//explicitly. The following declaration, therefore, will result
//in many errors by the compiler
Building oHouse; //this is illegal

//in order to use the methods from the Building object, you need
//to create a new one derived from Building
class Tower : public Building
{
  //snip
};

//The following declaration is then legal and allowed by the
//compiler
Tower oTowerOfHanoi;
```

You should notice two modifications in Listing 34.5. The first is that the virtual keyword has appeared in front of the destructor. As explained previously, the reason for this is to ensure the proper destructor is called when this object leaves scope. The other modification is that the PrintStats member function has become defined as a pure virtual, making it illegal to explicitly declare an instance of this class. In other words, to take advantage of what the ABC class offers your software, you need to directly extend the class with a new one.

SUMMARY

This chapter was an important component on learning the C++ language. Because of object-oriented design requirements, it is often necessary to model the classes within an application as a hierarchy of various object types that inherit properties from parent objects. The use of virtual functions presents a method of allowing the compiler to execute the appropriate member function of a class when used. You also learned about the importance of abstract data classes, and using the pure virtual keywords to signal to the compiler that this object cannot be instantiated directly. In the next chapter, you will learn various object-oriented techniques and design theory.

EXERCISES

34.1 What does the `virtual` keyword do?

34.2 What is the difference between early and late binding?

34.3 What is an abstract base class?

34.4 What does pure virtual mean?

34.5 What are interfaces?

35   Object-Oriented Analysis

In This Chapter

- What Is A Game Design?
- Classic Waterfall Software Design
- Iterative Software Design
- Introduction to the Unified Modeling Language
- Software Reusability
- Anatomy of a Game
- Creating a Basic Design Document
- Draft an Initial List of Timeboxes

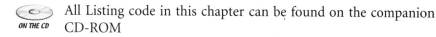 All Listing code in this chapter can be found on the companion CD-ROM

A basic understanding of some common design fundamentals can radically improve your project, but it is most often overlooked by beginning developers (of any language). Having a clear understanding of your design goals can reduce the amount of development time for your software by minimizing some of the risks involved.

WHAT IS A GAME DESIGN?

At the highest level of your game project, the game design details and defines how your game operates and responds to the player. The game design acts as a blueprint or structure that you and your team will use to work through to the completion of your game. It provides everyone with a central, single definition of what should occur within the game world, depending on what conditions exist or what input is received by the player. Design helps you map from the basic concepts of your game through implementation. It is also the central document that aids in coordinating tasks between team members. Design literally describes and entails the last word on everything involved with the game.

Skipping the game design process can contribute to massive delays in the project in the later stages. Programming by trial and error is not a manageable process. It is much more difficult to maintain a single vision without a central document or design, and can be nearly impossible to recruit any help without providing something the potential team member can browse through.

To help bring your gaming projects to fruition, you can take advantage of software design principles professional programmers use: the classic waterfall approach, or an iterative design.

CLASSIC WATERFALL SOFTWARE DESIGN

Although you might already be familiar with this type of approach, the *classic waterfall* method has been in use since the early days of software design. The waterfall model focuses on each phase of the design flowing into the next. This means that as you complete one phase of the design, you move into the next through implementation and testing phases, cascading down through the creation process like a waterfall. Figure 35.1 demonstrates this method.

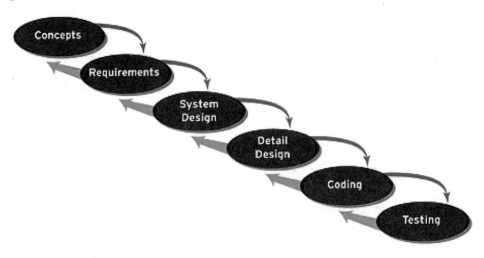

FIGURE 35.1   Classic waterfall design process.

Some programmers and software engineers working on applications swear by this design method in the real world, but it is not always the best model to follow for game development. During the implementation phase of a project, for example, you might realize that there are some flaws in the design based on some earlier (now erroneous) assumptions. After being perhaps months in development, it is often far too late to return to your client and/or project manager to ask for more time to rebuild a section of the code base.

What if the current target market demographic suddenly changes, and your marketing team demands some alterations to the game? What if technology changes much more quickly than anticipated, and new hardware or effects become available to implement in your game?

These are only a few of the pitfalls that you or your team can encounter during the project; therefore, you should have one or more contingency scenarios defined.

ITERATIVE SOFTWARE DESIGN

Because of some of the problems associated with the waterfall design approach, most game programmers (some unknowingly) tend to follow a much more iterative design process. This style of design allows for much more fluidity and adaptation to the project if necessary.

Most of your gameplay is iterative in nature and difficult to envision without the benefits of building tests to see how the different rules of your game and/or universe interact with each other. If after testing, you decide that some of the rules need more tweaking or should be removed, the iterative method allows you to adjust the design as necessary. In the waterfall method, objects within each phase are pretty much set in stone, as they depend on objects created in the previous phase; therefore, any real tweaking is never allowed or even acceptable. Figure 35.2 provides an overview of the iterative process.

The "spiral" process underscores the continued process of requirements gathering, making adjustments and client feedback that forms the heart and soul of iterative design.

As you begin the overall design process, you are responsible for setting a schedule that represents the timeline of the project to the best of your knowledge at the present time. Along the way, you should mark project *milestones*, in which you and your team have the opportunity to do a mini-evaluation on the project so far. If you need to make any alterations or adjustments because of recommendations by the marketing department, or if you discover any serious problems with the design in general, this is a feasible approach to follow. Each milestone should have a subset

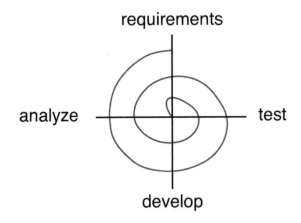

FIGURE 35.2   Iterative "spiral" design process.

of goals that you and your team are looking to accomplish. Again, during each milestone period, the team can also readjust any or all of the upcoming goals.

Principles of Agile Design

During the 1990s, the forming of Agile design methodologies was a direct response to models such as the waterfall approach, which was regarded by some as a cumbersome, bureaucratic, and slow process of creating useful software. Initially, the methods proposed by the Agile designers were collectively known as "lightweight" techniques. In 2001, some prominent members of the iterative software design community met to form the Agile Alliance. Their first task was to create the Agile Manifesto, which grouped these lightweight principles under the universal Agile brand. This has become an extremely popular design process within the industry and benefits software designers of nearly every type of application. The core principles behind the Agile design methodology are:

- Minimize project risk by developing your software in short iteration periods, known as *timeboxes*, which last between one and four weeks.
- Each timebox of the project is within itself a project of its own and includes all of the tasks behind releasing any updates to the main project. This includes new planning, new requirements, gathering and analysis, coding, implementation, and updating documentation.
- The Agile method emphasizes personal communication involving face-to-face discussions with the client. Agile stresses the fact that meetings or discussions with the client should always overshadow the written documentation on the project. Agile teams are usually formed within close proximity of their actual

clients. For Agile purposes, *clients* are defined as the people who have defined the project to begin with. External customers and project managers are some good examples.

■ The progress of an Agile project is measured by the amount of functioning code at the end of every timebox.

■ Agile welcomes requirement changes by the client, even late in the project, for the client to maximize any competitive advantage.

■ To the newcomers of this type of software design methodology, there is sometimes confusion between an Agile design approach and a pure *ad-hoc* practice in which the developers simply work through the project in any direction they choose with little restrictions. Since Agile methods emphasize continuous feedback along with rigorous and disciplined processes, however, it creates a successful environment with a clear direction and target.

 Agile methods are focused around minimizing risk in the project. You are still working from a larger picture but can prune any features from the project based on your timebox progress.

One of the foundation principles of Agile is that the design is test driven in nature. Agile developers create small tests to iteratively drive the project forward. Although it is one of the principles of proper Agile design, creating a test framework is outside the scope of this book.

INTRODUCTION TO THE UNIFIED MODELING LANGUAGE

As you are learning about software design techniques, it should be apparent that rarely does the project immediately shift into implementation and/or coding. Regardless of which software design model you prefer, after you have created the design document, it can save you a lot of time and hassle to transcribe your document into a modeling language. The Unified Modeling Language (UML) is an attempt to bring the concept of blueprints to the world of software design and implementation. The language of UML consists of a number of different graphical components that can be used to describe the architecture of your software. The benefit of this technique is that you now have a common graphical representation of your application that you and your team can follow. It becomes immediately apparent which component relies on which other component; this can alert you to any possible problems that might occur during the development phase of your project.

Although the UML is not the only modeling language, it is becoming the most widely accepted standard. In other words, this has major communication benefits with the other developers on your team in regard to understanding the overall design and architecture of your system.

Basic Class Notation

Within UML, a simple rectangle is the basic notation for representing a class. The rectangle is usually segmented into three sections. The uppermost section contains the class name, usually bolded. The middle section contains any attributes for the class, and the lowermost section contains any operations that the class can perform. Figure 35.3 demonstrates this.

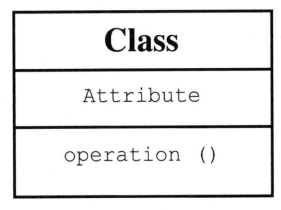

FIGURE 35.3   UML class notation.

 UML has a fairly strict differentiation between operations and methods of the class. Within a UML context, an operation is a service that you can request from any object of a class, and a method is a specific implementation of the operation.

Visibility Notation

Within UML, you can also provide an overview of the *visibility* of any attribute or operation of the class. Since you are working with C++ for this book, this is equivalent to the usage of the public, private, and protected declarations. The characters -, #, and + declare the attribute or operation as private, protected, or public. Figure 35.4 details visibility.

Comment/Note Notation

Within the UML is also a notation convention used to display or provide any additional comments the designer might have. This is provided via the Note model,

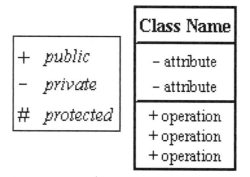

FIGURE 35.4   UML visibility notation.

which can also be referred to as a *comment*. Figure 35.5 details a comment notation in action.

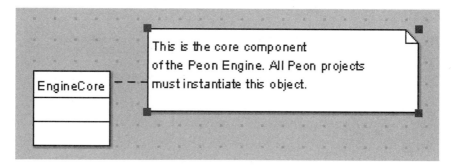

FIGURE 35.5   UML comment notation.

Modeling Class Relationships

As you are well aware, classes never exist by themselves in a vacuum. They are interconnected with other objects within the system. UML provides several *relationships* between objects, which are defined as connections between two or more notational elements. Within UML, there are three relationship types provided: a *dependency*, an *association,* and a *generalization.*

Dependency Relationship

One of the simpler relationships to model, the dependency provides a mechanism for one object to depend on another object's interface.

Association Relationship

A relationship that runs a little deeper than the dependency, the association provides a mechanism for one object to contain another object. The UML provides two types of associations to further help define your relationships: aggregation and composition.

Aggregation Association

An aggregation association is responsible for modeling a "has-a" relationship among peer objects. The *has-a* wording means that one object contains another. A *peer* means that one object in the association is no more important than the other. Figure 35.6 provides the UML notation of an aggregation association.

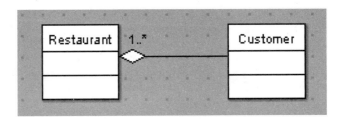

FIGURE 35.6   UML aggregation association.

A real-world example of an aggregation association can be the relationship between a franchise such as any fast food restaurant and the everyday customer. In this relationship, clearly the fast food outlet and the customer can operate independently of each other. If the franchise outlet goes out of business, the customer will still exist and can buy his favorite food product from another store. Likewise, if the customer no longer purchases from the outlet, the store will still remain in business.

Composition Association

Composition associations are more rigid than the aggregate. The difference between the two is that a composition is not a relationship among peer objects. In other words, the objects are not interdependent on each other. Figure 35.7 provides the UML of a composition.

A real-world example of a composition association is any typical food franchise such as *FastFoodInc*. A central office oversees and manages every *FastFoodInc* franchise outlet. These outlets cannot exist independently of the central office. The composition association signals to you that if the *FastFoodInc*'s central office goes out of business, then so must each franchise outlet (since they can no longer represent the *FastFoodInc* brand). However, the converse is not true. If a franchise outlet closes, the central office might still remain operational.

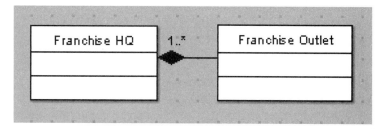

FIGURE 35.7   UML composition association.

Generalization Relationship

The generalization relationship models the inheritance of one object to another. In other words, it is a relationship between the general (interface) and the specific. For this reason, you can substitute any child object for the parent class. Figure 35.8 details the UML representation of a generalization.

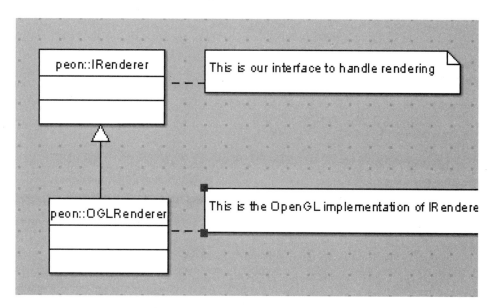

FIGURE 35.8   UML generalization relationship.

The generalization is a physical manifestation of the *is-a* relationship that you should be familiar with in C++.

SOFTWARE REUSABILITY

Reusability is another important concept to understand in all areas of development, including games. For the purposes of this chapter, reusability can be defined as both *code reuse* and *design reuse*.

Code Reuse

Code reuse is a fairly obvious concept for most game programmers, but it is nevertheless an important aspect of reusability that can save you months of work.

As you build your experience in game programming, you will usually encounter situations in which you are redeveloping the same functions, methods, or objects. All of this code needs to be properly tested before being migrated into your game, and so you should only be redeveloping what is necessary in any new project. Generic modules, such as interfacing with the operating system, creating a window, and so on should be coded and tested one time and placed into a central library or code repository for future projects. The small library you work with in this book makes use of the STL (Standard Template Library), which is a good example of code reuse.

It can be typical for your first game to take longer than subsequent ones. After all, you might be learning how to do things for the first time, along with building a small set of common functions and objects with which to work. Subsequent titles can take advantage of these objects, which allows you to focus more quickly on implementing the higher level objects in your game. The only caveat here is to be careful of over specification. Reuse done properly should reduce the amount of code size and complexity. Reuse done incorrectly can lead to heavyweight frameworks in which only a small fraction of objects are used.

Design Reuse

Although not as obvious as the code reuse aspect of software, *design reuse* refers to the common problems of software engineering that are solved a repeated number of times. This is evident in most game programming circles or newsgroups, in which the same types of questions are discussed again and again. If you abstract the approaches to solve these repeatable problems, you will get what are known as *design patterns*. Design patterns aid in describing the optimal design solution to a common problem. You will learn some of the more common design patterns that can help you get past any hurdles in your game. Only a small selection of helpful design patterns will be presented for use with your project. You should take the time to find some other quality design patterns that can be implemented as well.

With the Internet at your fingertips, there is no need to reinvent the wheel.

Pattern 1: The Object Factory

The object factory is a class whose sole purpose is to allow the creation of families of objects. This usually implies that all of the objects that can be instantiated by the factory are derived from the same abstract base class. Listing 35.1 demonstrates one example of an object factory pattern.

LISTING 35.1   Using an object factory.

```
//BaseObject – this is the lowest level object that we derive
//others from for this design pattern.
//In other words, an ABC (Abstract Base Class).
class BaseObject
{
public:
  BaseObject(){};        //constructor
  virtual ~BaseObject(){}; //virtual destructor
  float x, y, z;           //arbitrary member data
  virtual void doMethod(){}; //arbitrary method
};

//This is the ObjectA derived from BaseObject
class ObjectA : public BaseObject
{
  public:
    ObjectA(){};         //constructor
    ~ObjectA(){};        //destructor
    void doMethod(){}; //do some arbitrary thing
};

//This is the ObjectB derived from BaseObject
class ObjectB : public BaseObject
{
  public:
    ObjectB(){};         //constructor
    ~ObjectB(){};        //destructor
    void doMethod(){}; //do some arbitrary thing
};

//snip
//this demo ObjectFactory is used to generate new BaseObject
//instances.
//OBJECT_A – identifier for the ObjectA class
//OBJECT_B – identifier for the ObjectB class
BaseObject* ObjectFactory::create_object( int type )
```

```
{
  BaseObject* pObj = NULL;
  if( type == OBJECT_A)
  {
    pObj = new ObjectA();
  }else if(type == OBJECT_B)
  {
    pObj = new ObjectB();
  }

  if(pObj){ pObj->doMethod(); } //if object exists, call doMethod

  return pObj; //return our new object
}
```

Pattern 2: The Singleton

The singleton pattern ensures that one and only one instance of a particular object can exist in your application. This is helpful when you want to guarantee that you have only one instance of an object, such as the object encapsulating your audio or video hardware. Listing 35.2 details this popular design pattern.

LISTING 35.2 ISingleton.

```
//This object defines a template of Singleton
//You should not use this object directly, but derive other
//Singleton patterned-objects from this one
template <typename T> class ISingleton
{
protected:

    static T* ms_Singleton;

public:
    ISingleton( void )
    {
        assert( !ms_Singleton );
#if defined( _MSC_VER ) && _MSC_VER < 1200
        int offset = (int)(T*)1 - (int)(Singleton <T>*)(T*)1;
        ms_Singleton = (T*)((int)this + offset);
#else
    ms_Singleton = static_cast< T* >( this );
#endif
    }
    ~ISingleton( void )
        { assert( ms_Singleton );  ms_Singleton = 0;  }
    static T& getSingleton( void )
    {    assert( ms_Singleton );  return ( *ms_Singleton ); }
```

```
        static T* getSingletonPtr( void )
        { return ms_Singleton; }
};
```

As you can see in Listing 35.2, the ISingleton object makes use of a feature of the C++ language known as templates. Templates are explained in further detail in Chapter 45. In many cases, the singleton object is conceptually identical to an object (or variable) that is declared globally.

Pattern 3: The Façade Pattern

Known most of the time as a type of *manager* class, the façade design pattern enables you to provide a single object, which behaves as an interface to a group of similar related objects. One example of this pattern is to use a façade interface to communicate with your input or graphics subsystems. This object is especially useful at reducing the amount of *coupling*, or object interdependencies, in your application. By minimizing the amount of coupling in your code design, you reduce the amount of time spent on replacing any subsystems should there be a need to do so. Listing 35.3 provides some background behind the façade design pattern.

LISTING 35.3   Façade design pattern.

```
//This object contains our graphics device — say OpenGL
class GraphicsDevice
{
public:
  bool loadGraphics();

};

//This object encapsulates the texture resources used by our
//game.
class TextureManager
{
public:
  bool loadTextures();
};

//This object encapsulates the font resources used by our game
class FontManager
{
public:
  bool loadFonts();
};

//This "parent" object encapsulates the graphics device,
//texture manager and font manager objects. When you need
```

```
//access to one of those objects, you have to go through
//THIS one first.
class GraphicsSubsystem
{
private:
  GraphicsDevice m_oDevice;
  TextureManager m_oTexManager;
  FontManager m_oFontManager;

public:
  //This method demonstrates how useful the Façade pattern is.
  //We use it to indirectly work with lower-level objects.
  bool loadGraphicsSubsystem()
  {
    bool value = true;
    value = m_oDevice.loadGraphics();
    value = m_oTexManager.loadTextures();
    value = m_oFontManager.loadFonts();
    //obviously proper error checking is skipped. We're
    //just trying to demonstrate the design pattern here!
    return value;
  }
};
```

ANATOMY OF A GAME

Although games are incredibly complex and performance-intensive pieces of software, they can all be abstracted to some common runtime phases that are outlined and described here.

These phases are meant to outline the operational lifetime of your game while it is running for the player. This is not an abstraction to the entire process of creating a game in terms of management, product life cycle, support, and so on.

Initialization Phase

The *initialization phase* is the first phase involved in your game and obviously the most important. Within this phase, your program attempts to create interfaces to the underlying hardware available on the machine and perform any or all of the following list of actions:

■ Your video card is located and initialized to any desired resolution.
■ An interface to your sound hardware is created and opened.

■ Interfaces to your keyboard, mouse, and, optionally, the joystick are created.

■ Networking interfaces are loaded and initialized.

■ Any game-specific objects or data structures are loaded and initialized.

■ Game-specific graphics and audio resources are loaded and initialized.

When this phase is completed successfully, the game then proceeds to the *process phase*.

It is normally good practice to load as many objects and resources as possible for your game in this phase.

Process Phase

Throughout the course of the *process phase*, the game is responsible for updating all of the game world objects, and rendering (that is, drawing) them to the screen. You can, therefore, subdivide this phase into two subphases: *updating* and *rendering*.

Updating Phase

The updating phase is responsible for a host of actions along the lines of the following:

■ Updating all the game world objects for the current map, location, or level.

■ Processing any collision-detection calculations to test which objects have hit other objects to determine which ones are active or inactive within the game world.

■ Gather and process any input from the player to determine what your object (that is, the Avatar) is attempting to do.

■ Gather and process any network events to determine your relation to other players in the game.

■ Process any artificial intelligence routines for computer-controlled objects or players.

■ Start or stop any appropriate audio file.

Rendering Phase

The rendering phase is responsible for drawing all the game world objects to the screen. You must perform many chores here in terms of video object management, but the primary goal of this phase is to get everything on the screen as quickly as possible.

The game continues in the process phase until it has received a signal or message that you want to quit the game. It will then move into the *destruction phase*.

Destruction Phase

The overall goal of the *destruction phase* of your game is to clean up any object or hardware device used during the lifetime of your game. You will need to perform tasks like the following:

- Clean up all the audio resources and the audio hardware.
- Deallocate all the video resources and the video hardware.
- Clean up all the input devices used.
- Shut down and cancel any further network communication and/or device interfaces.
- Clean up any object memory allocated during the lifetime of the game.

Just about every game moves through these phases in one fashion or another, and understanding these basics will help to provide an overview to how things are supposed to work in your game projects.

CREATING A BASIC DESIGN DOCUMENT

Design documents created using the waterfall model often can be notoriously large and complex. One immediate problem with this approach is that as the document grows to encompass the project, not everyone in the team will properly update it. Another issue is that some team members might not even reference it because they feel that some objects or design decisions that are documented might already be outdated. In an attempt to create a design document that is both useable and maintainable, you can benefit from some of the Agile design techniques to create the project's design documentation. Although the Agile design approach is tailored for working with a customer to keep the project moving and updated, you will need to wear two hats during development of this basic document, as you are your own client.

Drafting a Project Overview

The initial project overview should contain a one- or two-line description of the overall game. This should be an exciting description of the whole purpose of the game, which will attract any potential customers or players. Listing 35.4 details a sample project overview.

LISTING 35.4   Project overview.

```
Project Overview: The overall goal of this game is to collect as many
sunshine units as possible before the evil King of Ragnorok awakens
from his slumber.
```

What Type or Genre of Game Is It?

Now that you have defined an overview of what is taking place in your game, you need to decide what type or *genre* of game you are creating. Although this small list of game genres is an attempt to categorize or classify existing software, there are many examples of mutated types of games that blend together several different genres.

Action/Arcade: This type of game usually involves the player being really involved in the game world in order to win. Usually, an action game has the player performing many fast and repetitive actions such as shooting many enemies while simultaneously dodging hails of lasers or bullets.

Strategy: A strategy game gives the player the ability to plan his moves, which usually centers on directing your resources to defeat the other players. For strategy games, you can usually spot two subgenres of this game type:

Real time: This type of strategy game forces players to make quick decisions where they cannot spend too much time planning their empires. Although they start out slowly, most real-time strategy (or RTS) games quickly ramp up the action, forcing players to frantically move their units around the game world.

Turn based: These types of strategy games are much slower than RTS experiences and give players as much time as they need to decide what action to perform next. These games usually work by dividing the play into rounds or turns. Usually, at the start of each round, the player is given a certain number of resources with which to work. After the player has used up these resources, the turn usually ends.

Adventure: Although these types of games are not released much anymore, adventure games revolve around the player experiencing a story through the game. They usually involve some type of quest for the player to accomplish. For the most part, they are single-player games that involve the player interacting with the environment to complete tasks or quests that reveal clues on how to proceed within the adventure toward the final goal.

Puzzle: Puzzle games are very popular among players who enjoy being presented with a problem they must solve. They are enjoyed by a wide range of players and typically have a difficulty of play that ranges from beginner to advanced as the player moves through the game. Puzzle games vary tremendously in gameplay, as some are slow paced but others build the action at a frantic pace.

Platform: Platform games are another popular category, where the goal of the game is to complete a journey or quest of some nature. You move your character through the game world by negotiating different levels or maps, and usually must collect items along the way to help you continue.

MMOG: Massively Multiple Online Gaming is becoming another huge vehicle for game design and development that focuses on thousands of people playing the game. While this type of game used to be for the more hardcore audience, several successful casual titles have made the MMOG experience a more accepted form of entertainment. While virtually anything can be done by the player in these online worlds, it is in the game designer's best interest to promote being involved in a community with other players in the game. Most MMOG titles have very large and epic storylines that players can feel a part of.

 Deciding on a game genre will also help describe the project to your friends and any other potential customers.

Who Is Your Audience?

This is a very important and critical question that needs to be answered as clearly and as early as possible in your project. The more detail you can provide here, the easier it will be to create a list of requirements for the game itself, along with providing some direction for the rest of the project. You need to decide who will benefit the most from your game. Within most people or companies who are developing their own games, the audience can be broken into two basic categories:

The casual gamer: This type of gamer composes the majority of the audience who typically supports many shareware titles on the Internet today. They represent an audience who enjoys playing games, but also has other priorities in their lives such as work or family. In other words, they are the type of player who wants to jump into the action for shorter periods of time. This type of gamer is also typically not very computer savvy. They are usually not very knowledgeable about upgrading any computer hardware, or even the basic risks or benefits behind upgrading their core software. In other words, to target a more casual type of player, you need to ensure that your game will run on older hardware with little to no configuration required to execute your game.

The hardcore gamer: This type of gamer is usually more computer savvy and enjoys the types of games that push their machine slightly harder than a casual game would (on average). This type of gamer would be more willing to sit down and play your software for a longer period of time or, at the very least, invest more into your game. They are usually not afraid to update any core software components such as applying new video drivers, and so on, to play your game properly. With the more hardcore crowd, you can afford to use slightly later technology, such as popular 3D graphics libraries like OpenGL or a version of Direct3D.

Why Make the Game?

Another critical question to answer at the beginning of the project is why you want to make this game. Instead of answering with a vague (and unmeasureable) response such as, "to make money" or "to have fun," it might be better used to describe why someone will choose your game over a similar product even if you have no intention of selling the game. There are many different clones of a game like Battleship available on the Internet, for example, so you should be prepared to discuss why a player might want to choose your version over another clone game. This is a very important part of the design process, as you will need to demonstrate to anyone that your game is different.

What Do You Want to See?

Although this can change during the project development or testing stages, describe here what you are envisioning as the outcome of your project. When the player launches the finished product, what should he see?

For example, in a game such as one similar to *Asteroids*, the player should be able to fly around in a section of space with the ability to blow up the encroaching asteroids to win the round. The player should be viewing the game world from an overhead bird's eye vantage point as he flies through a quadrant in space inhabited by asteroids and any enemy alien saucers.

What Does It Offer?

If a player were to download and purchase your game, what features does it offer that separates it from the others? This is definitely a follow-up question to the previous two. To help decide on a feature list that you want to promote for the game, begin by doing some basic market research. Now that you have chosen the genre of your game, along with what type of player you are targeting, you can spend some time on the Internet to find other comparable products and create a document detailing how they are similar and how they differ. Although you can find more resources through your favorite search engine, game portal sites such as *RealArcade.com* or *BigFishGames.com* provide a common gateway to hundreds of downloadable games. Although it is tough (that is, impossible) to find actual sales figures for these games, most of the game portal sites will have a ranking of some kind, which can help discern what is a popular sell. Select a few of the top-selling games that more or less match the type of game you want to create. Study the game(s) from a more analytical approach. What type of system requirements do they have? Is the gameplay between them all similar, or do they try to make a different experience?

DRAFT AN INITIAL LIST OF TIMEBOXES

After you finish answering the preliminary questions for your design document, you will then segment the project into several timeboxes to accomplish the overall goal of creating your game. At the end of each timebox, you can evaluate how the subsection fits into the overall project and verify that it does not need any modifications.

For a small project, you might only need three timeboxes:

Foundation and state timebox: The goal of this segment is to create the underlying objects to launch the game. This segment should also have some rudimentary states defined for the game, which you will fill in as the project progresses.

Graphics timebox: The goal of this segment of the project is to create the underlying objects necessary to create and display some of the basic graphics of the game, including any graphical user interface components.

Input and sound timebox: The goal of this segment is to create and add the components necessary to the game to provide audio feedback along with properly communicating with your input devices.

As you work through the timeboxes in any project, you will be constantly evaluating or updating the design document. If you are new to this type of design process, this type of rapid editing might feel "bad"; similar to people changing their mind too much during a project. However, most of the time, Agile relies on evolution of the original concepts.

The design document might seem a little on the lighter side, but you will be adding only what you need as you work through each timebox. This is a bit of a chicken-egg scenario—if this is your first game project, you will not be aware of what kind of components are needed in the game you are trying to design. As you work through each timebox or phase of implementation, you can make iterative adjustments to the design.

SUMMARY

In this chapter, you were introduced to a wide variety of common software engineering topics. You learned the differences between the classic waterfall and iterative design methods. You were also introduced to the concept of software reusability along with a short list of design patterns that are useful in solving some of the common design problems most developers face. Although brief, the introduction you were given covered using the Unified Modeling Language (UML) to learn more about documenting and designing your software. You also were provided with an introduction of the fundamentals of how a game operates and functions. Finally, you were introduced to the design document and how to create one that attempts to decrease the amount of time spent actually implementing your game. In the next chapter, you'll learn how to develop the foundation of the Battleship project that was introduced back in Part V.

EXERCISES

35.1. Within the UML, how do you design a class or method that is abstract?

35.2. Understand the advantages and disadvantages of the classic waterfall design method compared to the iterative process. Further investigate the design methodologies such as eXtreme Programming (XP) or Pair Programming techniques.

35.3. Although the waterfall process might not seem ideal for most game projects, discuss any situations in which the waterfall method might be necessary.

35.4. Take some time to research other useful design patterns that can help your code practices. Although not always the "magic bullet," design patterns can simplify many aspects of your application and improve your design and programming skills.

36 Battleship

In This Chapter

■ Object Hierarchy

All Listing code in this chapter can be found on the companion CD-ROM

I n the project related to Part VI of this book, you will be reworking most of the Battleship project used in Part V to take advantage of object-oriented programming techniques you have covered so far. With the knowledge of class hierarchies and virtual functions, you can separate much of the Battleship code into separate modules and objects, which can make the project itself far more readable and somewhat easier to maintain and modify.

You can follow along with this chapter by reviewing the source code contained in Project36_1.h and Project36_1.cpp on the companion CD-ROM.

OBJECT HIERARCHY

It is largely debatable if two unconnected objects can be considered a "hierarchy," but nevertheless this is where you will start with the object layout for the game.

FIGURE 36.1   Battleship object hierarchy.

The Piece class is meant to handle the different ship types available to you in the regular game of Battleship. Some pieces are only two units in length, while the Battleship is the full five. This feature should be considered as a property of the class.

The other class, GameBoard, is meant to encapsulate the functions you have been using so far to access the various battleship pieces, along with handling firing commands from the players. A common approach for this is to also create several different status flags for each square in the game grid. In other words, the square could be occupied with a ship piece, it could be a "hit" ship piece, or it could be a "missed" shot by a player, or finally an empty square.

The accompanying source code to the game provides the outlines of each class that was discussed here along with their implementation in the program.

SUMMARY

This concludes Part VI of this book. Congratulations on learning the basics behind object-oriented programming with C++! It is important to understand these basics, as the rest of your C++ knowledge will be built upon this background. Feel free to experiment and modify the project code in this chapter to see for yourself how much power and flexibility the C++ language brings to the table.

In Part VII, you will learn about accessing files, which is a crucial component of any game.

EXERCISES

36.1 Go through the Piece and Gameboard classes to determine if anything else can be removed and put into its own class definition.

Part VII

VII

Files and Streams

In the Part VI, you learned about object-oriented programming along with several key concepts behind object-oriented structuring. You learned how to create and define a class that is the definition of an object within your game world. You also were introduced to restricting access to your class via the security qualifiers that C++ provides. You had some lessons in how to overload both functions and operators in your class, and how to take advantage of the free store available to your program during runtime.

With the world of game programming, arguably one of the most important tasks is to load or store data within files. As your skill in C++ and game development grows, this is a critical task in any game. Your game world data such as model files from 3D authoring packages, or bitmaps created in your favorite paint software, need to be loaded and manipulated into any game. Part VII focuses on learning the groundwork with respect to manipulating files. You will learn how to leverage the power of the C++ iostream library to read and write text and data to a file. You will also learn how to add serialization to your C++ objects so you can read and write internal object data directly to binary files.

At the end of Part VII, you will be able to leverage the concepts learned to add serialization support to the Battleship game. Good luck, and happy loading!

37 Simple File Input and Output

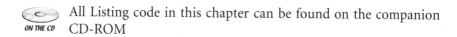 All Listing code in this chapter can be found on the companion CD-ROM

A ccessing data contained in files is arguably one of the most important aspects about game programming. Not only is it essential to be able to load and save critical data such as player information, for example, but most of your game's assets such as any images, models, and maybe even level data is all stored in a file format of some kind. Another use of a file is to create a way to log events that happen in your game, known as a *log file*. Log files allow you to trace events that can be used as the first method of debugging any problems with the game.

When working with file access, there are really only two kinds of data: text and binary.

TEXT STREAMS

As you might expect, text streams are human readable characters being loaded into (or written by) your programs. Since the discussion of sequential file access begins this section, you should understand that there are only three types of actions you can perform on a file:

- Writing data to a file
- Reading data from the file
- Appending data to an existing file

To illustrate working with text streams, you can begin with a simple example of writing some characters to a file as shown in Listing 37.1.

LISTING 37.1   Text stream output—Example37_1.cpp.

```
//simple io program to write characters to a file
//any file operations require us to include the fstream header file
#include <fstream>
#include <iostream>
using namespace std;

int main(int argc, char* argv[])
{
  //first open the file for output
  ofstream outfile("data.txt");

  //write some characters
  outfile.put('A');
  outfile.put('B');
  outfile.put('C');

  //the carriage return or newline feed
  outfile.put('\n');

  //we are finished sending characters to the file
  //so be sure to flush any leftover data and close
  //the file
  outfile.flush();
  outfile.close();

  return 0;
}
```

Listing 37.1 demonstrates the basics behind writing characters to a file. The standard C++ objects that come with the library include some objects to manipulate the file stream. The ofstream class is an object that is solely used to stream output data to a file. You first open the file when declaring the variable outfile, which is an instance of the ofstream class. Once that is successful, you can use the put method of the class to add text to the file. Once you have finished working with any file stream, it is always a wise habit to make sure all data is properly processed and the file handle closed. This is accomplished with the flush() and close() functions.

Back in Part I of this book, you worked with the >> and << operators to stream data to and from the console. These operators also exist within file manipulation and have been overloaded by the file stream objects to perform the equivalent type of actions. Listing 37.2 demonstrates how to use the << for another way of streaming text out to a file.

LISTING 37.2   Text streaming using the overloaded operator—Example37_2.cpp.

```
//demonstrates how to use << for text writing
#include <fstream>
#include <iostream>
using namespace std;

int main(int argc, char* argv[])
{

  ofstream outfile("data.txt");

  outfile << "This is another way " << " to input " << endl;
  outfile << "text in a more streaming fashion. " << endl;

  outfile.flush();

  outfile.close();

  return 0;
}
```

As you can see from Listing 37.2, you are opening the data file, which is handled by the outfile object. Using the << operator, you are then allowed to stream your output to the outfile much in the same way you have been streaming your output to the cerr or cout mechanisms.

Reading data from text files operates in a similar fashion. Whereas your output file stream was encapsulated by the ofstream handle, your file input object uses the ifstream class to gather input. Listing 37.3 details some use of the ifstream object.

LISTING 37.3   ifstream object.

```
//reads the input file created earlier and display it to the
//console
```

```
#include <ifstream>
#include <iostream>
using namespace std;

int main(int argc, char *argv[])
{
  ifstream infile("data.txt"); //declare an input stream named
                                         data.txt

  char outchar;                 //declare a value to store input
  while( infile.good() )        //while the file still has data
  {
    infile.get(outchar);        //read the char from the file into
                                  outchar

    cout << outchar;            //display outchar to the console
  }
  infile.close();               //close the file stream
  return 0;
}
```

Be careful when working with the >> operator when working with text file data. It skips over whitespace and tab characters, so your input will appear all scrunched together.

Listing 37.3 opens a new file handle to the text file and keeps it in the `infile` file handle. The small program then operates by reading the file character by character using the `get` method, and then displaying the content to the `cout` stream. Once the end of the file has been reached, the `while` condition will fail and the program will terminate.

You can also read string data from a text file line by line, which can be easier and far more efficient than only reading a single character at a time. Listing 37.4 details how this can be accomplished using the `getline` member function.

LISTING 37.4 Using `getline()`.

```
//reads the text file generated earlier using strings and displays
//it to the console
#include <ifstream>
#include <iostream>
using namespace std;

int main(int argc, char* argv[])
{
  ifstream infile("data.txt");    //declare an input file
  char nextline[256];             //array to store each line
  while( infile.good() )          //while the file has data
```

```
    {
      nextline.getline(nextline, 256); //read a line from the file
      cout << nextline << endl;        //stream the line to the
console
    }
    infile.close();                    //close the input file
    return 0;
  }
```

The getline() *function by default will read data up until the newline character is read from the file.*

The getline function works by reading up to *256* characters of the file into an array of char elements, which is used as a buffer. When the function encounters the end of a line, the buffer is closed off and the function returns.

Finally, you can append data to an existing file. This is generally important since there are many situations in which you may want to record a history of actions such as for a log file to trace any unwanted events in your game. Or perhaps you are storing the chat log for the current game into a file.

```
//appends to the text file created earlier
#include <fstream>
#include <iostream>

using namespace std;

int main(int argc, char* argv[])
{

  //define the file object
  fstream outfile;

  outfile.open( "data.txt" );
  if( !outfile.good() )
  {

    cerr << "There was a problem opening data.txt" << endl;
    return -1;
  }

  outfile << endl << "This data is appended." << endl;

  outfile.flush();
  outfile.close();

  return 0;
}
```

Binary Streams

While reading and writing to text files is the desired use of file input/output for some cases, there also exists the real need for a game programmer to add binary stream support to the code base. Perhaps you wish to record high-score information from the current player, which is used to calculate a ranking on a Web site somewhere. You certainly do not want this data modified or tampered with. Another case for needing binary file support is that most third-party applications that create game content load and store their data in binary form.

RANDOM-ACCESS FILES

So far, you have covered three modes of working with files: reading, writing, and appending. However, large blocks of data can often contain many different pieces of information. When you need to work with these large amounts of data, it becomes inefficient (and troublesome) to attempt to find a certain record and/or location within the file. Reading the file line by line to parse out the information you need is not your only option.

To access the file randomly, you need to learn how to manipulate the *file pointer*. File pointers to a file are equivalent to the subscripts you use to manipulate an array. To help you perform this type of access, you must make heavy use of the seekg function. It simply requires an offset and a starting position in the file. This offset value is simply how many bytes of data you want to access from the given position.

```
seekg( offset, startFileLocation )
```

The startFileLocation parameter can be one of three values:

ios::beg : The beginning byte in the file.

ios::end : The last byte in the file.

ios::cur : The current location of the file pointer.

Listing 37.5 details how you might take advantage of this function to access specific items within your inventory.

LISTING 37.5   Working with different inventory items randomly.

```cpp
#include <fstream>

class Item {
public:
  char ID[5];
  char description[20];
  float cost;
  void printItem(int entry){
    cout << "item entry: " << entry << endl;
    cout << "item id: " << ID << endl;
    cout << "item description: " << description << endl;
    cout << "item cost: " << cost << endl;
  }

};

int main(int arc, char* argv[]){

  fstream iofile;

  return 0;
}
```

SUMMARY

In this chapter, you learned more about the ability to read and write data in both ASCII format (text files) and binary format. This has many applications in game development for recording a log file of user actions to debug any problems with the game, and for many other aspects such as loading the data associated with a level in the game, perhaps any 3D model information, and so forth. In the next chapter, you will focus on object serialization: the ability for C++ objects to read and write data to and from files.

EXERCISES

37.1 How do you open a text file? Binary file?

37.2 Create a simple logger class that opens a file, appends text to it, and then closes it again.

38　Object Serialization

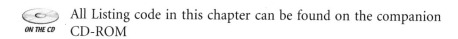

All Listing code in this chapter can be found on the companion
CD-ROM

OBJECT SERIALIZATION

In the previous chapter, you learned how to perform some simple file operations such as opening a text file and outputting some strings to a binary file. This might be more than enough for some tasks you might require in a game environment, such as recording game statistics to a file or recording any special game events. However, as your game world data becomes more complex, it can be a requirement to create an advanced system of loading or saving game objects. For example, a common task might be to load and store items the player has in his inventory. Or perhaps there needs to be a way to store the current state of everything in the game world.

Using the capabilities of the C++ language and the file stream objects, you are able to do much more than simply open and close text data. You also have the ability of your objects to *serialize* into and out of file streams. In other words, your objects can internally "know" how to load and save themselves to a file stream, which can save a lot of unnecessary typing and debugging if you were to do this by hand. This definitely presents a benefit to using the C++ language for your game!

When adding this type of capability to your application, there are a few things to be made aware of:

■ Objects are written to files in a compressed binary format. This makes it tougher for the average person to easily modify your game structures. It also creates a smaller file size for storage purposes.

■ To view the data stored in the files, you must write the necessary software to read the data into classes that are in the same structure and format as the class writing the data in the first place.

■ The class used to write the data to the file must match in the number and format of data members to the class used to read the data from the file. However, the member functions themselves do not need to match.

To provide some illustration of this concept, you will work with a small class that represents a player's inventory within a game. The inventory container is a common structure in a game that is capable of holding multiple items.

Listing 38.1 details how you might approach writing an object to a file.

LISTING 38.1   Object serialization (writing).

```cpp
#include <fstream>
#include <string>
#include <iostream>

using namespace std;

class Item
{
  char id[5];
  char description[256];
  float cost;
public:
  Item()
  {
    description[0] = '\0';
    id[0]          = '\0';
  }

  Item( char nid[], char ndesc[], float ncost) : cost(ncost)
  {
    strcpy( id, nid );
    strcpy( description, ndesc );
  }
```

```
};

class Bag
{
  Item items[5];   //can only hold 5 items
public:
  static int number_in_bag; //how many items we currently have
  Bag(){}
  void PushItem( char [], char [], float );
  void WriteToDisk();
};

int Bag::number_in_bag = 0;

void Bag::PushItem( char ID[], char desc[], float price )
{
  items[number_in_bag] = Item( ID, desc, price );
  number_in_bag++;
}

void Bag::WriteToDisk()
{
  ofstream outfile("INVENTORY.DAT");            /** open file for
  writing */
  outfile.write((char *)this, sizeof(*this));/** write item array
*/
}

int main(int argc, char* argv[])
{
  /** declare an instance of our Bag */
  Bag BagOfHolding;
  /** push two item objects into the bag */
  BagOfHolding.PushItem("1", "Potion of Healing", 1.4f);
  BagOfHolding.PushItem("2", "Big Sword", 10.0f);
  /** write the contents of the bag to disk */
  BagOfHolding.WriteToDisk();
  /** display a count of the items we have so far */
  cout << Bag::number_in_bag << " items were written. " << endl;

  return 0;
}
```

As you can see in Listing 38.1, when you instantiate the Bag instance, you are also creating a five element array of type Item. Although in Listing 38.1 you only add two items to the Bag instance, the entire array of five items is recorded to disk in the WriteToDisk() method.

When you add a new item to the bag container, you also increment the static item counter to prepare for the next item.

Do not forget to add bounds checking to the PushItem method to guard against more than 10 elements being added to the TenSlotBag.

In the WriteToDisk method of the object, you are dumping the contents of the this pointer, which is all 10 Items, to the disk. The write function you are using through the file stream only supports the input of char pointers. Therefore, any data being written to the stream must first be cast as a char pointer.

The INVENTORY.DAT file is in binary format, so you need to create a method within the TenSlotBag object to read items stored in a file. Listing 38.2 demonstrates what needs to be added to display your bag contents to the screen.

LISTING 38.2

```cpp
#include <iostream>
#include <fstream>
#include <string>

using namespace std;

/**
 * This object is used to track inventory items for us. While
   nothing
 * spectacular, it does allow us to handle basic serialization of
   reading
 * and writing to disk
 */
class Item
{
public:
    char id[5];                  /** id of our item */
    char description[256];       /** some friendly description */
    float cost;                  /** cost of the item */
public:
    Item()
    {
        description[0] = '\0';
    }

    Item( char nid[], char ndesc[], float ncost) : cost(ncost)
    {
        strcpy( id, nid );
        strcpy( description, ndesc );
    }
```

```
  };

  class TenSlotBag
  {
    Item items[10];              /** can only hold 10 items  */
  public:
    static int number_in_bag; /** how many items we currently have */
    TenSlotBag(){}
    void PushItem( char [], char [], float );
    void WriteToDisk();
    void ReadFromDisk();
    void PrintToScreen();
  };

  void TenSlotBag::ReadFromDisk()
  {
    ifstream infile("INVENTORY.DAT");         /** open the inventory
    file*/
    infile.read((char*)this, sizeof(*this) ); /** read into items
    array */
  }

  void TenSlotBag::PrintToScreen()
  {
    cout << "Here are the items in this container " << endl;
    int counter = 0;
    while(items[counter].id[0])
    {
      cout << "Item ID: " << items[counter].id << end;
      cout << "Item Description: " << items[counter].description <<
      endl;
      cout << "Item Cost: " << items[counter].cost << endl;
      counter++;
    }
  }

  int main(int argc, char* argv[])
  {
    TenSlotBag Bag;            /** our TenSlotBag instance */
    Bag.ReadFromDisk();       /** read the bag inventory from disk */
    Bag.PrintToScreen();      /** print it to the screen */
    return 0;
  }
```

Similar to the way you used the write method to record your objects to disk, the read method functions in the same way. The first parameter of the read function used in the readFromDisk member function is the this pointer casted to a char pointer. The second parameter is the size of the current `this` pointer. Since it is within the `TenSlotBag` object that has the array of `Items`, the `this` pointer will be large enough to store the object's contents even if all 10 slots were filled. If you run the Example38_2 program, you will see the output shown in Figure 38.1.

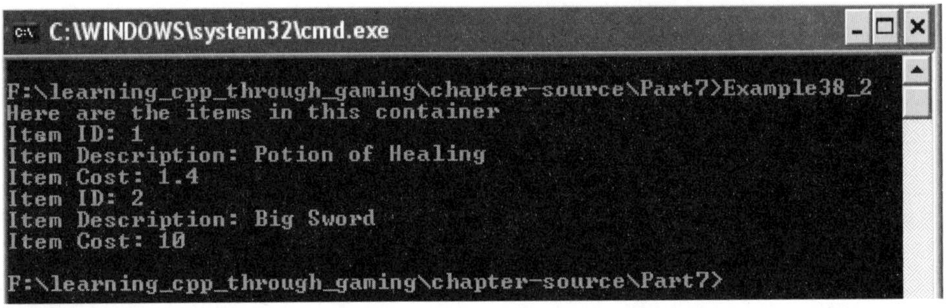

FIGURE 38.1 Example38_2.cpp output.

SUMMARY

The ability to read and write objects to and from the disk can be critical to the proper organization of your game world. This keeps your game data more hidden from prying eyes, and provides a method to load data into the appropriate game object. In the project for Part VII, you will learn how to leverage your object serialization skills to the Battleship game modifications that were created at the end of Part VI.

EXERCISES

38.1 What is serialization?

38.2 Create a simple `Player` class that contains three attributes: `name`, `level`, and `health`. Overload the necessary operators in this class to allow 10 `Player` objects be loaded or stored.

39

Adding Object Serialization to the Battleship Game

In This Chapter

■ Class Additions

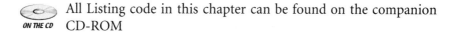 All Listing code in this chapter can be found on the companion CD-ROM

A t the end of Part VI, you explored using the C++ language to create some modifications to the Battleship game. Using the lessons learned in Part VII, you can now add a way to load and save your game to data files. To refresh your memory, this is also known as *object serialization*.

For the purpose of this modification to the existing Battleship code base, the goal of this project is to load and store a "*state*" of the game. In other words, you will be able to load or save the game at any given point during a session.

You can follow along by reviewing the source code contained in the Project39_1.h and Project39_1.cpp files on the companion CD-ROM.

CLASS ADDITIONS

The first step involved in adding some serialization support to the game, is to identify exactly what data you wish to serialize. Even though there are numerous ways to approach the issue of serialization support, you will first take a more basic approach. You will simply add some member functions to the Gameboard class definition originally created in Project36 from Chapter 36.

Throughout this section of the material, you have already learned the necessary methods to implement these serialization member functions, so only small snippets of code need to be presented.

Listing 39.1 displays the new loading and storing member functions to the Gameboard object.

LISTING 39.1 Gameboard definition with new member functions.

```
class Gameboard
{
  //snip!

  /**
  * toDisk — This method saves our game state into the
  * battleship.dat file. The key is the *this pointer!
  */
  void toDisk(){
    //define an output stream to write the game data to
    ofstream gamefile("battleship.dat");
    //use the write method to dump the contents of this object
    gamefile.write((char*)this, sizeof(*this));
  }
  /**
  * fromDisk — This method loads our game state from the
  * battleship.dat file. Note that we could add a mechanism
  * to load data from any given dat file, but this is good for now.
  */
  void fromDisk(){
    //define an input stream to load the game data to
    ifstream gamefile("battleship.dat");
    //use the read method to pull in the conents of the file into
    //this object
    gamefile.read((char*)this, sizeof(*this));
  }
}
```

That was easy!

The only addition(s) you really needed to make for this part of the Project, was displayed in Listing 39.1. If you recall from your introduction to the *this pointer in Chapter 31, it is added by the compiler as a parameter to each and every class member function. For proper handling by the input or output file streams, you read or write the class data by using the member functions of the file stream to either load the binary data from the file into the current *this pointer, or you save the contents of the current *this pointer to a binary data file.

Although you provided some basic loading and storing support to the current Battleship project, there are many other tasks within the scope of serialization that you can implement.

Multiple data files—The goal of this task is to allow the player to specify where to load and store any game data. This can be just a parameter to the game, specifying a path to the desired data file.

Data verification—Although it only takes one or two lines of C++ code to load or store your game data, you are not performing any data verification whatsoever. In other words, when you are loading in game data, you are working under the assumption that the data in the given file is the same size, structure, and format of the classes defined in your project. Add some verification checks to ensure that the loaded data is valid before you store it directly into your objects.

There are many other additions and modifications that can be made to the program, but for now they are left as "bonus" excercises for you.

SUMMARY

In this final chapter of Part VII, you learned how to add some basic object serialization to your Battleship project. Most of game programming today revolves around displaying some kind of information to the player in graphical form. As such, Part VIII revolves around discussion of using the Simple DirectMedia Layer to display some graphics to the player, and process keyboard commands.

EXERCISES

39.1 Currently the project creates binary data files during the serialization process. Alter the loading and saving somewhat by allowing the game to store everything in human readable text format.

39.2 If the game's data is stored in human readable text, then modify the program to ensure the data files being loaded are valid.

Part VIII

Graphics with Simple DirectMedia Layer

In Part VII, you learned how to work with the C++ `iostream` library to read and write text and binary data to file streams. You also learned how to add serialization support to your C++ objects, which allows you to load and save your object's internal data to binary file streams.

In Part VIII, you will shift your focus slightly to concentrate on a large portion of what goes into a game—the graphics. You will be using the Simple DirectMedia Layer (SDL) library to access your video, input, and sound hardware without much effort on your part. One of the many benefits of SDL is that it is a cross-platform library, meaning that the code you produce with this library is capable of running on the Windows, Linux, and MacOS platforms. You will learn how to create and work with basic sprite objects, and create a small OO hierarchy of your own to handle game projects.

At the end of this part of the book, you will be able to leverage these skills to focus on adding some rudimentary graphics support to the battleship game. Enjoy!

40

Introduction to Simple DirectMedia Layer (SDL)

In This Chapter

■ Setting up SDL

 All Listing code in this chapter can be found on the companion CD-ROM

A popular choice among game developers, both beginners and experts alike, is the Simple DirectMedia Layer. It is a cross-platform library that functions as a thin layer between your game and the underlying operating system. In effect, this makes it possible for a game written using SDL to run on various versions of Windows as well as other platforms such as Linux and the MacOS.

SETTING UP SDL

Contained on the accompanying CD-ROM is the latest installation of the SDL for the Windows platform.

If you are not running on the Windows platform, be sure to find the appropriate version of SDL for your operating system at www.libsdl.org, the SDL homepage.

When you launch the setup application, there will be a few install dialogs you can quickly read before continuing with the installation. By default, the SDL will be located at C:\SDL on your hard drive.

The next step is to ensure the necessary SDL header files are properly included in your IDE. Be sure to check with your IDE documentation to properly set the path in the IDE to point to the SDL directory containing the necessary header and library files, which are usually contained in C:\SDL\include and C:\SDL\lib folders.

When you compile any application using the SDL, you must also change a few settings. In the Visual Studio IDE for the Windows platform, you must ensure that your projects are using the multi-threaded DLL runtime.

The final thing to remember is that you will need to ensure that your application links with the SDL.lib and SDLMain.lib library files whenever you compile projects using the SDL.

For further clarification on setting up and configuring your compiler for use with SDL, consult the included documentation with the library.

Initializing SDL

Since SDL provides a layer for your application to go through when communicating with audio, video, or input devices, it is essential to let the SDL properly initialize the underlying hardware in your machine. By letting the SDL handle the mundane tasks of initializing video, input, and audio devices on your system, you are able to get to work on actually making your game. Initialization of the SDL is performed through the SDL_Init function outlined in Listing 40.1.

LISTING 40.1 SDL_Init.

```
int rc = 0;
rc = SDL_Init( SDL_INIT_EVERYTHING );
if(rc < 0)
{
  /** error initializing SDL */
  return false;
}
```

That is all you need to do to initialize the SDL subsystem layer! The SDL_Init function takes only one parameter depending on the subsystem you want to access during your program. Listing 40.2 outlines the other options available.

LISTING 40.2   `SDL_Init.`

```
int SDL_Init(Uint32 flags);
```

The flags parameter can be one or a combination of the following:

`SDL_INIT_TIMER:` This initializes the timer subsystem
`SDL_INIT_AUDIO:` This initializes the audio subsystem and devices
`SDL_INIT_VIDEO:` This initializes the video subsystem and internal devices
`SDL_INIT_EVERYTHING:` This initializes all of the timer, audio, video and joystick subsystems.

Although it might be obvious at this point, it is worth repeating that it is essential that you initialize the proper subsystem through SDL before using it.

Shutting Down SDL

Since SDL provides a layer for your application to go through when communicating with audio, video, or input devices, it is important to let SDL shut everything down and perform proper memory cleanup. This can be done at any location in your program; however, it is usually performed during the shutdown and cleanup operations of your game. To shut everything down, you simply need to call the `SDL_Quit` function as shown in Listing 40.3.

LISTING 40.3   `SDL_Quit.`

```
SDL_Quit();
```

You do not need any parameters, and the function does not return any error code to handle or inspect.

In short, it is very simple to initialize and shut down the SDL library!

Your First SDL Program

With the amount of information and detail you have learned on the SDL so far in this chapter, you should be ready to create your first full SDL application. Using the code in this chapter, you will initialize the SDL, create a video display surface, and then put the program into a continuous loop waiting for your input. Once you press the Esc key, the window will close, the SDL will be shut down, and control will be returned to the operating system.

To take advantage of the C++ language, you will create a very small set of C++ classes to use for this chapter and for the remaining chapters in the book. This will then allow you to quickly lay down the groundwork for any other game you want to build.

The `MainApplication` Object

The `MainApplication` object will be your first class designed to encapsulate the very basic necessities of communicating with SDL and starting up your game. For the class definition, look at Listing 40.4 which is also included on the accompanying CD-ROM.

LISTING 40.4 `MainApplication.h`.

```
class MainApplication
{
public:
  /** default constructor */
  MainApplication();
  /** virtual destructor */
  virtual ~MainApplication();
  /** perform the creation code for the entire application
  * @param const char* — title of window
  * @return bool — true if initialized properly
  */
  bool createApp(const char* strAppTitle);

  /** puts the application into the "main loop" which will only
  * return when the player quits the application
  * @return — any error code we want
  */
  int runApp();
  /** cleanup and destroy the application */
  void destroyApp();
  /** virtual function for creating game objects
  * @return bool — true if created ok
  */
  virtual bool createGame(){ return true; }
  /** virtual function for updating game objects
  * @param float — elapsed time since last update
  */
  virtual void updateGame(float){};
  /** virtual function for destroying game objects */
  virtual void destroyGame(){};
};
```

The basic theory behind the use of the `MainApplication` object will need to be understood to properly use it in your game. Whenever you want to use this object in your program, you will need to create a new application object, which is derived from the `MainApplication` class. Whenever you then use this derived object, you only need to override the `createGame`, `updateGame`, and `destroyGame` member functions. The rest are handled by the `MainApplication` base object. Listing 40.5 provides the derived object you will use for your first SDL application.

LISTING 40.5   MyApp.

```cpp
/**
* We want to use the MainApplication object but extend it to allow our
* own specific instance
*/
class MyApp : public MainApplication
{
protected:
  SDLCanvas* pCanvas;   /** pointer to the SDLCanvas */
public:
  /**constructor*/
  MyApp();
  /**destructor */
  ~MyApp();
  /** virtual function for creating game objects
  * @return bool — true if created ok
  */
  bool createGame();
  /** virtual function for updating game objects
  * @param float — elapsed time since last update
  */
  void updateGame(float);
  /** virtual function for destroying game objects */
  void destroyGame();
};
```

Seeing this object in the actual source code for your game might help clear up any confusion. HelloWorld.cpp contains the necessary use of the `MyApp` object and is provided in Listing 40.6.

LISTING 40.6   HelloWorld.cpp.

```cpp
int main(int argc, char* argv[])
{
  /** declare instance of MyApp */
  MyApp objApp;

  if(!objApp.createApp("Hello World"))
  {
    /** if MyApp failed to initialize, then return error code */
    return -1;
  }
```

```
        /** put MyApp into the "main loop" which only exits when game
quits */
        return( objApp.runApp() );
    }
```

Notice that you are just using the core member functions of the `MainApplication` object to start the system up and run everything. This is also known as a *driver* since it is responsible for setting up the application and making sure everything is continuously running properly. You will see more of the `MyApp` implementation later in this chapter once you are introduced to the rendering object. If you launch the `HelloWorld` example in this chapter, you will see a window appear with the title "`HelloWorld`" as shown in Figure 40.1.

FIGURE 40.1   HelloWorld output.

The SDL/Windows Event Queue

A main driving force behind the design of Windows is that it is an *event-driven* operating system. This means that as you perform an action in your application, either by clicking the mouse or resizing your application window, the corresponding event is being generated and posted to your application's main message queue by the operating system.

Figure 40.2 shows an overview of this process.

The SDL follows this same design philosophy, and every SDL application must define and use an event queue to listen for any specific events. Listing 40.7 displays the basic event queue that is contained within the `MainApplication::runApp` method.

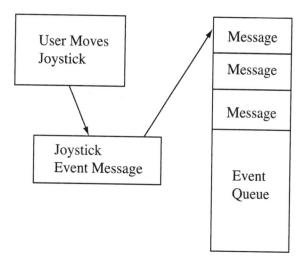

FIGURE 40.2   Event messages generated and passed to the queue.

LISTING 40.7   MainApplication::runApp.

```
int MainApplication::runApp()
{
  bool bDone = false;   // is main loop finished?
  SDL_Event event;       // temp variable to store current event

  // as long as our main loop is not done
  while(!bDone)
  {
    //check the event queue for the next message
    while( SDL_PollEvent(&event) )
    {
      // while we have an event message in the queue,
      // you need to determine what it is
      switch ( event.type )
      {

        case SDL_QUIT : // if user wishes to quit
          bDone = true; // this implies the main loop is done
        break;

        default: //default is to do nothing
          break;

      } //end switch
    } //end while( SDL_PollEvent )
```

```
        //update the game here since the events are done processing
        //ie. the Process Phase

    } //end while( !bDone )
    //the game is finished and is exiting. Do the garbage collection
    destroyApp();
    //no errors, return 0
    return 0;
}
```

The event queue in Listing 40.7 is a very basic method of structuring the main loop of your application. You are putting the program into a continuous loop, which is only responsible for listening to the SDL event queue. If there was a message received in the queue, test it to see whether it is the quit event. If it is, then signal to the main loop that you are ready to exit. If it is not the quit event or if there are no messages detected in the event queue, it is time to process one frame of your game. After one frame has been updated and rendered, the loop will start again at the beginning to test whether there is an SDL event message waiting in the queue.

SDLCanvas

The SDLCanvas object is next in line, and this will encapsulate some of the basic operations behind the interaction with the video hardware and SDL.

The SDLCanvas object is responsible for using the SDL drawing operations to interact with your video hardware.

This will become clearer as you proceed through this chapter and the rest of this book, and so you will begin by defining the SDLCanvas object shown in Listing 40.8.

LISTING 40.8   SDLCanvas definition.

```
    /** This object is used as an attempt to encapsulate the more
common
     * tasks or operations when working with graphics
     */
    class SDLCanvas
    {
    protected:
      SDL_Surface* pSurface; /** our SDL_Surface for drawing */

    public:
      /** constructor */
      SDLCanvas();
      /** destructor */
      ~SDLCanvas();
```

```
/** This function just creates the video surface according to our
 * needs
 * @param int    - width of video surface
 * @param int    - height of video surface
 * @param int    - bits-per-pixel of surface
 * @param bool   - windowed or fullscreen?
 * @return bool  - true if everything's ok
 */
bool createCanvas( int width, int height, int depth,
 bool windowed = true );
/** destroy our video surface */
void destroyCanvas();
};
```

You have seen code snippets throughout this chapter on how to initialize the SDL system for drawing, but for completeness, Listing 40.9 provides the details.

LISTING 40.9 SDLCanvas::createCanvas.

```
bool SDLCanvas::createCanvas( int width, int height,
  int depth, bool windowed)
{
  /** just use SDL to create our surface */
  pSurface = SDL_SetVideoMode( width, height, depth, SDL_SWSURFACE );

  //if there was an error during main surface creation, then return
  //an error code
  if( pSurface == NULL )
    return false;

  return true; //everything is okay!
}
```

Adding SDLCanvas to MyApp

Earlier in this chapter, you wrote the HelloWorld.cpp implementation and left the program there while the SDLCanvas object was discussed. Now it is okay to return to your MyApp class to add the use of the SDLCanvas object. Listing 40.10 provides some additional detail.

LISTING 40.10 MyApp::createGame.

```
bool MyApp::createGame()
{
  //SDL is already initialized for us at this point
  //Initialize the renderer
  pCanvas = new SDLCanvas();
```

```
        //create the windowed display screen in 640x480 using 32-bit
pixels */
        if(!pCanvas->createCanvas( 640, 480, 32, true ) )
        {
          //failure!
          return false;
        }

        return true;
    }
```

In Listing 40.10, you are creating the SDLCanvas object and attempting to create a windowed rendering surface of 640×480. If there are no errors, the MyApp object will next be launched into a continuous loop by the MainApplication driver until the Esc key is pressed.

To properly clean up the SDLCanvas object, you just need to put the necessary call to the delete operator within the destroyGame member function of the MyApp object. Listing 40.11 provides some clarification.

LISTING 40.11   MyApp::destroyGame().

```
    void MyApp::destroyGame()
    {
      if( pCanvas )
      {
        delete pCanvas;
        pCanvas = NULL;
      }
    }
```

The destructor of the SDLCanvas object handles the internal call to the destroy-Canvas function, which is responsible for performing all the garbage collection for any internal allocated memory.

There was a lot going on in this chapter, so make sure you take the time to go over the accompanying source code to understand how the objects in this small program are interconnected.

SUMMARY

Although there are many useful C++ libraries on the Internet to help the game developer, a popular choice is the SDL library. It is a small, lightweight utility library that allows you to run your programs on multiple operating systems and platforms. This chapter also demonstrated how to wrap the essentials of the SDL into a small set of C++ classes that will save you time for developing games. It demonstrates a clear benefit of virtual inheritance within an application, as it enables you to create a small object hierarchy that allows for improved readability and debugging. In the next chapter, you will learn more about working with surfaces in SDL; a key aspect behind making any images or graphics presented to the player in a high-performance application.

EXERCISES

40.1 What is SDL?

40.2 What platforms does SDL run on?

40.3 Who created SDL?

40.4 Explain what a video display is in SDL.

41

Working with Graphic Surfaces

In This Chapter

- Displaying TrueType Fonts with SDLCanvas
- Creating a Basic Sprite
- Displaying Images on Sprites
- Creating the SDLSprite

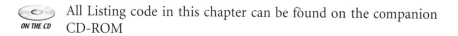 All Listing code in this chapter can be found on the companion CD-ROM

In Chapter 40, you learned how to initialize and create a video display surface using the SDL. You were able to request a video display size, with which SDL would attempt to create a surface for displaying your game content. In this chapter, you will focus on learning about basic TrueType font drawing, and working with basic objects that can be moved around the screen. In game programming terminology, the objects you manipulate to represent either the player or perhaps some monsters in your game are commonly referred to as *sprites*.

DISPLAYING TRUETYPE FONTS WITH SDLCanvas

When working with video surfaces through SDL, you may begin to wonder how a game (or any SDL application) notifies the player of any information. In other words, how can you print any status or debugging information to the main screen? A popular component developed and used by the SDL community is the SDL_ttf library, which is a basic wrapper for using TrueType Fonts.

On the Windows platform, the TrueType fonts were initially introduced with the release of Windows 3.1, and allowed you to easily scale your font size to almost any dimension, while still maintaining a crisp, sharp presentation. The underlying font presentation engine has evolved through the different versions of Windows, but the core concept of TrueType font presentation still remains today.

Adding TrueType Capability to SDLCanvas

As with every other SDL library you have been using so far, the main goal of the SDL_ttf library is to encapsulate and shield you from the necessary underlying layer of the font usage. Once initialized, it is simple to present any text to the player.

Rather than reprint the SDLCanvas object, you will only see the new additions made to the object to process text drawing. Listing 41.1 provides an updated version of the SDLCanvas class.

LISTING 41.1   Updated SDLCanvas.h/.cpp.

```
/** This object is used as an attempt to encapsulate the more
common
 * tasks or operations when working with graphics
 */
class SDLCanvas
{
protected:
  SDL_Surface* pSurface; /** our SDL_Surface for drawing */
  TTF_Font* pFont;       /** our TrueType font */
public:
  /** snip! */
  /**
   * This function is used to load the specified TrueType font for
   * use by our SDLCanvas object. For now it only supports one font
   * at a time
   * @param char* - font family we want (ie. Arial )
   * @param int   - size of the font (ie. 8, 10 or 12 )
   * @return bool - true if we're gtg
   */
  bool createFont( char* strFontFace, int size )
  {
```

```
        if( TTF_Init() < 0 )
        {
          //error loading the library
          return false;
        }
        pFont = TTF_OpenFont(strFontFace, size);
        if (pFont == NULL)
        {
          //error loading font!
          return false;
        }

        return true;
    }
```

That is all you need to start the SDL_ttf library. If you did not perform any error checking, you can reduce the initialization to one line!

Printing Text

The SDL_ttf font library layer is now initialized, so you can begin rendering any text you want to the video surface being presented to the player.

Again, since the SDL_ttf library handles the majority of the heavy lifting for you, you only need to add one more function to the SDLCanvas object to allow for rendering. Listing 41.2 has more details.

LISTING 41.2   Printing text through SDLCanvas.

```
    /** This object is used as an attempt to encapsulate the more
common
    * tasks or operations when working with graphics
    */
    class SDLCanvas
    {
    protected:
      SDL_Surface* pSurface;          /** our SDL_Surface for drawing */
      SDL_Surface* pFontSurface;      /** our SDL_Surface for fonts */
      TTF_Font* pFont;                /** our TrueType font */
    public:
      /** snip! */
      /** This method just prints the desired text to the screen
      * using the true-type library
      * @param fgR, fgB, fgB, fgA - the foreground color to use
      * @param bgR, bgB, bgB, bgA - the background color to use
      * @param strText* - the text to draw
      * @param textquality - solid, blended or shaded
      */
```

```
        void printText(char fgR, char fgG, char fgB, char fgA,
          char bgR, char bgG, char bgB, char bgA,
          char* strText, textquality quality )
      {
        SDL_Color fgColor = {fgR,fgG,fgB,fgA};
        SDL_Color bgColor = {bgR,bgG,bgB,bgA};

        if (quality == solid)
        {
          *pFontSurface = TTF_RenderText_Solid(pFont, strText,
fgColor);

        } else if (quality == shaded)
        {
          *pFontSurface = TTF_RenderText_Shaded(pFont, strText,
fgColor,
            bgColor);
        }
        else if (quality == blended)
          *pFontSurface = TTF_RenderText_Blended(pFont, strText,
fgColor);

      }
```

That is all there is to writing and displaying text to the screen.

Although every version of the Windows operating system has its own TrueType system fonts, it is against the license agreement of Windows to distribute the fonts with your game. In other words, you can refer and load them from your game; however, you cannot include the *.ttf files with your project without the end user being obligated to agree to the end-user license for the fonts provided by Microsoft. However, one can obtain many free-to-distribute TrueType fonts available from the Internet.

CREATING A BASIC SPRITE

Before you can learn how to create fantastical monsters or super powerful boss enemies for your game, you first need to learn the basics behind using a sprite. As such, it is best to start with a basic sprite that simply positions itself where you tell it to. Using the SDLCanvas you created in Chapter 40, you can create a small object to handle sprite objects. You can start with a base object called SDLSprite that you can use as the basic sprite to manipulate in your program. Listing 41.3 provides a definition of the SDLSprite class.

LISTING 41.3   SDLSprite.

```
class SDLSprite
{
public:

  int posx; /** x position of the sprite */
  int posy; /** y position of the sprite */

  int dimx; /** how wide the sprite rectangle is */
  int dimy; /** how tall the sprite rectangle is */

public:
  /** constructor */
  SDLSprite()
  {
    posx = posy = 0;
    dimx = dimy = 0;

  }
  /** virtual destructor */
  virtual ~SDLSprite(){};
  /** Easy way to set the position of your Sprite
  * @param x, y - x and y positions
  */
  void setPos(int x, int y){ posx = x; posy = y; }
  /** Easy way to set the dimension (width, height) of the Sprite
  * @param x,y - width and height of sprite
  */
  void setDim(int x, int y){ dimx = x; dimy = y; }
};
```

As you can see, there is a setPos member function, which is responsible for setting the position of your sprite on the screen. The setDim member function is responsible for setting the dimensions of the sprite. To work properly with a sprite, either to set its position or change its dimension, it is necessary to discuss the basics of coordinate systems.

If you recall from mathematics, the Cartesian Coordinate system involves segmenting the world into a grid aligned on two axes (actually three, but you only need to worry about two dimensions for now); the x and y axes. The x-axis travels horizontally and the y-axis segments the world vertically. Figure 41.1 provides some clarification.

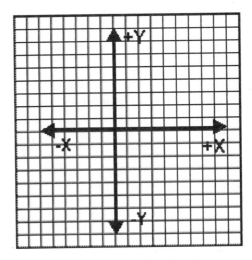

FIGURE 41.1   2D Cartesian Coordinates.

Sprite Movement/Animation

Now that you have learned how to position your sprites on the screen, the next step to making them appear in a game situation is to discuss how to actually move a sprite.

When you are moving any kind of sprite object around in your game, it is necessary to perform basic animation techniques with the help of the SDL to provide the illusion of smooth animation.

At its foundation, making sprites appear as if they are moving and exploding in your game world is actually an easy process. In Chapter 40, you were introduced to the concept of surfaces during the explanation about the creation of the video device. When you created the SDLCanvas device capable of handling the drawing on your screen, you also created a double buffering surface mechanism for fast animation.

Double Buffering

To help provide fast graphics and high-speed animation, games use the concept of double buffering to draw the game. When you create the surface used for the video device in the SDLRenderer object, the library is internally setting up two video surfaces to work with in memory. This creates what is known as a *surface chain*. The front buffer, or *primary surface*, is what appears to the player on screen. Due to design constraints of the underlying operating system and video hardware, you can never modify the contents of the front buffer directly. To change what is being displayed, it is first necessary to modify the other surface in the chain; the back buffer. The back buffer is usually another surface contained in memory that is the same size as the front buffer. To perform an update of the front buffer, follow these steps:

1. Clear the back buffer. This erases all of the previous content and then sits patiently waiting you to paint on it.
2. Draw your object(s) to the back buffer. Now that it has been cleared, position your objects that you want to see in the next frame and then draw them to the back buffer.
3. Once this is finished, signal the front buffer to exchange (or flip) itself with the back buffer.
4. Known also as *page flipping*, you draw the contents of the next frame for your game on the back buffer and then signal the two buffers need to be flipped. The front buffer becomes the new back buffer, while the existing back buffer containing the next frame of your game is promoted to the front. When done fast enough, it provides the illusion of high speed within your game. Figure 41.2 details how this process works.

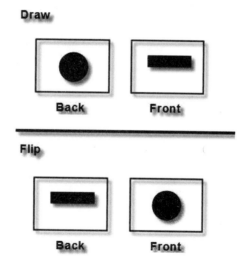

FIGURE 41.2   Page flipping.

Adding to SDLCanvas

Since you will need a mechanism to clear the back buffer and signal a page flip, these are good candidates for member functions of the SDLCanvas object. Listing 41.4 provides the additions to the object.

LISTING 41.4 Adding to SDLCanvas.

```
/** This object is used as an attempt to encapsulate the more
common
 * tasks or operations when working with graphics
 */
class SDLCanvas
{
protected:
   SDL_Surface* pSurface;        /** our SDL_Surface for drawing */
   SDL_Surface* pFontSurface;    /** our SDL_Surface for fonts */
   TTF_Font* pFont;              /** our TrueType font */
public:
   /** snip! */
   /** This function merely clears our back buffer */
   void clearCanvas();
   /** This function initiates the page flipping process */
   void flipCanvas();
```

For some actual implementation code, Listing 41.5 details the necessary SDL compatible code to add to the SDLCanvas object to implement the clearCanvas and flipCanvas functions.

LISTING 41.5 SDLCanvas additions.

```
bool SDLCanvas::clearCanvas()
{
  //if we can get a lock on the surface before drawing
  if(SDL_MUSTLOCK( pSurface ) )
  {
    if(SDL_LockSurface( pSurface ) < 0)
      return false;
  }
  //fill the surface with our chosen background color
  SDL_FillRect(
    pSurface,
    NULL,
    SDL_MapRGB(pSurface->format, 0,0,0 ) );

  return true;
}

void SDLCanvas::flipCanvas()
{
  //our video surface is still locked. Unlock it before doing
  //any flipping operations otherwise we incur huge performance
  //penalties
  if(SDL_MUSTLOCK( pSurface ))
  {
```

```
        SDL_UnlockSurface( pSurface );
    }
    //Finally, flip the surface chain!
    SDL_Flip( pSurface );
}
```

Locking Surfaces

As you may have noticed from Listing 41.5, there are calls to the SDL_LockSurface and SDL_UnlockSurface functions. When the front and back buffers of memory are created by SDL during the initialization of your video device, they are internally communicating with the video driver that they need a space large enough in the video card's onboard memory to store the front and back buffers. As your video hardware processes the hundreds or thousands of drawing calls every second, it must optimize the location of its internal buffers. This video memory is highly volatile and you cannot rely on where your own resources are at any given moment. As such, before you can begin to draw on your back buffer, you need to make a request to the underlying video hardware to lock down a section of memory for you to draw to using the SDL_LockSurface function. Once you are finished drawing your objects to the back buffer, you must also remember to tell the underlying video hardware that it can release this lock via the SDL_UnlockSurface function.

Forgetting to release this lock can cause serious performance problems and the possibility of strange behavior in other applications.

DISPLAYING IMAGES ON SPRITES

In every game using sprites, you will always need to use some kind of artwork or image that is overlaid onto your sprite object. This artwork is another tool used to create your compelling game for the player. In a game of checkers, for example, you will need to load the artwork the game uses to display the pieces of each player, along with the checkerboard the game is played on.

Earlier in this chapter, you learned some basics behind surface manipulation. You were introduced to the concepts of double buffering, which is used to create high-speed animation. Another use for surfaces is to create temporary storage areas for artwork and images. As you work with sprites in this chapter, this will become clearer.

Loading Artwork

The default image format supported by the SDL is the BMP (or bitmap) format most commonly used on the Windows platform. If you do some digging in any search engine, you will be able to learn more about image formats and the BMP extension. However, it is not the focus of this text to explain these details. For the moment, when you wish to load any of your favorite images into a game using the SDL, just be sure these images are saved with the BMP extension (supported by every paint program). The first step to using the artwork is to load up the image data into an SDL surface. Listing 41.6 details how this is done.

LISTING 41.6 Loading a bitmap.

```
SDL_Surface *pImage;
SDL_Surface *pTemp;

pTemp = SDL_LoadBMP("image.bmp");
if(pTemp == NULL)
{
  cout << "unable to load bitmap" << endl;
  return -1;
}

pImage = SDL_DisplayFormat(pTemp);
SDL_FreeSurface(pTemp);
```

In Listing 41.6, you are declaring two SDL_Surface pointers—one is used as a temporary working surface, while the other contains the final image data of the artwork you wish to load. The SDL_LoadBMP function is used to load the given image data into a temporary SDL_Surface object. If the image data fails to load, an error message is displayed for the player. Once the image has been properly loaded, it is then necessary to ensure that the image data properly matches the video surface format you are using to display your game to the screen. This is handled internally for you, with the SDL_DisplayFormat function, which converts the contents of one SDL_Surface into the final surface used by your game. The image data stored in the temporary SDL_Surface is then cleaned up with the execution of the SDL_FreeSurface function.

Displaying Image Data

Once the image data is loaded into an SDL_Surface object, it is available to be used in your game. To display the image on your screen is an easy task. Since the front and back buffers used for displaying your game are SDL_Surfaces, the process of displaying images is to simply copy the contents from the SDL_Surface containing the image data to the SDL_Surface used in your buffer chain. This is all accomplished with the SDL_BlitSurface function. Listing 41.7 details how this is done.

LISTING 41.7   Using SDL_BlitSurface.

```
SDL_Rect source, target;

//the source SDL_Rect structure is the size of the SDL_Surface
//containing the original image data (for this example)
source.x = 0;
source.y = 0;
source.w = image->w;
source.h = image->h;

//the target SDL_Rect structure contains the width and
//height dimensions of where on the screen we wish to
//display the image data
target.x = 100;
target.y = 100;
target.w = image->w;
target.h = image->h;

//Finally, use the SDL_BlitSurface function to copy the
//data defined by the contents of the source SDL_Rect,
//to the location on the screen defined by the other SDL_Rect
SDL_BlitSurface(pImage, &source, pScreen, &target);
```

CREATING THE SDLSprite

With the lessons learned in sprite manipulation thus far with the SDL, along with the concepts covered in this book, it makes logical sense to create a class definition that allows you to work with sprites. This is covered in the SDLSprite object located on the companion CD-ROM for this chapter. Feel free to follow along in the source code, as you will only cover the basics here.

ON THE CD

Listing 41.8 outlines the SDLSprite class.

LISTING 41.8   SDLSprite.

```
/**
* This object is used to encapsulate one or two useful ways of
drawing
* sprites to the main display
*/
class SDLSprite
{
```

```
public:
  SDL_Surface* pSurface; /** SDL_Surface to hold any data */
public:
  /** constructor */
  SDLSprite(){}
  /** virtual destructor */
  virtual ~SDLSprite(){}
  /** snip! */
};
```

To render the SDLSprite contents to the screen, you can modify the SDLCanvas object to handle the new sprite manipulation class. Listing 41.9 adds the necessary function to the SDLCanvas.

LISTING 41.9 SDLCanvas **modification.**

```
/** This object is used as an attempt to encapsulate the more
common
 * tasks or operations when working with graphics
 */
class SDLCanvas
{
protected:
  SDL_Surface* pSurface;        /** our SDL_Surface for drawing */
  SDL_Surface* pFontSurface;    /** our SDL_Surface for fonts */
  TTF_Font* pFont;              /** our TrueType font */
public:
  /** snip! */
  /** Draw the given SDLSprite object to our main SDL_Surface!
   * @param pSprite - pointer to our SDLSprite
   * @param x, y    - location of sprite on our main screen
   */
  void drawSprite( const SDLSprite* pSprite, int x, int y )
  {
    SDL_Rect dstRect;
    dstRect.x = x;
    dstRect.y = y;
    SDL_BlitSurface( pSprite->pSurface, NULL, pSurface, &dstRect );
  }
```

SUMMARY

This chapter introduced you to one of the foundations of computer gaming—sprites. Sprites allow you to graphically present and manipulate the data structures in your game, such as the player, and the monsters, along with any object in the game world. You modified the SDLRenderer class in order to work with the new SDL-Sprite object, which draws basic sprites that contain bitmap images. In the next chapter, you will tackle more critical components of any game; reading and processing the user's input, and playing music or sound effects audio through the sound hardware.

EXERCISES

41.1 What is a sprite?

41.2 What is double buffering? How does it help the graphics?

42

Using SDL for Input and Sound

In This Chapter

■ Handling Input
■ SDL Mixer

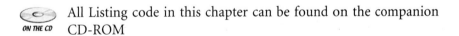 All Listing code in this chapter can be found on the companion CD-ROM

Y ou have covered quite a few concepts of SDL, and until now have just been focusing on displaying a bitmap (or sprite) to the screen. Since a game also requires the occasional input from the player to direct action on the screen, you will learn about processing input from the keyboard.

HANDLING INPUT

There is not too much to worry about for handling input from the keyboard. Since the SDL is a cross-platform library that provides a layer of abstraction, it handles the grunt work of creating and initializing your input devices.

Processing Keyboard Messages

As you learned during the introduction to SDL in Chapter 40, the library functions by providing an event queue that is constantly listening and processing SDL-related messages sent from your application. One such event is when the keyboard detects any action by the player. When the player presses or releases a key, an SDL_Event message is generated and posted to the event queue. Listing 42.1 details what is contained in this message.

LISTING 42.1   SDL_Event.

```
typedef struct
{
  Uint8 type;        //is SDL_KEYDOWN or SDL_KEYUP
  Uint8 state;       //is SDL_PRESSED or SDL_RELEASED
  SDL_keysym keysym; //the data containing the scan code and name
} SDL_KeyboardEvent;
```

To process what the player actually pressed or released, you just need to do some basic digging through this event structure posted to the queue. Listing 42.2, taken from Example 42.1, on the companion CD-ROM, contains a small function that prints out the received message.

ON THE CD

LISTING 42.2

```
void DisplayKeyInfo( SDL_KeyboardEvent *key )
{
  char keyInfo[256];
  char tempInfo[256];
  // Is it a release or a press?
  if( key->type == SDL_KEYUP )
    strcpy(keyInfo, "Release:- ");
  else
    strcpy(keyInfo, "Press:- ");

  // Print the hardware scancode
  sprintf( tempInfo, "Scancode: 0x%02X", key->keysym.scancode );
  strcat( keyInfo, tempInfo );

  // Print the name of the key
  sprintf( tempInfo, ", Name: %s\n",
    SDL_GetKeyName( key->keysym.sym ) );

  strcat( keyInfo, tempInfo );
  cout << keyInfo << endl;
}
```

SDL MIXER

As you learned through using SDL to process your input from the keyboard, another SDL library exists to help the management and playback of your audio effects. Since it is SDL compatible, the SDL Mixer library is also a cross-platform agent assigned the sole task of providing an abstraction layer between your program and the management of the underlying audio hardware. With SDL Mixer, you are able to play two types of audio files: digitized sound effects and music data.

Some Basic Audio Concepts

Although the SDL Mixer library successfully encapsulates most of the audio management for you, it can be helpful to understand some of the common nomenclature behind audio programming.

All sound waves are composed of two common characteristics:

Amplitude: On your basic wave figure, amplitude is the measure of the height of your sound wave from the base to the crest.

Frequency: Frequency is defined by the number of cycles per second the sound wave "pulses." This can also be known as the pitch of the sound and is measured in Hertz (Hz).

When you record or store your sound effect into digitized form for playback, you are telling the computer that you wish to record the amplitude of the sound. How often you record this amplitude is known as the *sampling rate*. In other words, the higher the sampling rate of a sound effect, the more the digitized form matches the amplitude of the original sound effect. A higher sampling rate does come at a storage cost.

To provide an example, CD-audio quality has a sampling rate of 44,000 Hz. This means that the computer has made 44,000 measurements of the amplitude per second while recording the sound. Taking fewer measurements per second will lower the size of the resulting audio file, but will lower the quality of your sample.

Initializing SDL Mixer

Now that you have covered some of the basic audio terminology, initializing the SDL Mixer library is not difficult, and is well contained within just two or three lines of code.

Listing 42.3 details how to initialize your audio layer using SDL Mixer.

LISTING 42.3 SDL Mixer initialization.

```
int audio_rate     = 22050;     //a 22050 Hz frequency rate
Uint16 audio_format = AUDIO_S16; // 16-bit stereo
int audio_channels  = 2;
int audio_buffers   = 4096;
//This is where we open up our audio device.
//Mix_OpenAudio takes as its parameters the audio format
//we'd *like* to have.
if(Mix_OpenAudio(audio_rate, //frequency
  audio_format, //audio format
  audio_channels, //2 for stereo, 1 for mono
  audio_buffers)) //bytes used per output sample
{
  return false;
}
//query the audio layer to see what we really ended up with
Mix_QuerySpec(&audio_rate, &audio_format, &audio_channels);
```

Working with Sound Effects

SDL Mixer provides an easy and effective layer to the loading and playback of sound effect files. Commonly, your sound effect data is stored in the WAV format, which is completely handled by the SDL Mixer library.

Loading Your Sound Effect

The actual loading of WAV audio data is a simple and painless process thanks to SDL Mixer. You use the Mix_Chunk object, which does the necessary work for you as shown in Listing 42.4.

LISTING 42.4 Loading with Mix_Chunk.

```
Mix_Chunk* pLaser = NULL;
pLaser = Mix_LoadWAV("laser.wav");
if(pLaser == NULL)
{
  //there was a problem loading the audio resource
  //display an error message, and return a failure code
  cerr << "Error loading laser sound effect" << endl;
  return -1;
}
```

That was easy.

Playing Your Sound Effect

The playback of your loaded `Mix_Chunk` object is also just as simple. You only need to let the object know how you want to play the sound effect, and it will worry about the rest. Listing 42.5 clarifies how this is done using the `Mix_PlayChannel` function provided by the library.

LISTING 42.5   `Mix_PlayChannel`.

```
//use the Mix_PlayChannel function to play the audio
//resource.
Mix_PlayChannel( -1, //use the first free channel
  pLaser,           //the audio resource to play
  -1 );             //number of times to loop the sound
                    //(-1 loops infinitely)
```

Sound Effect Cleanup

As with the other C++ objects you have created that are dynamic in nature, you need to ensure you properly clean them up when you no longer need the `Mix_Chunk` object. Listing 42.6 demonstrates how to use the `Mix_FreeChunk` function.

LISTING 42.6   `Mix_FreeChunk`.

```
//first you need to signal the audio library to stop playing
//all the samples. Using the -1 in the Mix_HaltChannel function
//stops playback of every channel
Mix_HaltChannel( -1 );

//free up any allocated memory for this resource
Mix_FreeChunk( pLaser );
```

Working with Music

Just about every game has some kind of accompanying background music or maybe even some incidental music as the player accomplishes some goal. SDL Mixer gives you the tools to play your own music file to enhance any and every aspect of your game. A popular audio type for music is currently the Ogg-Vorbis format. It has a similar type of compression that the popular Mpeg-3 (MP3) files have; however, there is one key difference. You do not need to pay for licensing to use Ogg-Vorbis, whereas with MP3 files you do.

Loading Your Music

The `Mix_Music` object within the library is responsible for handling your music files. Listing 42.7 provides the necessary steps behind loading an Ogg-Vorbis file.

LISTING 42.7 Loading `Mix_Music`.

```
Mix_Music* pMusic = NULL;

//load up the music
pMusic = Mix_LoadMUS("music.ogg");
if( pMusic == NULL )
{
  //there was a problem. Display an error and return an
  //error code
  cerr << "Error loading background music " << endl;
  return -1;
}
```

As you can see in Listing 42.7, you only need to use the `Mix_LoadMUS` function of the library to handle the work of loading your music data.

Playing Your Music

To play the loaded music object, you only need to use the `Mix_PlayMusic` function, which is responsible for communicating with your audio hardware. Listing 42.8 details how this function is used.

LISTING 42.8 Playing music.

```
//Mix_PlayMusic takes 2 parameters. The Mix_Music object that
//contains the music data, as well as how you would like this audio
file
//played.
//0 means you only want the music played one time through
//-1 signals that you want the music to loop continuously
Mix_PlayMusic( pMusic, 0 );
```

Music Cleanup

As with cleaning up your sound effect `Mix_Chunk` object, the destruction of the `Mix_Music` object is just as simple. Listing 42.9 shows how this is done.

LISTING 42.9 `Mix_FreeMusic`.

```
Mix_HaltMusic();          //halt all the music
Mix_FreeMusic( pMusic );  //free any allocated memory
Mix_CloseAudio();         //shutdown audio library
```

SUMMARY

The input and audio handling of your game is just as critical as the need to display graphics. In this chapter, you covered how to use and listen to the SDL event queue to receive messages from the keyboard. You also learned how to use the SDL Mixer library to help you with the playback of audio files, which is capable of supporting both WAV and OGG audio samples. In the next chapter, you arrive at the project for Part VIII that focuses on adding graphical SDL support to the Battleship game you have been working with so far.

EXERCISES

42.1 What is SDL_Mixer? What file formats does it support?

42.2 What input objects do I need to load up for use in SDL?

42.3 Modify the sample programs for this chapter to play a sound. Use a key to start and stop the sound being played.

43 Graphical Battleship

In This Chapter

■ Rendering the Graphics

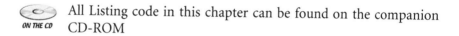 All Listing code in this chapter can be found on the companion CD-ROM

Building on the knowledge you gained in learning how to use SDL, you can re-visit the Battleship game developed in Part VII with the purpose of adding some simple graphics. Using your newfound discovery of SDL, putting some graphics into the game will be a snap!

 Much of the source code will be commented on during this chapter. To follow along, browse through the same source code on the companion CD-ROM contained in the /Chapter43 folder.

In theory, you should be able to leave your game logic and basic gameplay as they are. You are only concerned with the actual presentation of the game board and playing pieces. Using the SDL toolkit, you will be able to draw some sprites, and learn how to capture the player's input from the keyboard.

RENDERING THE GRAPHICS

For adding some new graphics to your Battleship game, you should first draft a list of tasks you will probably need to perform.

- Initialize and create our game window using SDL.
- Load any sprite images to use for the game.
- Draw the appropriate sprite for each object in the game.

ON THE CD

For this sprite management, you can reuse the SDLSprite object you learned about in Chapter 41. You just need to use a small array of them to represent the various objects within your Battleship game field, as outlined in more detail in the accompanying source code on the companion CD-ROM.

Capturing the Player's Input

In Chapter 42, you also learned how to manipulate and work with the SDL event queue to read the input messages generated by the player. You are not doing anything new for the Battleship game, and so the accompanying source code should provide more than enough detail in working with the keyboard messages sent by the player.

SUMMARY

This project concludes Part VIII, which introduced you to using the SDL to create and display images on the screen. This chapter also focused on demonstrating how input is taken from the player and how sound is played back. In the next and final part of this book, you will learn some more advanced topics of the C++ language. The section of the book then culminates with a simple shooter game demonstrating more C++ techniques.

EXERCISES

43.1 When the game is launched, allow the player to specify the window size of the game. Typically, graphical games use sizes such as 640 pixels wide by 480 pixels high (640×480 for short), 800×600 and 1024×768. Either present a small text menu before the screen is displayed to allow the player to choose between the three, or simply allow them to choose their desired size from the command line.

Part

IX

Advanced C++ Topics

In Part VIII, you learned how to leverage the SDL library to present simple sprites to the screen, and work with basic keyboard input and audio playback.

Although you have learned a lot from this book and are building experience with your C++ skills, there is always more to learn to help you develop into a better programmer. In this part of the book, you will learn some slightly more advanced techniques to help you on your game programming adventures. You will learn some basic data structures such as a linked list, and working with preprocessor statements to only compile sections of the code you need. You will also learn more about the Standard Template Library (STL), which has a large collection of well-developed and tested objects to help reduce any errors with your code.

At the end of Part IX, you will take these skills, along with everything else you have learned to this point, and create a basic side scroller game. Engage!

44 Introduction to Linked Lists

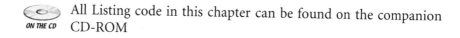 All Listing code in this chapter can be found on the companion CD-ROM

I f you recall in Chapter 14, you learned to use arrays to manipulate a program's data that could be stored in a collection. Arrays are acceptable for certain types of data storage; however, you also saw that as the array grows, it can take longer to find the particular element you need to work with. You can use a sorting mechanism to ensure your array is optimized for quicker access; however, that too can have some drawbacks. Resizing and/or constantly updating array pointers with each new addition can get intensive, and it is easy to make a mistake with the pointer manipulation, costing you time and effort to finding the bugs.

SINGLE LINKED LIST

As an alternative, a popular choice among game developers is to use a data structure known as a *linked list*. As you might infer from the name, a linked list is a collection of nodes containing items. Each node must also contain a pointer to the next node in the list; hence the name "linked list." As you update the list, you only need to add (or remove) a node to the list, making it much easier to grow or shrink in size as required. Figure 44.1 provides a graphical representation of a linked list.

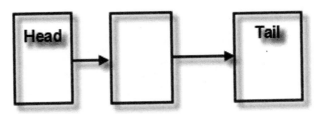

FIGURE 44.1 Single linked list.

Each node can be created using a `struct` that in itself contains a pointer to the next data block in memory. By now you are more than familiar with pointers, so you will recall that each node's pointer contains the address of the next block of data in the list. The first node in the list is known as the *head* node, while the last node is referred to as the *tail* node.

To protect the list, the tail node's pointer is set to NULL. This helps you when determining if you are at the end of the list, and prevents the pointer for the next node (which there is none) to be garbage data that might cause problems.

Listing 44.1 outlines a linked list example that details this concept.

LISTING 44.1   First linked list.

```
#include <iostream>

using namespace std;

struct sNode        /** sample node for linked list */
{
   int age;         /** store age of something */
   char name[80];   /** store name of something */

   sNode* pNext;    /** pointer to next sNode in the list */
};

int main( int argc, char* argv[] )
{
   sNode* pRoot = new sNode; /** create the first node */
   pRoot->pNext = NULL;      /** set the next node to NULL */

   return 0;
}
```

While not that exciting for now, you have taken some small and important steps to working with linked lists. In Listing 44.1, you defined the basic node structure sNode, which contains a pointer to the next node structure in the list. You are then declaring the root node in the linked list along with setting the pNext pointer to NULL (since this is the first and last node in the linked list so far). A linked list with only one node is not very useful or educational. The next topic you will learn about is adding a new node to the list.

Adding a Node to the List

Obviously, a primary action you would need to handle is when you would like to add a new node to the linked list. Since you have learned a lot about using pointers, you will have no trouble adding the logic to handle the addition of new nodes to the list. It is only a matter of making sure the pointers are updated so the current tail node points to your new node instead of NULL. Then, update the pointer from your new node to the NULL value. Listing 44.2 details how to add a new node to the list.

LISTING 44.2 Adding a new node.

```cpp
#include <iostream>

using namespace std;

struct sNode        /** sample node for linked list */
{
  int age;          /** store age of something */
  char name[80];    /** store name of something */

  sNode* pNext;     /** pointer to next sNode in the linked list */
};

sNode* AddNode( sNode* pList, sNode* pItem )
{
  /** if the given list or node to be added isn't null
  if( pList != NULL || pItem != NULL )
  {
    pItem->pNext = NULL;     /** the pItem is the new tail */
    pList->pNext = pItem;    /** attach pItem to the linked list */
  }
  return( pList );           /** return the linked list */
}

int main( int argc, char* argv[] )
{
  sNode* pRoot = new sNode; /** create "head" node */
  sNode* pObj  = new sNode; /** create a node to add */
```

```
            pRoot = AddNode( pRoot, pObj ); /** add pObj to tail of pRoot */
            return 0;
        }
```

As you can see in Listing 44.2 you are creating two sNode objects; one is the head node, and the other becomes the tail. Once the head node exists, you just need to update its pointer to attach the tail node.

Linked List Traversal

Because of their layout and design, it is impossible to sort a linked list in the same way as an array. This is due largely in part because of their composition. There is no guarantee that they are sequential in memory, since the pointer to the next node in the list is just an address. This address is assigned by the computer, which denies you the ability to specify its location.

As such, the only way to traverse the linked list is to start at the head node and move through each node in the list by following the pointer to the next node. Once you determine that the next node in the list is NULL, you have arrived at the tail of the list.

Listing 44.3 provides some clarification on this algorithm.

LISTING 44.3   Linked list traversal.

```cpp
#include <iostream>

using namespace std;

struct sNode          /** a sample node for linked list use */
{
  int age;            /** store the age of something */
  char name[80];      /** store the name of something */
  .
  sNode* pNext;       /** pointer to the next sNode in the list */
};

int main( int argc, char* argv[] )
{

  sNode* pRoot = new sNode;       /** create our root node */
  sNode* p1    = new sNode;       /** create node 1 */
  sNode* p2    = new sNode;       /** create node 2 */

  pRoot = AddNode( pRoot, p1 );   /** add node 1 to the root */
  pRoot = AddNode( pRoot, p2 );   /** add node 2 to the root */

  sNode* pTemp;                   /** create a temporary list
  pointer */
```

```
        pTemp = pRoot;                      /** assign it the address of our
root */

        while(pTemp != NULL)                /** while the temp node is not
null */
        {
           while(pTemp->pNext != NULL )  /** while the next node is not
null */
           {
             /** display the stored name and age of temp node */
             cout << pTemp->name << " is " << pTemp->age
                  << " years old. " << endl;
           }
           pTemp = pTemp->pNext;/** update the temp node to point to next
node*/
        }
        return 0;
    }
```

Listing 44.3 outlines a small sample list traversal. You first begin by defining the list item, which you have seen before. You are then creating three new sNode elements and setting their internal data variables to various names of random age values. Once that is done, you create the linked list by first taking the pointer to the head node and assigning the pointer to the next node to the p1 node. Then, you assign the next list item pointer from p1 to p2. Finally, ensure that the tail node in the list (in this case, p2) is pointing to NULL.

The traversal is done within a while loop, which demonstrates the algorithm that was previously explained; a temporary pointer of an sNode is used to move through each node in the linked list displaying its properties. This temporary pointer is needed for linked list traversal to ensure you do not accidentally "lose" the actual list you are supposed to be traversing!

Removing Items

As you learned in Chapter 32, when using dynamically allocated memory, you must remember to clean up everything you created. Linked lists are no exception. Since there are pointers to the next node in the list, you cannot simply delete each node. Otherwise, you run the risk of losing the memory address of the next node in the chain, thus leaving hanging nodes throughout the system. Generally, the algorithm you need to use is to traverse the list with a temporary pointer. As you remove the list nodes, you must update the temporary pointer with the next address of a node so you do not lose the nodes remaining within the entire chain. Listing 44.4 provides some clarification for this method of removing nodes.

LISTING 44.4 Removing nodes.

```cpp
#include <iostream>

using namespace std;

struct sNode        /** sample sNode used for linked list */
{
  int age;          /** store age of something */
  char name[80];    /** store name of something */
  sNode* pNext;     /** pointer to next sNode in the list */
};

void DeleteNodes(sNode* pList)
{
  sNode* pTemp; /** temp pointer */

  for(sNode* p = pList; p != NULL; p = pTemp) /** loop through list
*/
  {
    pTemp = p->pNext;  /** use the temp node to store the next node
*/
    delete( p );       /** delete the allocated memory for this
node*/
  }
}

int main( int argc, char* argv[] )
{
  sNode* pRoot = new sNode;        /** create root node */
  sNode* pObj1 = new sNode;        /** create obj1 */
  sNode* pObj2 = new sNode;        /** create obj2 */
  sNode* pObj3 = new sNode;        /** create obj3 */

  pRoot = AddNode( pRoot, pObj1 ); /** add obj1 to list */
  pRoot = AddNode( pRoot, pObj2 ); /** add obj2 to list */
  pRoot = AddNode( pRoot, pObj3 ); /** add obj3 to list */

  DeleteNodes( pRoot );            /** remove all nodes */
  return 0;
}
```

SUMMARY

In this chapter, you learned about the use of the linked list data structure to dynamically add and remove elements to a list in memory. This can be a useful data structure to use in your program, as it can only create list items as needed instead of reserving a large block of data in memory. This can be directly useful in any game that requires keeping track of player or computer controlled units.

The next chapter focuses on the ability to use templates that allow you to abstract certain functions and/or methods to reduce the amount of code you need to write and maintain.

EXERCISES

44.1 What is a linked list?

44.2 How does a linked list differ from an array?

44.3 Explain how to traverse the list.

45 Discussion of Templates

In This Chapter

- Defining Templates

ON THE CD

All Listing code in this chapter can be found on the companion CD-ROM

DEFINING TEMPLATES

You have learned many different data structures and OO mechanisms that the C++ language provides for the game developer. Another useful feature of C++ is the support of *templates*.

Before a discussion on the definition of the term *template*, it might be easier to understand templates by using an example first. In a program, it might become necessary to create a function to sort an array of 10 integer values. You might therefore start with a function similar to Listing 45.1.

LISTING 45.1 Sorting integers.

```
#include <iostream>
using namespace std;
void sortValues(int nums[], int number)
{
```

```
        int temp, i, j; //used for swapping during the sort
        for(i = 0; i < number; i++)
        {
            for(j = i; j < number; j++) /** the inner "core" of the
swapping */
            {
                if(nums[i] > nums[j]) /** if current element bigger than next
one*/
                {
                    temp = nums[i];      /** store the current element */
                    nums[i] = nums[j];   /** put the next element into current
one */
                    nums[j] = temp;      /** next element then becomes the
stored  */
                }
            }
        }
    }

    int main(int argc, char* argv[])
    {
        /** define a randomized array of integers */
        int myArray[] = { 1, 8, 3, 5, 2, 9, 4, 5, 9, 1 };
        /** sort them! */
        sortValues( myArray, 10 );

        return 0;
    }
```

As you can see in Listing 45.1, you are iterating through the array and comparing each value with the value of its neighbor. If the value at the current position is larger than the value at the next position in the array, the positions are swapped. This process continues until you have gone through each element in the array. The result is an array of integers sorted from lowest value to highest.

You continue to work on the program using this function until you decide that it would be nice to create a similar mechanism to sort an array of float values. Listing 45.2 outlines a function you could use that is similar to Listing 45.1.

LISTING 45.2   Sorting float values.

```
    #include <iostream>
    using namespace std;

    void sortValues(float nums[], int range)
    {

        int i, j; //used for swapping during the sort
```

```
        float j;
        for(i = 0; i < range; i++)
        {
          for(j = i; j < range; j++) /** the inner "core" of the swap */
          {
            if(nums[i] > nums[j])    /** if element is bigger than next
one */
            {
              temp = nums[i];        /** store current element */
              nums[i] = nums[j];     /** put next element into current
index */
              nums[j] = temp;        /** put the stored element into next
one*/
            }
          }
        }
    }

    int main(int argc, char* argv[])
    {
      /** a randomized array of float elements */
      float myArray[] = { 1.0f, 8.0f, 3.3f, 5.5f, 2.2f, 9.8f,
                          4.4f, 5.4f, 9.2f, 1.0f };
      /** sort them! */
      sortValues( myArray, 10 );

      return 0;
    }
```

As with the integer sorting example shown in Listing 45.1, this does essentially the same thing with an array of floats; you are comparing and swapping values in the array to produce a sorted array of float values.

What if there was a desire to sort an array of other data types such as doubles or char values?

Since the code from Listings 45.1 and 45.2 is so similar, you would more than likely cut and paste these functions and add support for the other data types if needed. This process can be troublesome to maintain, since the fix for any bug in one function would likely need to be replicated among the others.

This is where a template would be useful. A *template* can be defined as an outline or blueprint from which other things are created or generated.

A template is similar to a pattern that is used to define a set of functions to the compiler. Then, when your program is compiled, the template functions are automatically internally generated, which can save you a lot of typing and error checking. All template functions (or classes) begin with the template keyword, followed by the function name. Based on the previous two code listings, you are already familiar with the sortValues function, which is a good candidate to be rewritten in template form as shown in Listing 45.3.

LISTING 45.3   Using templates for sortValues().

```
template <class T> void sortValues(T nums[], int range);
```

It is a simple task to rewrite the sortValues function using templates to reduce the amount of code in the application. Listing 45.4 provides a demonstration.

LISTING 45.4   Rewrite sortValues to support using templates.

```
template <class T> void sortValues(T nums[], int range)
{
  T temp;
  int i, j; //used for swapping during the sort
  for(i = 0; i < range; i++)
  {
    for(j = i; j < range; j++)
    {
      if(nums[i] > nums[j])
      {
        temp = nums[i];
        nums[i] = nums[j];
        nums[j] = temp;
      }
    }
  }
}
```

By reducing the three sorting programs down to one, you have reduced the amount of code in the application, and have lowered the amount of code you will need to maintain. In other words, in a future version of our application, you might discover a logic error in the sortValues function, or you might decide that you need to add other code to the function body.

NOTE

While templates are a valuable addition to your arsenal, some programmers tend to get carried away and overuse them. They should be considered as just another helpful tool, not a way to design or pattern your entire code base.

SUMMARY

In this chapter, you learned the value and benefits of using template functions. We explained how templates can reduce the amount of code in a program, along with lowering the amount of maintenance that would be required if any modification needed to be made. In the next chapter, another important topic is discussed that provides a mechanism for actively guarding your game for error exception handling.

EXERCISES

45.1 What is the difference between an overloaded function and a template?

45.2 What is the difference between the parameter in a function and the parameter in a template?

45.3 Create a small template function to swap two variables.

46

Introduction to Assert and Exception Handling

In This Chapter

- Using Assert Statements
- Exception Handling

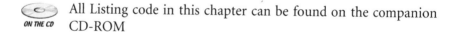 All Listing code in this chapter can be found on the companion CD-ROM

With the examples and code you have been working through so far, it has been relatively simple to debug any errors. Four to ten lines of code do not present too much difficulty if a problem should arise. It is when you move to the larger projects such as a game, which can have several hundred or thousand lines of code, that you need more effective ways of tracing the root cause of bugs or program crashes.

The C++ language standard library thus provides you with two useful mechanisms to add to the debugging arsenal: Assert statements and exception handling.

USING Assert STATEMENTS

The assert macro is designed to test a statement in your program. If the statement is proven false, the assert macro will alert you that this test has failed. In most cases, it is used to evaluate if an object or pointer is NULL. One advantage to using the assert mechanism for testing objects, is that if you are building the final release version of your program, then within the preprocessor stage of compilation your Assert tests are collapsed to produce no code; the result being no performance penalty on your final program, nor does it increase the size of the executable output. Listing 46.1 provides a sample use of assert.

LISTING 46.1 Simple assert.

```
#include <assert.h> //include the assert macro header file
#include <cstdio>

void WriteToLog( char* strMessage )
{
    /**
    * use Assert to ensure that our string we want to write
    * to our log file is not NULL
    */
    assert( strMessage != NULL );

    /** write the string to our log file */
    /** snip! */
}

int main(int argc, char* argv[])
{

    /** A stub function for preparing our log file for use */
    OpenLogFile("debug.log");

    /** dump a string to the log file */
    WriteToLog( "Making games is fun" );

    /** uncomment the following to produce an assert error */
    //WriteToLog(NULL);

    //*snip*

    /** do other things, but always close our log file when finished
    */
    CloseLogFile();

    return 0;
}
```

As you see in Listing 46.1, you must remember to include the assert.h header file before the assert macro is available. In this small program, you are using assert to test if the string pointer in the WriteToLog function is NULL before writing it to a log file. In the first case, the assert function is testing the "Making games is fun" string, which successfully passes. In the next use of the function, however, you are passing a NULL value into WriteToLog(). It will cause the assert function to fail, and you will see a dialog box similar to Figure 46.1.

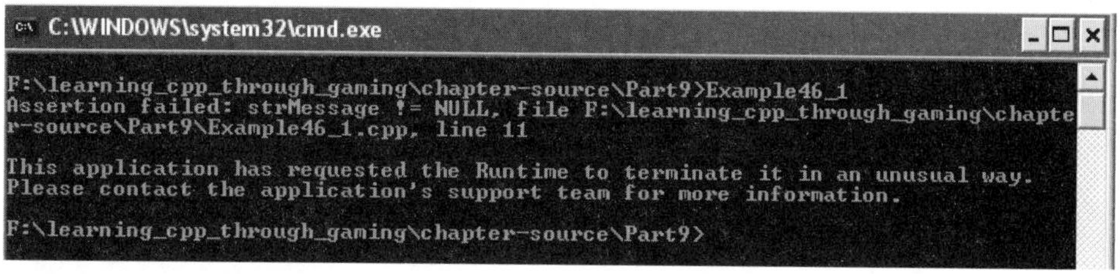

FIGURE 46.1   Failing assertion.

EXCEPTION HANDLING

Although the assert macro is a very powerful tool to aid in finding program errors, it can only really be used to find programming-related problems such as inadvertently setting a pointer to NULL. If your program receives bad data, is unable to physically open a file, or generates out-of-memory errors, you need something more powerful than assert.

Another popular tool for debugging a program is the exception handling tools the C++ language provides. Exception handling is most often used in sections of code that has a potential of failing, and can disrupt the operation of the rest of the program should it fail. Thus, if the guarded block of code fails, you are alerted and can respond quicker to tracing the error down to its root cause.

This is done with the use of the try and catch keywords. They surround the target code and act as guards to handle any problems as a result of the execution of the code within them. Listing 46.2 clarifies the use of exception handling in a code module.

LISTING 46.2   A simple Try–Catch Block.

```
/**
 * in most cases, file access is generally surrounded with try-catch
 * exception handling blocks, since they can have a higher
probability of
 * failing. Perhaps our local hard drive is full (or corrupted).
Perhaps
 * the path to our desired file does not exist, etc …
 */
```

```
try
{
  //perform some file operation such as opening a file
  throw "error opening file";

}catch( char* strError )
{
  cerr << "Caught Exception: " << strError << endl;
}
```

If Listing 46.2 is executed within some code, the console will display the message:

```
"Caught Exception: error opening file".
```

If a section of code bound by a `try` clause does not generate an exception, the statements in the `catch` clause are not executed. However, when an exception is generated, the compiler will search for a `catch` clause that can handle the same operand type that was thrown. This is where the flexibility of this exception handling mechanism can provide many benefits to your code base. If you can throw different exception errors depending on the action that has failed, you can provide refined `catch` blocks. Listing 46.3 provides some additional clarification on using a small block of multiple operands.

LISTING 46.3 Try–Catch with Multiple Operands.

```
/**
 * This small try-catch block just demonstrates some basics of
 * exception handling by illustrating the different operands we
 * are able to throw as errors
 */
try
{
    /**
  * The try block just has various tasks which can raise exceptions
    */

}catch( char* strError )
{
  /** this catch block is waiting for string data
   *    to be thrown by this block
   */
  cerr << "Caught Exception: " << strError << endl;
}catch( int error )
{
  /** this catch block is waiting for integer data
   *    to be thrown by this try block
```

```
   */
   cerr << "Caught Exception of error code: " << error << endl;
}catch( … )
{
   /** this is known as the default handler. In other words, if
   *   the operand thrown by the exception is not caught (for
example the
   *   operand is not a char* or int), then it is handled in this
   *   default block
   */
   cerr << "Default handler caught exception " << endl;
}
```

In Listing 46.3 is a small system of catch blocks that are capable of listening for different operands thrown within the try block of instructions. This way, you can throw a string describing the generated exception, or some kind of error code. In possible cases where the thrown operand does not find an associative catch block, the program will execute the code within the default handler block.

SUMMARY

In this chapter, you were introduced to two common methods of finding or tracing problems in a program: the assert macro and try-catch exception handling. Both are exceptional tools in debugging and should not be overlooked. The next chapter covers the use of preprocessor statements within a program, which can help include or ignore specific blocks of your program depending on your target application's requirements during the compilation stages of your source code.

EXERCISES

46.1 Explain why you are using exceptions to handle errors instead of dealing with them as they occur in each instruction.

46.2 Does the exception generated by the application need to be caught in the same location as the try-catch block that created it?

46.3 Create a simple program to handle exceptions raised if you insert more than five items into an array.

46.4 How does the final section complete a try-catch exception block?

47

Preprocessor Directives

In This Chapter

■ Macro Definitions (#define and #undef)

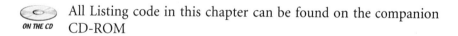 All Listing code in this chapter can be found on the companion
CD-ROM

As you gain more experience with the C++ language, you also pick up and learn new techniques and methods of speeding up either project development time and/or the time spent on bug hunting. You have also been introduced to using the `assert` macro and the `try-catch` exception handling blocks. These are excellent techniques for finding problems with the code.

Another useful feature available to you is the use of preprocessor directives. These statements are always preceded by the pound (#) sign and are executed even before your code is generated by the compiler. They also only can contain one line of code and do *not* end with a semicolon (;). Each time you run your program through the compiler to build your final output, the compiler does not work directly with the source code you are presently viewing. Instead, the compiler sends your program first through the preprocessor, where any preprocessor directives are evaluated first. Depending on your preprocessor instructions, this can result in a modified version of your source code, which is used as the input source code for the compiler.

This intermediary file that represents the source code that will be sent to the compiler is normally not saved in any form. It is possible, however, to instruct the compiler to save this intermediary file in a format you can view. Be sure to reference your compiler documentation for more information.

MACRO DEFINITIONS (#define AND #undef)

To define a preprocessor statement, you use the #define macro. It is of the format shown in Listing 47.1.

LISTING 47.1   #define.

```
#define <identifier> <replacement>

#define USE_CAR      1
#define USE_BOAT     2
```

When the preprocessor statements are found and executed by the compiler, it finds all occurrences of the identifier and replaces them with the replacement.

This replacement can be just about anything: an expression, a statement, or even a block of code.

The preprocessor does not "understand" the C++ language. Therefore, if you try to #define an invalid or illegal code statement, an error will not be generated until your program is run through the compilation phase.

To demonstrate this preprocessor statement in action, inspect Listing 47.2.

LISTING 47.2   #define—Example47_1.cpp.

```
#include <iostream>

using namespace std;

#define FINDMAX(a,b) ((a)>(b)?(a):(b))

int main(int argc, char* argv[])
{
  int x=5, y;
```

```
      /** this will be replaced with ((a)>(b)?(a):(b)) during
compilation */
      y = FINDMAX(x,2);

      cout << y << endl;
      /** this as well will become ((a)>(b)?(a):(b)) */
      cout << FINDMAX(7,x) << endl;
      return 0;
   }
```

You first used the #define directive to create a small max function. If the first operand is larger than the second, it is the largest; otherwise, the second operand must be larger. During the compilation of this program, the compiler will first process Listing 47.2 and replace all findmax function calls with the statement ((a)>(b) ? (a) : (b)).

The #undef directive is used to undo a directive which has been previously declared with #define. Listing 47.3 provides a further example to using the #undef directive.

LISTING 47.3   Using #undef.

```
      #include <iostream>
      #define MAX_NUM 100          /** first define MAX_NUM to be 100
*/
      using namespace std;
      int main(int argc, char* argv[])
      {
         int array_one[MAX_NUM];    /** declare an int array of 100
elements*/
         #undef MAX_NUM            /** undefine the MAX_NUM label */
         #define MAX_NUM 150       /** redefine MAX_NUM to be 150 */
         int array_two[MAX_NUM];   /** declare an int array of 150
elements*/

         return 0;
      }
```

Conditional Directives (#ifdef, #ifndef, #if, #endif, #else, and #elif)

While the use of #define / #undef might enable you to get around certain situations with your program, it is not optimized unless there was a way you could create a preprocessor conditional block. In other words, it would be more useful to only execute certain #define directives in one situation, and a different set of #define directives in another. Listing 47.4 is an example of using these conditional directives to modify the output shown in Example 47_2.

LISTING 47.4 Example47_2.cpp.

```cpp
/** this sample demonstrates using conditional directives */
#define TRIAL_VERSION
#define APP_WIN32

#include <iostream>
#ifdef APP_WIN32         /**only include win32 header if building
for */
    #include <windows.h>  /**windows
*/
#endif
using namespace std;

int main(int argc, char* argv[])
{
    cout << "Deciding on which version of software this is.." <<
endl;
    #ifdef TRIAL_VERSION
      cout << "This is the trial/demo version of our software " <<
endl;
    #else
      cout << "This is the full-blown registered version " << endl;
    #endif

    #ifdef APP_WIN32
      cout << "This build is targeting the Windows platform " <<
endl;
    #else
      cout << "This build is targeting the MacOS platform " << endl;
    #endif
    return 0;
}
```

Be sure to run the example a few times and play around with commenting and uncommenting the various #define directives to see its output in the program.

SUMMARY

In this chapter, you covered the use of preprocessor directives, which gives you a way to restrict sections of code depending on the needs of the game. A common use for preprocessor directives is to add extra debugging information during nonrelease (or beta) compiles of the software, and to keep them removed from the final release version of the application.

In the next chapter, you will learn about the Standard Template Library (STL), which contains a useful collection of common objects that are available for high-performance use in games.

EXERCISES

47.1 What is a preprocessor directive?

47.2 When is it called?

47.3 Create a small program that uses preprocessor statements to either include or ignore a function.

48 Introduction to the Standard Template Library (STL)

In This Chapter

- What are Containers?
- What are Iterators?
- The string Container
- The vector Container
- The list Container
- The map Container

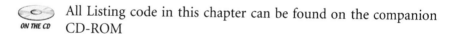 All Listing code in this chapter can be found on the companion CD-ROM

One of the basic foundation tenants of the C++ language is the concept of object reuse, while game programming also requires fast application performance. In many situations, C++ programmers are often faced with a library that seems to oppose these two goals. Either the library is a perfect shining example of object-oriented design and reuse, but is too slow for the heavy requirements of a game, or conversely, the design of the library is fairly poor but performs at a fast enough level for a game.

In many game projects, the developers involved usually have their own custom library of objects that allow them to save implementation time when starting a new project. Because of the ability of C++ to reuse objects, experienced game developers can quickly move past the initial stages of testing well-used classes and/or components. In almost every case, this custom library usually has a generic linked list or resizable array class.

However, an alternative exists for the game programmers who would like to use a standardized library of functions that is both generic enough to handle almost any object they create, and is more than fast enough to be able to handle game situations. The Standard Template Library (STL) has been created for this very purpose; to devise a group of generic container objects that can also be used where maintaining a fast speed is critical. The STL has also been around long enough, and has matured to a very stable and well-tested library.

At the heart of the STL lie the basic principles that it was built upon: containers and iterators.

WHAT ARE CONTAINERS?

Within the context of STL, a container is a powerful object designed to manipulate and store collections of other objects. Within the STL library, there are generally only two types of containers you will be working with: *sequence* and *associative* containers. Sequence containers hold a sequence of a single element type in a linear fashion. This is similar in nature to working with string data and/or arrays. In this chapter, you will learn about the vector and list containers that are sequential. Associative containers are specialized objects that are optimized for fast object retrieval given a specific key value. Later in this chapter, you will learn about the map container, which is associative.

WHAT ARE ITERATORS?

To manipulate the objects that are stored in the containers, the STL provides an iterator mechanism. An *iterator* is an object that is used to point to an individual object within the container. For example, all the STL containers support a `begin()` member method, which returns an iterator to the first element in the container. Similarly, containers also have a member method `end()`, which returns an iterator pointing to the last element in the collection. You can access the specific element by dereferencing the iterator with the star (`*`) operator, in the same way you can dereference a pointer.

To obtain an iterator to an STL container, you would use the syntax outlined in Listing 48.1.

LISTING 48.1 Iterator syntax.

```
std::class_name<template_parameters>::iterator name
```

The `name` represents the variable name you wish to assign the iterator. The `class_name` is the class name of the element pointed to in the container.

The `template_parameters` are the parameters used to declare objects that will work with this iterator. Listing 48.2 contains some sample iterator declarations.

LISTING 48.2   Sample iterators.

```
/** This defines a vector container for storing float elements */
std::vector<float> vecResizeableArray;
/** This defines an iterator compatible with a container of floats
*/
std::vector<float>::iterator itResizeableArray;
```

Using the `iterator` will become clearer as you work through each STL container type outlined in this chapter, so do not panic if you are still a bit confused.

NOTE

A "gotcha" when using iterators is that if the container being pointed to by the iterator changes significantly, it is possible that the declared iterator will be trashed and you will need to request a new one.

THE `string` CONTAINER

Arguably one of the most famous objects within the STL is the `string` container.

It is a replacement within the C++ language to the "C-style" workings of handling strings as `NULL` terminated `char` arrays. Listing 48.3 demonstrates how easy it is to declare and initialize a string container.

LISTING 48.3   String initialization.

```
#include <iostream.h>
#include <string>  /** the STL string header file */

using namespace std;

int main(int argc, char* argv[])
{
  /** declare a string initialized with some text */
  string galaxy = "the Milky Way";
  string planet = "";
  /** reassign planet with new string data */
  planet = "Earth";
  /** create a new string which is composed of other string data */
  string myPlanet = planet + " in " + galaxy;
```

```
/** send the new string to the output stream */
cout << myPlanet << endl;
return 0;
}
```

As you can see, there are many ways you are using the string container already in Listing 48.3. You are declaring the galaxy variable, which you are immediately assigning string data to. It is also possible to initialize the string with nothing as shown with the planet variable. The declaration of the myPlanet variable demonstrates that you can use the overloaded plus operator (+) to construct a final string by concatenating existing string data. Finally, the myPlanet string is displayed to the console.

Using c_str

A special member function of the string container provides a mechanism for converting the internal string data to a "C-style" string in the event you are working with another object or function that can only accept chars as a parameter. Listing 48.4 provides a code sample of using this "legacy" conversion function.

LISTING 48.4 c_str.

```
#include <iostream>
#include <string>  /** the STL string header file */

using namespace std;

int main(int argc, char* argv[])
{
  /** declare a string */
  string filename = "autoexec.bat";
  /** display the string to the console */
  cout << "using filename := " << filename << endl;
  /** display the same string in a different (valid) way */
  cout << "or we can use filename := " << filename.c_str() << endl;
  return 0;
}
```

Using the [] Operator

A method for accessing individual elements within a string object is through the use of the overloaded square bracket ([]) operators. This allows you to treat the string data as if it were a char array to access elements. Listing 48.5 provides some clarification.

LISTING 48.5   Using the [] Operator.

```
#include <iostream>
#include <string> /** the STL string header file */

using namespace std;

int main(int argc, char* argv[])
{
  /** initialize a string with some data */
  string dialog = "You there! Check out that noise!";
  /** access an element from the string using the [] */
  char c = dialog[10];
  /** display it to the console */
  cout << "c := " << c << endl;
  /** set a new value to a specific element in the string using []
*/
  dialog[10] = 'e';
  cout << dialog << endl;
  return 0;
}
```

The use of the [] operator can cause boundary problems, as there is no check on where you are accessing by STL. Make sure you do not specify a position outside of the string data!

THE vector CONTAINER

Another popular container you will learn about in the STL is the vector class. This class can be thought of as a type independent resizable array. In other words, it is a container that behaves like an array that you can dynamically grow or shrink in size depending on how many objects you are working with. vector objects are typically more powerful than just using arrays because you have many options in terms of functions available to the container. Listing 48.6 provides a small sample of declaring a vector container to hold float elements.

LISTING 48.6   Declaring a vector.

```
#include <iostream>
#include <vector>  /** the STL vector header file */

using namespace std;

int main(int argc, char* argv[])
```

```
   {
     /** declare a vector container to store float elements */
     vector<float> vecStats;

     return 0;
   }
```

Adding Elements

Elements can be added into a vector object by using the push_back member method, which is common to most STL container objects. Listing 48.7 provides a sample of adding elements to the vector, along with using the size member method to display how many items are in the container.

LISTING 48.7 Using push_back.

```
   #include <iostream>
   #include <vector>  /** the STL vector header file */

   using namespace std;

   int main(int argc, char* argv[])
   {
     vector<float> vecStats;      /** declare a vector for float
   elements*/

     vecStats.push_back( 45.0f );/**push 45.0f to the end of the
   container*/
     vecStats.push_back( 20.0f );/**push 20.0f to the end of the
   container*/
     vecStats.push_back( 10.0f );/**push 10.0f to the end of the
   container*/

     /** verify the elements were stored, by displaying the number
     * of elements in the vector */
     cout << "There are " << vecStats.size() << " items in the
       vector." << endl;

     return 0;
   }
```

Using a vector Iterator

More often than not, you will need to iterate through each item in your vector container. You learned about iterators previously in this chapter; however, now you will get some more exposure to using them in real code. Listing 48.8 demonstrates how to use an iterator to display each element in the vector container.

LISTING 48.8   Iterating through a vector.

```cpp
#include <iostream>
#include <vector>  /** include the STL vector header */

using namespace std;
int main(int argc, char* argv[])
{
  vector<float> vecStats;        /**declare a vector for floats */

  vecStats.push_back( 45.0f ); /**push 45.0f in the vector */
  vecStats.push_back( 20.0f ); /**push 20.0f in the vector */
  vecStats.push_back( 10.0f ); /**push 10.0f in the vector */

  /** verify how many elements are in the vector by displaying
  * a count */
  cout << "There are " << vecStats.size() << " items in the
      vector." << endl;

  /** create a float iterator and assign it to the first element
* in the float vector. Keep looping through each element using the
* Iterator until there are no more
*/
  for( vector<float>::iterator it = vecStats.begin();
    it != vecStats.end(); it++)
  {
     //"it" is a pointer to the current element in the iterator,
     //so you need to dereference the it pointer so we can
     //determine the actual value
     cout << "displaying value: " << *it << endl;
  }
  return 0;
}
```

Working with Custom Objects

Until now, you have been adding and iterating through basic data types. However, in most game situations where vector containers are used, the vector is storing collections of custom objects used in the game world; perhaps to track the player's inventory or spell list, to track skills and professions, and so forth.

This is handled in the same manner you have been using when working with vectors. The only difference is that you will be creating a container for storing pointers to your objects. Listing 48.9 provides an example of this.

LISTING 48.9   Adding objects to vectors.

```cpp
#include <iostream>
#include <vector>  /** include the STL vector header file */
```

```
using namespace std;

/**
 * Create a small dummy object that we can use to demonstrate
 * Object manipulation within a vector
 */
class IObject
{
public:
  int x;
public:
  IObject(){ x = 0; }  /** default constructor */
  virtual ~IObject(){} /** virtual destructor  */
};

int main(int argc, char* argv[])
{
  /** declare a vector to store POINTERS of the IObject class */
  vector<IObject*> pObjects;
  /** just create a loop to add 10 new IObject pointers to the
   *  Container */
  for(int i = 0; i < 10; i++)
  {
    IObject* pTemp = new IObject();/** create a new pointer      */
    pTemp->x = i;                  /** assign a data member to i */
    pObjects->push_back( pTemp );  /** push the pointer into the
vector*/
  }

  //print out results
  for( vector<IObject*>::iterator it = pObjects.begin();
    it != pObjects.end(); it++)
  {
    //"it" is a pointer to the element in the iterator,
    //so *it dereferences it so we can get the value
    cout << " x :=  " << *it->x << endl;
  }

  return 0;

}
```

Cleaning up Objects

Listing 48.9 demonstrates how to create and use a vector containing pointers to a collection of IObject* items. After declaring the vector, the program enters a small for loop of 10 iterations, which just creates a new IObject instance on the free store and adds it to the vector. Once this is finished, it uses an iterator to display the x member variable of each IObject instance in the vector. One problem with this sample is that there is no cleanup before the program exits. As such, the memory created on the free store is left dangling when the program terminates—not good.

The STL containers support a member function called clear(), which is responsible for cleaning up the internal data. Since the vector contains nothing but a collection of pointers, using clear() will remove these pointers but will not clean up the dynamic memory being pointed at!

For this to happen, you have to iterate through each object in the container and manually delete it. Listing 48.10 demonstrates how this is done, taken from Example 48_1.cpp (See CD-ROM).

ON THE CD

LISTING 48.10   Adding garbage collection.

```
#include <iostream>
#include <vector>

using namespace std;

class IObject
{
public:
  int x;
public:
  IObject(){ m_x = 0; }
  virtual ~IObject(){}
};

int main(int argc, char* argv[])
{
  vector<IObject*> pObjects;

  for(int i = 0; i < 10; i++)
  {
    IObject* pTemp = new IObject();
    pTemp->x = i;
    pObjects->push_back( pTemp );
  }

  //print out results
  for( vector<IObject*>::iterator it = pObjects.begin();
    it != pObjects.end(); it++)
  {
      //"it" is a pointer to the element in the iterator,
      //so *it dereferences it so we can get the value
      cout << " x :=  " << *it->x << endl;
  }
```

```
for( vector<IObject*>::iterator it = pObjects.begin();
  it != pObjects.end(); it++)
{
   //clean up the allocated memory on the free store
   //for this object with the delete operator
   delete *it;
}
//finally call the clear method to clean the pointers
pObjects.clear();
return 0;


}
```

THE list CONTAINER

In Chapter 44, you learned how to create and use your own linked list data structure as a flexible alternative to using arrays. Although they can be used in many different situations, the linked list approach has two costs associated with it:

■ If you are creating your own, it is error prone. Since you are manipulating pointers to control the members of the list, it easy to make a typo or nonobvious bug that directly affects the performance of the list.

■ Being a linear data structure, the only reliable way to find elements is by moving through each node from head to tail.

There are improvements to the linked list data structure, such as the double linked list. In this type of linked list, each node has a pointer to the next node in the list and a pointer to the previous node. This can make accessing the list much more efficient.

The STL has a double linked list container class known as list. Listing 48.11 provides some detail from the Example48_2.cpp file.

LISTING 48.11 Example48_2.cpp.

```
#include <iostream>
#include <list> /** the STL linked list header file */
using namespace std;
int main( int argc, char* argv[] )
{
   /** declare an STL linked list container for storing integers */
   list<int> mylist;
   /** add several int elements */
   mylist.push_back( 4 );
   mylist.push_back( 5 );
```

```
      mylist.push_back( 6 );
      mylist.push_back( 10 );
      /** create a for loop with an iterator to display the values
stored in
      * the list */
      for(list<int>::iterator list_iter = mylist.begin();
        list_iter != mylist.end(); list_iter++)
      {
        cout << list_iter << endl;
      }
      mylist.clear();
      return 0;
    }
```

THE map CONTAINER

Another useful data structure for game programmers is the hash map (also known as a hash table). Since it is an STL container, it has almost all of the same member functions the vector and list containers possess. The map container functions more or less as a 2D array. It is filled with keys that are used to index this table of the location of the actual data being stored. It is a very quick process to retrieve your object via the key, which is why this is a popular container to use. Listing 48.12 details the code found in Example 48_3.cpp

LISTING 48.12   Example 48_3.cpp.

```
#include <iostream>
#include <string>  /** STL string header */
#include <vector>  /** STL vector header */
#include <map>     /** STL map header */
using namespace std;

/**
* define a simple monster object that we can use to help
demonstrate
* using a map container
*/
struct sMonster
{
  string name;  /** monster name */
  int health;   /** monster health */
};

int THAL_KEY = 1;    /** define a key for the THALs */
int KALED_KEY = 2;   /** define a key for the KALEDs */
```

```cpp
int main(int argc, char* argv[])
{
  /** declare a map container of sMonster pointers which are
  * indexed by unique int values. */
  map<int, sMonster*> oMonsters;
  sMonster* mon1 = new sMonster();
  sMonster* mon2 = new sMonster();

  //set some basic properties for the monsters
  mon1->name = "Thal";
  mon1->health = 100;
  mon2->name = "Kaled";
  mon2->health = 50;

  //insert them into the map container using a key
  //value that we can use to find them later
  oMonsters.insert(make_pair(THAL_KEY, mon1));

  //the following assignment is also legal
  oMonsters[KALED_KEY] = mon2;

  //we want to find the Thal monster to we need an
  //iterator object to enumerate the map elements
  map<int, sMonster*>::iterator iter;

  //find the element matching the key value
  iter = oMonsters.find(THAL_KEY);
  if (iter == oMonsters.end())
  {
    //can't find it!
    cout << "The Thal has been exterminated!" << endl;
  }else
  {
    cout << "The Thal has " << iter->second->health
    << " health left. " << endl;
  }
  //clean up. Note that since you are storing pointers to sMonster
  //objects which are allocated on the memory heap, you need
  //to clean up and deallocate this memory before calling the
  //clear() method of the container.
  sMonster* pObj;
  for(map<int, sMonster*>::iterator it = oMonsters.begin();
    it != oMonsters.end(); it++)
    {
      delete it->second;
    }
  }
  //clear the map of the sMonster pointers
```

```
        oMonsters.clear();
        return 0;
}
```

SUMMARY

Although brief, in this chapter you were introduced to the basics behind the powerful concepts of containers and iterators. Using the Standard Template Library (STL) drives home the very core principles and tenants of the C++ language: object reuse. The STL is a strong, proven library of containers and iterators that has been tested and refined 100 times and more. In the next chapter, you will see the STL in a small game situation as you encounter the final project for this book: a simple side scroller.

EXERCISES

48.1 What does STL stand for and why is it important?

48.2 What is a container? What is an iterator?

48.3 Can the STL containers be used in a game?

49

A Simple Action Scroller Using SDL

In This Chapter

- The SSS Design
- Configuring the Display
- Parallax Scrolling
- Adding the Player Sprite
- Adding the Enemy Sprites
- Adding Laser Sprites
- Adding Collision

 All Listing code in this chapter can be found on the companion CD-ROM

You have been steadily working through various game projects at the end of every part of this book. Apart from Part VIII, they have all focused more on the actual underlying mechanics of the game instead of requiring any kind of graphics feedback to the player.

In this chapter, you now place all the focus on drawing graphics for a simple game to illustrate the techniques used throughout this entire book. Using the SDL and the objects you created in Part VIII, you will work on a very small game known as a "side scroller." All you will see is a scrolling background, some text to the player, moving sprites for the player and enemies, and a laser shot or two. That will be all you will cover here, but it will hopefully ignite some passion inside you to extend the game into a fully fledged title!

Much of the source code will be commented on during this chapter. To follow along, browse through the same source code on the companion CD-ROM contained in the /SSS folder.

THE SSS DESIGN

Although you may know what you want to see for the Simple Side Scroller game, it is a great opportunity to create a very small design document, which you learned about in Chapter 35. It will be a very trimmed down document that is just going to be a plan of attack for what you will end up with by the end of this chapter.

The rest of the document is up to you to fill out and create as you either extend the work you will do in this chapter, or make your own different game entirely.

CONFIGURING THE DISPLAY

With the simple graphics you added to the Battleship project back in Part VIII, you will have no trouble in this section of the SSS project. The only goal of this small section is to ensure the graphics device and underlying SDL is initialized properly. Working with the `MainApplication` object you created in Part VIII, you can create a new instance of the class as shown in Listing 49.1.

LISTING 49.1 MyApp.h.

```
#include "MainApplication.h"
class MyApp : public MainApplication
{
public:
  MyApp();
  ~MyApp();

};
```

There is nothing different with this implementation in comparison with how you started the Battleship graphics. You are just creating a new main driver object to keep the game updating and drawing.

PARALLAX SCROLLING

Most side scroller games usually involve some very basic drawing "tricks" to create the illusion that you are traveling very fast through a star field or other such phenomenon. For the SSS project, you will create a triple-layered star field. Creating three different layers of stars will allow you to update them at different rates to create the illusion that the player's ship is traveling very fast through space. The bottom layer will have stars that move fairly slowly down the screen. The middle layer of stars will travel at a medium pace, and the top layer, which is closest to the player, will move at a very fast rate from the top of the screen to the bottom. This gives you the illusion that you are flying through a huge expansive environment filled with stars.

The sStar struct contains the necessary position and plane information to keep the star moving at the right speed depending on how far into the screen it is from the player. In reality, all of the stars are drawn on the same level; however, the plane variable allows you to trick the eyes of the player by updating at different rates to appear as if it was further into the screen.

This also demonstrates how to create the different sStar items that are stored in a vector container. You are randomly generating an x and y location to display the star, along with a random choice of which plane the star lives on: the far, middle, or near plane.

You are then iterating through the vector container to display each sStar item using different levels of "brightness" to simulate the various levels of a scrolling background of stars.

ADDING THE PLAYER SPRITE

With the Starfield object successfully added and drawing itself properly to the background, you can work on the next important thing: adding the player sprite. This is not difficult, since you are well versed in sprite manipulation at this point in the material. You just need to use an SDLSprite object that you created in Part VIII to represent the piece the player moves around and controls.

Controlling the Player Sprite

In Part VIII, you learned how to use SDL to capture the input from the keyboard. For controlling the player's position, all you need to do is work with the input received from the keyboard to create movement multipliers. If the player is moving to the right or upward, these are counted as positive movement. If the player is moving to the left or downward, the movement is multiplied by a negative multiplier to properly position the ship. Chapter 42, which discussed how to poll the SDL queue for input, also details what is needed to support the input from the player.

ADDING THE ENEMY SPRITES

The player sprite has been added to the SSS demo and can be manipulated by the keyboard to move left or right, up or down. To add some conflict to the demo, you can now add enemy objects that stand between the player and his final goal of survival.

You are simply creating more SDLSprite instances and will just spawn them in random positions at the top of the screen. They will then move in a very "dumb" way down to the bottom. They will have no artificial intelligence to speak of, so they will not bother the player if the player does not bother them.

ADDING LASER SPRITES

The player and enemy sprites can move around but cannot do much more than that. The next goal of the SSS demo is to add the ability for the player to fire some lasers at the enemy sprite objects. This is a rather unfair demo, as the player can fire at the aliens, but the aliens are defenseless. The approach you will take is quite basic, but will get the job done and demonstrate how to add various effects. If the program detects that the player has fired the weapon, the game will spawn a new laser sprite at the player's current position. It will then update itself independently of the player as it travels upward through the game world. They will appear in their own vector container, which will remove them once the laser moves past the top of the screen.

ADDING COLLISION

The final task involved in the SSS demo is to add some basic collision detection. *Collision detection* is a fancy phrase for a very basic task: to detect if one object has struck another. This requires some rudimentary mathematics, but it is not difficult to envision what needs to be done. This works by computing the distance between the two objects being tested. If an object has struck another, you just need to remove the laser sprite and the affected enemy sprite from their respective lists.

SUMMARY

In this final part of the book, you took the various knowledge and lessons covered throughout this book and directly applied it to a basic game example. The goal here was to illustrate some aspects of game programming, and the effectiveness and flexibility of the C++ language.

As a final note, I would like to extend kudos to you, the reader, for the willingness to learn the C++ language. I hope this gives you the necessary tools to enjoy any project you undertake in the future, whether it is game related or not. Happy gaming!

EXERCISES

49.1 Currently the small SSS demo only allows the player to fire anything at the aliens. Add some small logic or random way for the aliens to fire back at the player. It can be very simple, such as randomly firing a laser every 2 seconds.

49.2 The input system for the SSS demo only processes commands from the player's keyboard. Add some small functionality to handle input from the mouse as well.

Appendix
A
SDL API Reference

Note: This is an abridged version of the SDL documentation available on the main SDL Web site and maintained by the following contributors:

- Sam Lantigua
- Martin Donlon
- Mattias Engdegård
- Julian Peterson
- Ken Jordan
- Maxim Sobolev
- Wesley Poole
- Michael Vance
- Andreas Umbach

SDL GENERAL REFERENCE

SDL_Init

Prototypes

```
void SDL_Init( Uint32 flags );
```

Parameters

flags: Descriptor(s) to signal to SDL which hardware subsystem to create. If more than one subsystem needs to be created, these values should be OR'd together.

SDL_INIT_TIMER: Initializes the timer subsystem.

SDL_INIT_AUDIO: Initializes the audio subsystem.

SDL_INIT_VIDEO: Initializes the video subsystem.

SDL_INIT_CDROM: Initializes the CD-ROM subsystem.

SDL_INIT_JOYSTICK: Initializes the underlying joystick subsystem.

SDL_INIT_EVERYTHING: Initializes all of the underlying subsystems described above.

Description

This function must be called before any other SDL function is attempted. It is responsible for creating and setting up any underlying hardware. To keep things simple, just stick to specifying the SDL_INIT_EVERYTHING flag.

Errors

Returns a −1 if there is an error, or 0 if everything initialized successfully. The exact error message can be discovered using SDL_GetError().

Sample

```
if(SDL_Init( SDL_INIT_EVERTHING ) < 0 )
{
  cerr << "Unable to initialize SDL" << endl;
  exit(1);
}
```

SDL_Quit

Prototype

```
void SDL_Quit( void );
```

Parameters

None.

Description

This function is responsible for performing any underlying subsystem cleanup according to the subsystems used during the program. This will also clean up the main application window with the underlying window manager.

Errors

None.

Sample

```
//cleanup all your application objects
//then cleanup SDL
SDL_Quit();
```

SDL_GetError

Prototype

```
char* SDL_GetError( void );
```

Parameters

None.

Description

This queries the current error string within the SDL subsystem. This error string contains the last recorded SDL error.

Errors

None.

Sample

```
char strError[256];
if (SDL_Init(SDL_INIT_EVERYTHING) == -1)
{
  sprintf(strError, "SDL initialization failed: %s\n",
    SDL_GetError());
  cerr << strError << endl;
  exit(1); //or any other exit code you may have
}
```

SDL VIDEO REFERENCE

The following functions available to the developer via the SDL are important for configuring and displaying graphics and/or images on an SDL_Surface.

SDL_GetVideoSurface

Prototype

```
SDL_Surface *SDL_GetVideoSurface(void);
```

Parameters

None.

Description

This function attempts to return a pointer to the current SDL_Surface of the primary (front) display.

Errors

Returns NULL on any internal error.

SDL_SetVideoMode

Prototype

```
SDL_Surface *SDL_SetVideoMode(int width,
                              int height,
                              int bitsperpixel,
                              Uint32 flags);
```

Parameters

width: Width of the desired video surface.

height: Height of the desired video surface.

bitsperpixel: Bits per pixel of the desired video surface. Most common values are 15, 16, and 32.

flags: Additional descriptors can be specified here for the video surface creation.

SDL_SWSURFACE: Create the video surface in system memory.

SDL_HWSURFACE: Create the video surface in hardware memory.

SDL_DOUBLEBUF: Enable hardware double buffering. This descriptor must be used in conjunction with SDL_HWSURFACE. During a surface chain flip, the surfaces are then flipped from front to back in hardware. Otherwise, if this hardware double buffering mechanism could not be created, then a call to SDL_Flip will internally use the SDL_UpdateRect function.

SDL_FULLSCREEN: SDL will attempt to use a full-screen video mode that is compatible with the given video surface dimensions.

Description

This function is responsible for setting up and initializing the underlying video device swap buffer chain. You are able to specify a width, height, and bit depth of your surface along with some other specifications. Note that the surface chain created by this function need not be explicitly released by you; SDL_Quit will internally clean them up.

Errors

This function returns a pointer to the newly created SDL_Surface, or NULL if there is an error.

Sample

```
int width = 640;
int height= 480;
int bpp = 16;
int flags = SDL_SWSURFACE;
pSurface = SDL_SetVideoMode(width, height, bpp, flags);
if(pSurface == NULL)
{
  sprintf(strError, "SDL initialization failed: %s\n",
    SDL_GetError());
  cerr << strError << endl;

  return -1;
}
```

SDL_UpdateRect

Prototype

```
void SDL_UpdateRect(SDL_Surface *screen,
                    Sint32 x,
                    Sint32 y,
                    Sint32 w,
                    Sint32 h);
```

Parameters

screen: The video surface to update.

x: The upper-left corner x pos of the rectangle specified to update.

y: The upper-left corner y pos of the rectangle specified to update.

w: The width of the rectangle to update.

h: The height of the rectangle to update.

Description

This function is used to update the specified rectangle on a given SDL_Surface. This rectangle must exist and be confined within the borders of the screen, since no surface clipping will be performed. If x, y, w, and h parameters are all 0, the entire screen will be updated.

Errors

None is returned from this function.

Sample

```
//pScreen is the main SDL_Surface used for displaying any graphics.
//Obviously it needs to be created prior to using SDL_UpdateRect on
//it

//draw some new pixels to the back buffer

// Tell SDL to update the whole screen
SDL_UpdateRect(pScreen, 0, 0, 640, 480);
```

SDL_Flip

Prototype

```
int SDL_Flip(SDL_Surface *screen);
```

Parameters

Screen: The pointer to the primary SDL_Surface in the swap buffer chain.

Description

This function is used to update the video surfaces used in the swap buffer chain for the game. On video hardware that supports double buffering, this function sets up the internal flip and then returns. On hardware that does not support this double-buffering mechanism, this is equivalent to executing SDL_UpdateRect(screen, 0, 0, 0, 0); .

Errors

This function returns a *0* if everything was successful; otherwise, an error is signaled by a *-1*.

Sample

```
//do any surface blitting or filling any rects
//to the back buffer SDL_Surface object
//when you have drawn your new display objects
//signal SDL you want the buffers flipped
SDL_Flip( display_buffer );
```

SDL_FreeSurface

Prototype

```
void SDL_FreeSurface(SDL_Surface *surface);
```

Parameters

surface: SDL_Surface pointer to clean up and deallocate.

Description

This function is responsible for cleaning up and deleting the underlying video surface specified in the SDL_Surface pointer. If the surface parameter value is NULL, the function will do nothing and return.

Errors

No errors are returned with this function.

Sample

```
//load our bitmap into a surface
SDL_Surface *pShip = SDL_LoadBMP("alien_ship.bmp");

//use the surface to display our big alien ship!

//free the surface (in our cleanup code) as we no longer need it
SDL_FreeSurface(pShip);
```

SDL_LockSurface

Prototype

```
int SDL_LockSurface(SDL_Surface *surface);
```

Parameters

surface: The video SDL_Surface to lock.

Description

This function is used to set up the SDL_Surface for preparation of directly accessing the pixel data of the surface. Between matching pairs of SDL_LockSurface and SDL_UnlockSurface, the surface->pixels data structure can be read and written to using the format stored in surface->format. Once you are done accessing this surface, you must remove the lock by calling SDL_UnlockSurface.

Errors

This function returns *0* or *-1* if the surface could not be locked.

Sample

```
//our main display SDL_Surface
SDL_Surface *pScreen;

//don't forget to create it with SDL_CreateSurface

if(SDL_LockSurface(pScreen) >= 0)
{

 //now you can access the pixel data of the main display directly

 //when finished, remember to unlock it
 SDL_UnlockSurface( pScreen );
}

// Tell SDL to update the whole screen
SDL_UpdateRect(pScreen, 0, 0, 640, 480);
```

SDL_UnlockSurface

Prototype

```
void SDL_UnlockSurface(SDL_Surface *surface);
```

Parameters

Surface: An SDL_Surface that has been locked by SDL_LockSurface.

Description

This function unlocks a previously locked SDL_Surface by the SDL_LockSurface function. Every surface that is locked must have a corresponding call to SDL_UnlockSurface.

Errors

None is returned from this function.

Sample

```
//our main display SDL_Surface
SDL_Surface *pScreen;
```

```
//don't forget to create it with SDL_CreateSurface

if(SDL_LockSurface(pScreen) >= 0)
{

  //now you can access the pixel data of the main display directly

  //when finished, remember to unlock it
  SDL_UnlockSurface( pScreen );
}


// Tell SDL to update the whole screen
SDL_UpdateRect(pScreen, 0, 0, 640, 480);
```

SDL_ConvertSurface

Prototype

```
SDL_Surface *SDL_ConvertSurface(SDL_Surface *src,
                                SDL_PixelFormat *fmt,
                                Uint32 flags);
```

Parameters

src: The SDL_Surface you would like to convert to.

fmt: The desired format of the new surface.

flags: The desired creation flags that are internally used during the creation/copy of the new SDL_Surface.

Description

This function is used to create a new SDL_Surface of the given format, along with a copy of the given SDL_Surface. It is useful for converting different surface formats and cloning surfaces.

Errors

This function returns a pointer to the SDL_Surface if successful; otherwise, a NULL value.

Sample

```
//pSprite is defined as an SDL_Surface
//pScreen is the previously created display surface

//load our bitmap into a temporary surface
SDL_Surface *pTemp = SDL_LoadBMP("alien_ship.bmp");

//convert it to match the surface format of the display surface
pSprite = SDL_ConvertSurface(pTemp, pScreen->format,
                             SDL_SWSURFACE);

//free the temp surface as we no longer need it
SDL_FreeSurface(pTemp);
```

SDL_BlitSurface

Prototype

```
int SDL_BlitSurface(SDL_Surface *src,
                    SDL_Rect *srcrect,
                    SDL_Surface *dst,
                    SDL_Rect *dstrect);
```

Parameters

src: The source SDL_Surface to copy from.

srcrect: The source rectangular area to copy. If NULL is specified for this value, the entire src contents are copied.

dst: The destination SDL_Surface to copy to.

dstrect: The destination rectangular area to copy to. If this value is NULL, the destination upper-left corner is set to *(0, 0)* of the dst SDL_Surface.

Description

This function performs a fast "blit" from the source surface to the target surface. In other words, it copies the pixel data from the defined source rectangle over to the destination surface to the defined coordinates.

Errors

If an error is detected during this process, a *-1* is returned and the error can be discovered using `SDL_GetError`. Otherwise, a *0* denotes a successful blit.

Sample

```
//load a bitmap of our spaceship
SDL_Surface* bitmap = SDL_LoadBMP("ship.bmp");

// Part of the bitmap that we want to draw – our
//loaded bitmap could have several tiles on it for example
SDL_Rect source;
source.x = 20;
source.y = 60;
source.w = 60;
source.h = 50;

// Part of the screen we want to draw the sprite to
SDL_Rect destination;
destination.x = 200;
destination.y = 100;
destination.w = 60;
destination.h = 50;

//do the blitting!
if(SDL_BlitSurface(bitmap, &source, screen, &destination) < 0)
{
    //handle error checking
}

//flip the back buffer to the front to display new frame
SDL_Flip(screen);
```

SDL_LoadBMP

Prototype

```
SDL_Surface *SDL_LoadBMP(const char *file);
```

Parameters

file: The Windows BMP file you wish to load into an `SDL_Surface`.

Description

This helper function is used to load a Windows BMP image file into an SDL_ Surface.

Errors

This function returns the newly created SDL_Surface, or a NULL value if there was an internal error.

Sample

```
//SDL makes it so easy to load images, that it is reduced
//to a single API call
SDL_Surface* pBitmap = SDL_LoadBMP("sprite_image.bmp");
if(pBitmap == NULL)
{
    //handle error checking here
}
```

SDL_WM_SetCaption

Prototype

```
void SDL_WM_SetCaption( const char *title, const char *icon );
```

Parameters

title: The text to change the window title to.

icon: The text to change the window title to (when app is minimized).

Description

This function attempts to set the name of the window along with the iconic text that appears if the window is minimized.

Errors

None.

Sample

```
//create the window display surface, before changing the caption
int width = 640;
int height= 480;
int bpp = 16;
int flags = SDL_SWSURFACE;
pSurface = SDL_SetVideoMode(width, height, bpp, flags);
if(pSurface == NULL)
{
  sprintf(strError, "SDL initialization failed: %s\n",
    SDL_GetError());
  cerr << strError << endl;

  return -1;
}

//now that we have a working display surface, change the caption
SDL_WM_SetCaption( "SDL Roxx", "SDL Roxx" );
```

Appendix

B Exam Answers (Odd)

CHAPTER 1

1.1 A human language may contain inconsistencies and ambiguities. A computer cannot handle either, so computer languages are syntactically and grammatically formalized in such a way that inconsistency and ambiguity are impossible. Any departure from the accepted form of the computer language will be rejected at compilation time.

1.3 A compiler takes source code, written in a programming language like C++, and transforms it into object code the computer can execute.

CHAPTER 2

2.1 a) Invalid: A constant must be initialized.
   b) Valid.
   c) Invalid: "C+" isn't a single character.
   d) Valid.
   e) Valid.
   f) Valid.
   g) Valid.
   h) Invalid: There is a space in the middle of "score 3," and identifiers can't contain blank spaces.
   i) invalid: There are two type names in this declaration.
   j) invalid: goto is not a valid variable name because it is a reserved keyword.

2.3 A literal is an item that doesn't have a name, like the number 5. A constant is an identifier used to give a name to a literal.

2.5 The code snippet will not compile because the second line refers to MyAge, which is undefined. Remember that C++ is case sensitive, and myAge and MyAge aren't the same identifier.

CHAPTER 3

3.1 This snippet uses the extraction operator with cout. Replace the extraction operator >> with the insertion operator << and the snippet will work.

3.3 The program won't compile because the names of the iostream entities endl and cout aren't declared. You can fix the program by inserting the line:

```
using namespace std;
```

3.5

```
/***********************************
Learn C++ by Making Games
Solution to Exercise 3.5
***********************************/

#include <iostream>
using namespace std;

int main()
{
  // Prompt the user for data
  cout << "Type in three integer numbers:" << endl;

  // Read in the three values
  int a, b, c;
  cin >> a >> b >> c;

  // Print out all permutations
  cout << "Here are the permutations:" << endl;
  cout << a << " " << b << " " << c << endl;
  cout << a << " " << c << " " << b << endl;
  cout << b << " " << a << " " << c << endl;
  cout << b << " " << c << " " << a << endl;
  cout << c << " " << a << " " << b << endl;
  cout << c << " " << b << " " << a << endl;

  // And we're done!
  return 0;
}
```

CHAPTER 5

5.1 Instead of the assignment operator =, the statement contains the equality operator ==. It will generate an error at compilation.

5.3 The value is 3. The assignment in the fourth line erases the results of everything that preceded it, and the fact that the fifth line increments foundPotions has no impact on numPotions.

5.5 When both of a division's operands are integer values, C++ automatically applies integer division. If you want the true floating-point quotient, you must transform at least one of the operands into a floating-point value, and static_cast is the recommended way to do so.

5.7

```
/***********************************
  Learn C++ by Making Games
   Solution 5.7: Equations
 ***********************************/

#include <iostream>
using namespace std;

int main()
{
  // First, get the data from the user
  int a, b, c;
  cout << "Please type in the three numbers:" << endl;
  cin >> a >> b >> c;

  // Calculate the equations
  int eq1 = a * a + 2 * a * b * c + b * b - 4;
       int eq2 = a * b * c + 2 * c * ( a - b ) + a * c / b - a;

  // print the results
  cout << "Equation 1 = " << eq1 << endl;
  cout << "Equation 2 = " << eq2 << endl;

  return 0;
}
```

CHAPTER 6

6.1 No. Either a variable is local to a certain block, or it is global.

6.3 Variables that go out of scope are erased from the computer's memory and can no longer be accessed. As far as the program is concerned, they no longer exist.

CHAPTER 7

7.1 A do-while loop's test condition is checked at the end of each iteration, so its code block will always be executed at least once. A while loop's test condition is checked at the beginning of the iteration, so it is possible that the code block will not be executed at all if the test condition is false from the start.

7.3 The break statement always tells the computer to terminate the current block.

7.5 An infinite loop! The semicolon at the end of the while statement tells the compiler the while block is empty; therefore, this block contains no way to change the variable iter.

7.7

```cpp
/************************************
Learn C++ by Making Games
Solution 7.7 - Super divination
************************************/

#include <iostream>
using namespace std;

int main()
{

    // Let's define the number that we want the
    // player to guess as a constant
    const int magicNumber = 8;

    // Then, ask the player to guess until he
    // gets it right
    cout << "Guess which number between 1 and 100 "
            << "I'm thinking about...\n";

    int playerGuess;

    // Loop until the player gets it right
    do
    {
```

```
    cin >> playerGuess;
    if( magicNumber == playerGuess )
      cout << "You're right! Congratulations!\n";
    else if( magicNumber < playerGuess )
      cout << "Lower..." << endl;
    else
      cout << "Higher..." << endl;
  } while( magicNumber != playerGuess );

  // And we're done!
  return 0;
}
```

CHAPTER 9

9.1 C++ will attempt to perform an automatic type cast to make the arguments fit what the function expects. Sometimes, this will work properly; other times, it will result in improper argument values or generate a compilation error if there is no way to perform the type cast.

9.3 No. These two functions differ only in their return type, which is illegal.

CHAPTER 10

10.1 There is a semicolon at the end of the first line, which makes it a function prototype. The following block is not attached to the function, which the compiler will therefore consider undefined.

```
/************************************
    Learn C++ by Making Games
  Solution 10.1: Score assessment
*************************************/

#include <iostream>
using namespace std;

    void assessment( int playerScore )
{
 if( playerScore >= 1000 )
   cout << "Excellent performance! Good job!";
  else if( playerScore >= 800 )
    cout << "Pretty good, you're getting better!";
      else if( playerScore >= 600 )
```

```
      cout << "Not bad for a rookie...";
    else if( playerScore >= 300 )
      cout << "Well, at least you're not getting fired...";
    else
      cout << "Did you fall asleep during the game?";

        cout << endl;
  return;
}

int main()
{

  // Let's read the score
  cout << "What score did you get?" << endl;
  int playerScore;
  cin >> playerScore;

  // Give an appropriate assessment
  assessment( playerScore );

  // And we're done!
  return 0;
}
```

10.3 The `return` statement terminates a function and returns control to its caller. When `return` has an argument, it passes it back to the caller as the function's return value.

10.5 You should give the function the return type `void`.

CHAPTER 11

11.1 A value parameter is copied and manipulated locally, so any changes made to the parameter are not propagated back to the caller. A reference parameter is an alias for the variable being passed as an argument by the caller, so any changes made to the parameter within the function will be propagated back to the caller.

11.3 No. Overloaded functions must differ in their parameter types; otherwise, the compiler wouldn't be able to choose which one to call.

11.5 Of course, as long as it is a by-value parameter.

11.8

```
/************************************
  Learn C++ by Making Games
  Solution 11.8: Non-Taxable Potions
 ************************************/

#include <iostream>
using namespace std;

// The tax rate function
double potionPriceCalculator( int potions,
                              double unitPrice,
                              bool isTaxable = true,
                              double taxRate = 0.07 )
{
  if( isTaxable )
    return( potions * unitPrice * ( 1.0 + taxRate ) );
  else
    return( potions * unitPrice );
}

int main()
{
  // First, a case where we want the standard tax rate to
  // apply. We can use the default values for isTaxable
  // and for taxRate.
  cout << potionPriceCalculator( 12, 3.0 ) << endl;

  // Now, let's show a call for a non-taxable potion
  // We override the default value for isTaxable
  // We leave the default tax rate unchanged, since
  // we don't use it
  cout << potionPriceCalculator( 10, 5.0, false ) << endl;

  // Finally, a case where we need to change the tax rate
  // We must specify all 4 parameters, including isTaxable
  // even if the value we supply is identical to the
  // default, because we want to override the default
  // value for the 4th and last parameter
  cout << potionPriceCalculator( 2, 8.0, true, 0.10 ) << endl;

  return 0;
}
```

CHAPTER 12

12.1 No. Some functions can't be inlined, in which case they will perform exactly like normal functions.

12.3 For programmer-defined headers, the file's .h extension must be specified explicitly and the filename must be wrapped in double quotes.

12.5 extern means that a variable that will be referred to in a source file is a global defined elsewhere in the program, possibly later in the same source file, possibly in another.

12.7

```
/*************************************
  Learn C++ by Making Games
  Solution 12.7: Non-Taxable Potions
  Header file
 *************************************/

#ifndef SOLUTION12_1_H
        #define SOLUTION12_1_h

#include <iostream>
using namespace std;

// The tax rate function's prototype
double potionPriceCalculator( int potions,
                              double unitPrice,
                          bool isTaxable = true,
                          double taxRate = 0.07 );


#endif;
/*************************************
  Learn C++ by Making Games
  Solution 12.1: Non-Taxable Potions
  Source file
 *************************************/

#include <iostream>
        #include "solution12_1.h"

using namespace std;
```

```
int main()
{
  // First, a case where we want the standard tax rate to
  // apply. We can use the default values for isTaxable
  // and for taxRate.
  cout << potionPriceCalculator( 12, 3.0 ) << endl;

  // Now, let's show a call for a non-taxable potion
  // We override the default value for isTaxable
  // We leave the default tax rate unchanged, since
  // we don't use it
  cout << potionPriceCalculator( 10, 5.0, false ) << endl;

  // Finally, a case where we need to change the tax rate
  // We must specify all 4 parameters, including isTaxable
  // even if the value we supply is identical to the
  // default, because we want to override the default
  // value for the 4th and last parameter
  cout << potionPriceCalculator( 2, 8.0, true, 0.10 ) << endl;

  return 0;
}


// The tax rate function
// Note that the default values are defined in the prototype,
// not here
double potionPriceCalculator( int potions,
                              double unitPrice,
                              bool isTaxable,
                              double taxRate )
{
  if( isTaxable )
    return( potions * unitPrice * ( 1.0 + taxRate ) );
  else
    return( potions * unitPrice );
}
```

CHAPTER 14

14.1 MyArray[0] and MyArray[41]
14.3 The '\0'

CHAPTER 15

15.1 `<Datatype> <variable name> [number_of_elements]`

15.3
```cpp
for(int i = 0; i < 10; i++){
    for(int j = 0; j < 10; j++){
      myBigArray[i][j] = 0;
    }
}
```

CHAPTER 16

16.1 `int myarray[5] = { 0, 0, 1, 1, 2 };`

16.3
```cpp
int add_up_array( int number_array[], int length ){
    int sum = 0;
    for(int i = 0; i < length; i++){
      sum = sum + number_array[i];
    }
    return sum;
}
```

CHAPTER 17

17.1
```cpp
/**
 * Modification of fib to add some cout statements
 */
int fib(int n)
{
  if( n < 3 )
  {
    cout << "reached stop condition" << endl;
    return 1;
  }
  else
  {
    cout << "entering another fib loop with n = " << n << endl;
    return( fib(n - 2) + fib( n - 1 ) );
  }
}
```

17.3
```
/**
 * Factorial function which computes the factorial without recursion
 */
long factorial(int n)
{

  long result = 1;

  for (int i = 2; i <= n; i++)
    result = result * i;

  return result;

}
```

CHAPTER 18

18.1 The dot (.) operator is used to select a member of a struct.

CHAPTER 20

20.1 A pointer allows you to point to a particular data type.

CHAPTER 21

21.1 Pointer arithmetic allows you to add or subtract the current position of a pointer in memory.

CHAPTER 22

22.1
```
void display_array( char* pArray, int length ) {
        for(int i = 0; i < length; i++){
          cout << "[" << i << "] = " << pArray[i] << " ";
        }
      }
```

CHAPTER 23

23.1 `int (*myFunction)(float param1, float param2);`

CHAPTER 24

24.1 A pointer is used to point to a particular memory location and can be updated to point to any new memory location, whereas a reference is much cleaner to use than a pointer but cannot be modified.

CHAPTER 26

26.1
```
class Cat {
      char name[80];
      };
```
26.3 Encapsulation is the process of hiding class member data at a lower level.

CHAPTER 27

27.1 A member function or data declared as `private` is not accessible from outside the class. A `protected` member function or data is fully visible to the object as well as any derived object. A member function or data declared as `public` is fully accessible by anyone.

27.3 Getter and setter member functions are accessors to internal class data members.

CHAPTER 28

28.1 A constructor is called when an object first appears within the current scope of the program.

28.3 Any operation that throws an exception of some kind (such as opening or closing a file) should not be put into a constructor.

CHAPTER 29

29.1 Function overloading is the process of executing different function implementations depending on the parameters.

CHAPTER 30

30.1 Operator overloading allows you to provide a more intuitive approach to the design and implementation of your objects.

30.3

```
class Rectangle
{
public:

  //snip!

  Rectangle operator* (const Rectangle& p1)
  {
    return Rectangle( width * p1.width, height * p1.height );

  }


  //doesn't make much sense to divide the area of one rectangle
  //by another, but perhaps you want a way to calculate how many
  //rectangles fit into a larger rectangle?
  Rectangle operator/ (const Rectangle& p1)
  {
    return Rectangle( width / p1.width, height / p1.height );

  }

}
```

CHAPTER 31

31.1 The this pointer is used internally within each object's member function for the object to be able to determine the source object executing the function. Since the C++ language is polymorphic in nature, this is a critical key for each object to determine which object in a hierarchy is executing what.

CHAPTER 32

32.1 A memory leak occurs when you allocate and reserve some memory on the heap, and do not clean it up and return it when you are finished. This creates "dangling" memory, which is inaccessible by other programs and usually cannot be cleaned without a reboot of the machine.

32.3 If a new directive fails, the object pointer returned is NULL.

CHAPTER 33

33.1 Polymorphism is the process of defining multiple forms or implementations of a single object or member function. This allows you to have a base "common" function that you can extend with any children objects.

33.3 The access qualifiers of private, public, and protected allow you to control how the member variables and functions are received by a new object that is derived from an existing one.

CHAPTER 34

34.1 The virtual keyword allows you to provide different function implementations of class members, which are evaluated at the runtime of the object with the help of the this pointer.

34.3 An abstract base class is usually at the lowest levels of your class library. It provides you with a generic interface that you use to design other objects. You can never explicitly declare a direct instance of an ABC; instead, other objects must be derived from it.

34.5 Interfaces are usually used to restrict the behavior of an object without actually being an object itself. An example might be using an ATM machine. You follow a certain sequence of actions to deposit and withdraw money, but these actions are not restricted to that ATM machine. If you visit a different ATM, you can perform the same actions to produce the same results. These actions (in this case) could be the interface to a way of standardizing what is and isn't allowed at an ATM.

CHAPTER 35

35.3 In reality, the only time you would explicitly choose waterfall over an iterative approach is when the publisher demands or restricts you to a waterfall approach.

CHAPTER 37

37.1 Opening a text file.
```
ifstream infile;
infile.open("C:\\temp\\datafile.txt");

infile.close();
```

CHAPTER 38

38.1 Serialization is the process of reading or writing bytes from/to a file source.

CHAPTER 40

40.1 SDL is an abstraction layer for dealing with the multimedia hardware in your system such as video and sound devices, without needing to worry about the implementation lower level specifics of each of these devices.

40.3 Sam Lantigua created SDL while working at Loki Software. Since then, he has departed for Blizzard, and the SDL is now actively maintained by Sam and other exceptional developers within the community.

CHAPTER 41

41.1 A sprite is a simple abstraction for an object that is drawn or positioned on your display. For example, your mouse cursor is a sprite.

CHAPTER 42

42.1 SDL Mixer is an SDL-compatible library that provides an abstraction layer for the audio hardware. The upshot of this is that you do not need to know (or care) about the individual commands needed to set up the audio devices.

CHAPTER 44

44.1 A linked list is a way to dynamically organize and gather data in a collection. The advantage of this is that you can grow or shrink the list during the lifetime of your program as you need to add or remove objects.

44.3 Traversing the list is very simple. You create a temporary pointer to a node in the list. You then assign it to the head (first node) in the list. Using the internal pointers to the next node in the list, you can follow the chain of nodes all the way to the end.

CHAPTER 45

45.1 An overloaded function does allow you to handle different data types with the same function name; however, you are still maintaining multiple bodies of code. Templates give you an "almost-write-once-run-anywhere" approach.

45.3

```
template <class T>
void MySwap(T a, T b){
  T res;
  res = a;
        a = b;
  b = res;
        }
```

CHAPTER 46

46.1 Exception handling in blocks allows you to group together a collection of function calls of a common task. It helps you isolate the problem, and reduces the work of the developer to individually check every function execution for errors.

46.3
```
int myarray[5];
try{
  for(int i = 0; i < 6; i++){
    myarray[i] = 2;
  }
}catch( const char* strError ){
  cout << "\nException raised! " << strError << "\n";
}
```

CHAPTER 47

47.1 A preprocessor directive allows you to create and specify actions or code branch executions based on these directives, which are processed during the compilation phase of your code.

47.3
```
#define use_function 1
void do_something(void){
  #ifdef use_function
    cout << "I'm in the ifdef block!\n";
  #else
    cout << "I'm a regular block\n";
        #endif
}
```

CHAPTER 48

48.1 Standard Template Library contains a library of commonly used container components.

48.3 Yes, the STL container classes are perfectly suited for games.

Appendix

C About the CD-ROM

SYSTEM REQUIREMENTS

To compile the accompanying source code provided on this CD-ROM, you will need a PC capable of compiling C++ modules. To run the sample code, you will need any version of Windows (newer than NT4.0) with at least 1 GHz CPU and a minimum of 256 MB of RAM. The sample projects are created in a format compatible with Microsoft's Visual Studio 6.0; however, any newer version of the Microsoft Visual Studio product line is capable of working with this format.

FOLDERS

Figures: All of the figures from the book, organized in folders by chapter.

SDL: Simple DirectMedia Layer—the main SDL libraries, including SDL and SDL Mixer of this popular open source cross-platform game creation toolkit.

Projects: The game projects from the book, organized by the corresponding chapters.

Source Code: All of the source code for this book is contained within a single installer, which will expand to a chosen location on your hard drive.

SOFTWARE

The following software products have been included on the CD-ROM:

Simple DirectMedia Layer *http://www.libsdl.org*

Index